# Understanding PISA's Attractiveness

**New Directions in Comparative and International Education**
Edited by Stephen Carney, Irving Epstein and Daniel Friedrich

This series aims to extend the traditional discourse within the field of Comparative and International Education by providing a forum for creative experimentation and exploration of alternative perspectives. As such, the series welcomes scholarly work focusing on themes that have been under-researched and under-theorized in the field but whose importance is easily discernible. It supports works which theoretical grounding is centered in knowledge traditions that come from the Global South, encouraging those who work from intellectual horizons alternative to the dominant discourse. The series takes an innovative approach to challenging the dominant traditions and orientations of the field, encouraging interdisciplinarity, methodological experimentation, and engagement with relevant leading theorists.

Also available in the series

*Resonances of El Chavo del Ocho in Latin American Childhood, Schooling, and Societies*, edited by Daniel Friedrich and Erica Colmenares

Forthcoming titles in the series

*Education in Radical Uncertainty*, Stephen Carney and Ulla Ambrosius Madsen
*Internationalization of Higher Education for Development*, Susanne Ress

# Understanding PISA's Attractiveness

## Critical Analyses in Comparative Policy Studies

Edited by
Florian Waldow and Gita Steiner-Khamsi

BLOOMSBURY ACADEMIC
LONDON • NEW YORK • OXFORD • NEW DELHI • SYDNEY

BLOOMSBURY ACADEMIC
Bloomsbury Publishing Plc
50 Bedford Square, London, WC1B 3DP, UK
1385 Broadway, New York, NY 10018, USA

BLOOMSBURY, BLOOMSBURY ACADEMIC and the Diana logo are trademarks of
Bloomsbury Publishing Plc

First published in Great Britain 2019

A catalogue record for this book is available from the British Library.

A catalog record for this book is available from the Library of Congress.

ISBN: HB: 978-1-3500-5728-9
ePDF: 978-1-3500-5729-6
eBook: 978-1-3500-5730-2

Series: New Directions in Comparative and International Education

Typeset by Newgen KnowledgeWorks Pvt. Ltd., Chennai, India

To find out more about our authors and books visit www.bloomsbury.com
and sign up for our newsletters.

# Contents

# Notes on Contributors

**Søren Christensen** is an associate professor at the Department of Education, Aarhus University, Denmark. Among his main research interests is the interplay between educational globalization and changing conceptions of educational competition in Singapore and East Asia. Recent publications on this topic include "Healthy Competition and Unsound Comparison: Reforming Educational Competition in Singapore" (*Globalisation, Societies and Education*, *13*(4), 2015).

**Jaakko Kauko** is a professor of education policy at the Faculty of Education and Culture, Tampere University, Finland. His research is situated in the fields of education policy and comparative education. In 2017, he published a monograph together with Hannu Simola, Janne Varjo, Mira Kalalahti, and Fritjof Sahlström titled *Dynamics in Education Politics*: *Understanding and Explaining the Finnish Case*.

**Sonja Kosunen** is an assistant professor of education at University of Helsinki, Finland. Her main research interests are in the fields of sociology of education and urban studies. Kosunen's latest publications focus on urban and school segregation in cities (e.g., Kosunen, Sonja, Venla Bernelius, Piia Seppänen, and Miina Porkka. "School Choice to Lower Secondary Schools and Mechanisms of Segregation in Urban Finland." *Urban Education* (2016)).

**Yoonmi Lee** is a professor of education at Hongik University, Seoul, South Korea. She received her PhD at the Department of Educational Policy Studies (majoring in comparative history of education), University of Wisconsin-Madison. She served as president of the Korean Association for History of Education from 2011 to 2012. Her research interests include comparative and transnational history of modern education, education and state formation, and cultural politics of education, particularly in the East Asian context. Her publication includes *Modern Education, Textbooks, and the Image of the Nation: Politics of Modernization and Nationalism in Korean education 1880–1910* (2000).

**Bob Lingard** is Professorial Fellow in the Institute for Learning Sciences and Teacher Education, Australian Catholic University and Emeritus Professor at the University of Queensland, Brisbane. His most recent books include *Globalizing Educational Accountabilities* (2016), coauthored with Wayne Martino, Goli Rezai-Rashti, and Sam Sellar, and the sole-authored *Politics, Policies and Pedagogies in Education* (2014).

**Lluís Parcerisa** is a PhD candidate in the Department of Sociology at the Autonomous University of Barcelona (UAB). Since 2013 he has been a member of GEPS Research Center. His research interests include comparative education, cultural political economy, school autonomy with accountability reforms, and teacher professionalism. Together with Antoni Verger, he has published a background paper for the 2017/18 Global Education Monitoring Report on *Accountability in Education.*

**Vicente Chua Reyes Jr.** is with the School of Education, University of Queensland, Australia. He is a fellow of the Centre for Chinese Studies of the Republic of China and the National Taiwan Normal University and the University of Macau. He is also a visiting academic at the Institute of Education, University of London. His latest book with Routledge (2016) is entitled *Mapping the Terrain of Education Reform: Global Trends and Local Responses in the Philippines.*

**Risto Rinne** is a professor of education and Vice Dean in the Faculty of Education and Head of the Department of Education and in the Research Centre CELE at the University of Turku, Finland. His main interests relate to sociology of education, international comparative education, educational policy and history of education. His recent publications include, for example, *Cultural Capital, Equality and Diversifying Education* (2017), "The Paradox of Educational Race—How to Win the Ranking Game by Sailing to Headwind" (2013) and "National Policy Brokering and the Construction of the European Education Space in England, Sweden, Finland and Scotland" (2011).

**Nancy Green Saraisky** is a research associate in the Department of International and Transcultural Studies at Teachers College, Columbia University. She holds a PhD in comparative education and political science from Columbia University, where her studies were funded by the National Science Foundation. Her current work focuses on the relationships between data, politics, and policy as it relates to educational assessment, both domestically and internationally. She also researches education activism, most recently around the opt-out movement in the United States.

**Barbara Schulte** is an associate professor of education at the Department of Sociology, Lund University, Sweden. Her research focuses on the global diffusion and local appropriation of educational models and programs; on education, privatization, and consumerism; on new technologies/ICT, education, and techno-determinism; as well as on issues of education, aid and development, with particular focus on China. Recent and ongoing research projects include a study of private schools in urban China; an investigation into the challenges of the "digital society" in China and their implications for education and upbringing; and a project on ethnic minority education in Southwest China.

**Sam Sellar** is a reader in education studies at Manchester Metropolitan University. His current research focuses on large-scale assessments, data infrastructures, commercialization, and new accountabilities in schooling. Sam's recent books include *The Global Education Race: Taking the Measure of PISA and International Testing* (2017) and *Globalizing Educational Accountabilities* (2016).

**Piia Seppänen** is a professor of education, especially in comparative education and education policy at the University of Turku, Finland. Much of her scholarly work has focused on school choice policy, pupil selection, classed practices, urban social segregation, and comprehensive schooling systems. Seppänen has coedited the books *Lohkoutuva peruskoulu* (2015) [Segmenting Compulsory School in Finland] and *Contrasting Dynamics in Education Politics of Extremes: School Choice in Chile and Finland* (2015). Her current research focuses on private actors in public education systems and their connections to global education industry.

**Kirsten Sivesind** is an associate professor in the Department of Education, University of Oslo, Norway. Her publications include, "Transnational Policy Transfer over Three Curriculum Reforms in Finland: The Construction of Conditional and Purposive Programs (1994–2016)," *European Educational Research Journal*, coauthored with Azita Afsar and Kari Bachmann. Her research interests center on curriculum history, European didactics and comparative education policy. Currently, she coordinates the research project "Policy Knowledge and Lesson Drawing in Nordic School Reform in an Era of International Comparison" (NRC, 2018–23).

**Gita Steiner-Khamsi** holds a dual academic appointment as a professor of comparative education at Teachers College, Columbia University, New York (since 1995) and more recently at the Graduate Institute of International and Development Studies, Geneva, where she also serves as Director of NORRAG. Past president of the Comparative and International Education Society (USA), she is editor or co-editor of three book series (Routledge, Teachers College Press, E. Elgar) and author of several books and journal articles on comparative policy studies, globalization and education, and public-private partnerships in education. Her most recent edited book is entitled *The State, Business and Education: Public-Private Partnerships Revisited* (with Alexandra Draxler, 2018).

**Youl-Kwan Sung** is a professor and a dean of the Graduate School of Education at Kyung Hee University in Seoul, South Korea. His research interests include comparative approaches to neoliberal education reform, the politics of policy borrowing, and social justice education. He has published various articles and book chapters on political aspects of the curriculum and educational policies to such journals as *Comparative Education, Asia Pacific Journal of Education, Oxford Review of Education*, and many others.

**Charlene Tan** is an associate professor at the National Institute of Education, Nanyang Technological University, Singapore. She has published widely on education policy in China and Singapore; her recent books include *Learning from Shanghai: Lessons on Achieving Educational Success* and *Educational Policy Borrowing in China: Looking West or Looking East?*. Her forthcoming book is on high-performing educational systems in East Asia. Her latest book is *Comparing High-performing Education Systems: Understanding Singapore, Shanghai, and Hong Kong*.

**Antoni Verger** is an associate professor at the Department of Sociology of the Universitat Autònoma de Barcelona, and general deputy of the European master program Education Policies for Global Development. A former post-doctoral fellow at the Amsterdam Institute for Social Science Research (University of Amsterdam), his research analyzes the relationship between global governance institutions and education policy. He has specialized in the study of public-private partnerships, quasi-market mechanisms and accountability policies in education, and has published extensively on these themes. Currently, he coordinates the ERC-funded research project REFORMED—Reforming Schools Globally: A Multiscalar Analysis of Autonomy and Accountability Policies in the Education Sector.

**Florian Waldow** is a professor of comparative and international education at Humboldt University, Berlin, Germany. Among his main research interests is studying the role of "reference societies" in education policy-making. Together with Gita Steiner-Khamsi, he has edited the 2012 World Yearbook on Education on *Policy Borrowing and Lending in Education*.

# Series Editors' Foreword

The field of comparative and international education requires its researchers, teachers, and students to examine educational issues, policies, and practices in ways that extend beyond the immediate contexts with which they are most accustomed. To do so means that one must constantly embrace engagement with the unfamiliar, a task that can be daunting because authority within academic disciplines and fields of study is often constructed according to convention at the expense of imagination and creativity. Comparative and international education as an academic field is rich and eclectic, with a long tradition of theoretical and methodological diversity as well as an openness to innovation and experimentation. However, as it is not immune to the conformist—especially disciplinary—pressures that give academic scholarship much of its legitimacy, we believe it important to highlight the importance of research and writing that is creative, thought-provoking, and, where necessary, transgressive. This series offers comparative and international educators and scholars the space to extend the boundaries of the field, encouraging them to investigate the ways in which underappreciated social thought and theorists may be applied to comparative work and educational concerns in new and exciting ways. It especially welcomes scholarly work that focuses upon themes that have been under-researched and under-theorized but whose importance is easily discernible. It further supports work whose theoretical grounding is centered in knowledge traditions that come from the Global South and welcomes perspectives including those that are associated with post-foundational theorizing, non-Western epistemologies, and performative approaches to working with educational problems and challenges. In these ways, this series provides a space for alternative thinking about the role of comparative research in reimagining the social.

*Understanding PISA's Attractiveness: Critical Analyses in Comparative Policy Studies* continues the critical thrust of the series. The role of international large-scale assessment studies such as Programme for International Student Assessment (PISA) in shaping globalizing education continues to be a major issue of attention for scholars, policy-makers and practitioners alike. This volume comes at an opportune time, furthering our understanding of the relations between transnational policy actors, national education systems, teachers and students and, most notably, the ways in which references to "the other" shape governance and accountability in education. Through concept development and well-chosen case studies, the volume makes clear that education is no longer the preserve of "local" policy-makers, if it ever was. Rather, we are now seeing a new era in education policy where political agendas are made in relation to what is reasonable, desirable or necessary in the eyes of others and in order to gain legitimacy and influence both at home and abroad. A new terminology is emerging here—reference societies, projection, scandalization, and envy— that complicates and extends earlier notions of excellence, success, and crisis. The volume requires that we rethink the political in education as well as our understanding of place, context, and political agency. There is little likelihood that the influence of data-driven policy will diminish. It is hoped, therefore, that this important collection may provide some tools to analyze and better understand its place in our educational landscape.

Stephen Carney, Irving Epstein,
and Daniel Friedrich

# Introduction: Projection in Education Policy-Making

Florian Waldow

## International large-scale assessments and education policy-making

Starting from humble beginnings in the late 1950s, international large-scale assessments (ILSAs) in education have undergone a tremendous expansion in number, frequency, and scope over the past few decades (Kamens and McNeely 2010; Pizmony-Levy 2013; Addey 2018). While in the beginning they were mostly driven by scientific curiosity, over the years ILSAs have increasingly developed into a tool of governance and accountability (Addey 2018). In addition, ILSA results have become an important point of reference and a legitimating argument in education policy-making.

By now, there is a substantial body of research looking at how large-scale assessments, especially PISA, are being used in education governance and policy-making (to name but a few important publications in this field: Grek 2009; Martens and Niemann 2013; Meyer and Benavot 2013; Bieber et al. 2014; Sellar and Lingard 2014; Hamilton, Maddox, and Addey 2015). Among other things, this body of research has shown that countries do not simply participate in ILSAs because they are interested in the results. Rather, according to Steiner-Khamsi (2017), participating in ILSAs can serve purposes of

> (1) coalition-building or, more precisely, . . . generating or alleviating reform pressure, (2) mobilising financial sources for the education sector, (3) demonstrating 'internationality' and, finally, (4) learning technical skills of how to measure student outcomes and system performance. (Steiner-Khamsi 2017, 444; see also Addey and Sellar 2017)

The fact that there is such a diverse range of purposes for participating in ILSAs means that the processes initiated by ILSAs in national education systems and education policy-making are a good deal more complicated than mere "lesson-drawing" from successful ILSA-league leaders.

This volume aims to take a fresh look at some of the changes the rise of ILSAs has brought about in education policy-making. It understands policy-making in a wide sense, also comprising media discourse and policy-relevant academic writings, which ultimately may feed back into the policy process proper. The contributors to this book focus on why and how national policy actors use the results from international large-scale student assessments for setting policy agendas, evaluating reform options, and formulating new policies. The analytic lens for this fresh look is provided by the concept of projection, which will be outlined below.

## Reference Societies, Scandalization, and Glorification

Before the concept of projection is introduced, it is necessary to revisit the concept of "reference societies," which the former concept builds on in a number of ways. The concept of "reference societies" was originally coined by the macro-sociologist Reinhard Bendix (1967, 1978). Bendix modeled his "reference societies" on the concept of "reference groups" as used in social psychology and sociology (see Hyman 1942; Merton and Rossi 1968).[1] Usually, the term "reference society" is used in the sense of a model nation from which to borrow elements (e.g., by Schriewer 1990; Arbeitsgruppe Internationale Vergleichsstudie 2003; Lingard and Rawolle 2011), that is, the concept denotes *positive* reference to another country.[2] However, arguably Bendix's (1978) definition of the concept allows for a wider analytic use of "reference societies." In his book *Kings or people*, he gives the following definition: "I shall use the term *reference society* whenever intellectual leaders and an educated public react to the values and institutions of another country with ideas and actions that pertain to their own country" (Bendix 1978, 292, emphasis in original). Bendix's definition leaves open whether reactions to "values and institutions of another country" are positive or negative, accepting or rejecting. Indeed, these reactions can take both a negative and a positive form (Waldow 2016). Reference societies can function as a way of presenting either a desirable model or an "anti-model." Both types of reference societies are frequently encountered in education policy-making and will feature in this book.

Reference societies are frequently invoked in the context of "scandalization" or "glorification" (see Steiner-Khamsi 2003), respectively. Gita Steiner-Khamsi (2003) defines "scandalization" as "highlighting the weaknesses of one's own educational system as a result of comparison" and, conversely, "glorification" as "highlighting the strengths of one's own educational system as a result of comparison" (Steiner-Khamsi 2003). It should be noted that "highlighting the weaknesses of one's own educational system *as a result of comparison*" is not the same as "highlighting the weaknesses of one's own educational system *as a result of low scores*." Comparison is a complex process of meaning-making, and scandalization can also occur if ILSA results are average, but lower than anticipated (see Martens and Niemann 2013). Scandalization can even occur when ILSA results are very good, for example, if there is a perception that these results have been bought at too high a price, as claimed by some observers, for example, in Korea (see Chapter 11 by Lee and Sung in this volume) or Shanghai (see Chapter 8 by Reyes and Tan in this volume).

When speaking of reference societies, Bendix speaks of "countries," that is, he tacitly assumes that reference societies are contained within the boundaries of nation states. However, this is not necessarily the case. Reference societies can encompass several nation states deemed to be similar or part of a region that is perceived as culturally homogeneous, for example, when the "Scandinavian" or "East Asian" education systems are invoked as a reference (e.g., see Chapter 3 on Germany and Chapter 4 on Australia in this volume).

What turns a society into a reference society for others? Researchers have identified various factors. The educational philosopher and historian R. Freeman Butts (1973), who used the term "reference society" for the first time in connection with education, identified countries that were particularly quick to modernize as potential reference societies for others. Bendix (1978) himself demonstrated how economic competitors and military rivals can become reference societies, citing among others Meiji-era Japan as an example. More recently, scholars have identified achieving high scores in ILSAs as a factor that can turn a country into a reference society for others (Wiseman 2010; Lingard and Rawolle 2011). Reference societies have also been actively promoted with reference to ILSA results by the Organisation for Economic Co-operation and Development (OECD) itself. For instance, OECD (2011) presents "[l]essons from PISA for the United States" by presenting a range of "[s]trong performers and successful reformers" (OECD 2011, title page). These not only include PISA top scorers such as Finland, Hong Kong, and Shanghai but also countries that are not top scorers, but supposedly show improvement and are presented as models for successful reform, such as Germany and Brazil. Finally, non-state commercial actors such as McKinsey & Company also promote reference societies in connection with high ILSA results (Barber and Mourshed 2007).

It is important to note that economic competition, military rivalry, and success in ILSAs are "in the eye of the beholder," that is, they are not objectively given, but the result of perception and interpretation. This means that there can be different perceptions and interpretations in different places. ILSA success can lead to countries becoming reference societies in many other countries and lead to the emergence of new semi-global reference societies, Finland being a case in point. However, ILSAs and the data they produce resonate differently with different nationally or locally preexisting structures and discourses. As mentioned above, the processes involved are more complicated than merely promoting league leaders to the status of global models. How ILSA participation and results (of one's own country and other countries) are processed and interpreted and which consequences they have (if any) depend heavily on the context in which this takes place (see Martens and Niemann 2013; Baird et al. 2016). These processes of perception and interpretation and the broad range of reactions to them are an important part of what this book is about.

# Projection

Having clarified what reference societies are, we can now turn to the concept of "projection." In the following, it will be argued that some of the processes occurring in connection to the use of reference societies in education policy-making can usefully be conceptualized as "projection." The notion of projection has popped up now and then in the literature on education policy-making and educational transfer (e.g., Meyer 1986; Zeng and LeTendre 1999; Smithers 2004; Takayama 2010; Waldow 2010, 2016; You and Morris 2016), although researchers have often used terms other than "projection" to describe the phenomenon understood here as "projection" and have rarely discussed the phenomenon systematically, a gap this book attempts to fill at least to a certain extent.

## Reference as Projection

The concept of projection in education policy-making grows out of a tradition of research on education policy borrowing and lending grounded in the work of, among others, Schriewer (1990), Steiner-Khamsi (2004) and Zymek (1975).

One important insight from this line of research is that references to "elsewhere" depend mostly on the perspective prevalent in the context from which the referring is done, not the context that is being referred to. The concept of projection takes this insight one step further, stressing that actual conditions in the place that is being referred to are often of minor importance; the important thing is what observers *want* to see, to the extent that what is observed may not even exist in the place that is being referred to. Conceptions of "good" and "bad" education are being projected onto other countries or regions like a slide or a film are projected onto a projection screen. The ensuing image is mostly determined by the "slide," not by the "screen." The main function of these projections is the legitimation and delegitimation of educational policies and agendas in the place from which the projection is made.

The fact that the "slide" is more important for the image presented than the "screen" means reference societies will usually be depicted in a very selective way. Certain aspects may be inflated out of proportion, complex and contradictory situations may be presented in a simplified way, and important aspects of context may be neglected. In any case, projection radically reduces the complexity of actual educational conditions and situations.

In the most extreme case, the things that are visible on the projection screen will not even exist in the reference society that is being used as a projection screen. An example from the German media discourse may illustrate this: in an article published about half a year after the German "PISA shock," that is, the publication of the first round of PISA results in December 2001, the German newspaper *Die Welt* celebrated "all-day schooling" (*Ganztagsschule*) as the reason for Finnish PISA success and recommended this as a policy recipe for Germany to emulate (Gatermann 2002). At the time, there was an intensive discussion about all-day schooling in Germany. The fact that "all-day schooling" did not exist as a widespread phenomenon in Finland at the time the article was published (see Matthies 2002) was apparently unknown to the journalist, nor did presumably many readers notice that the journalist was projecting his own idea of a trait of the "good school" onto the Finnish case.

Not every potential reference society is equally suitable as a projection screen, a point that will be elaborated below. Established stereotypical assumptions and beliefs about reference societies play a role here. For purposes of projection, it may even be helpful if not too much is known about the reference society that is used as a projection screen, since a blank screen is particularly suitable for projection. In Chapter 2 in this volume on the Chilean case, Parcerisa and Verger note that other Latin American countries are conspicuously absent as reference societies in educational matters in Chile. They suspect that hidden local rivalries may play a role here. In addition, countries from the vicinity of one's own country may not be as suitable as countries that are further away because observers feel they know a lot about the former; therefore, the projection screen is not blank and it is more difficult to project (positive or negative) images on to it than in the case of a country that is widely unknown in the context from which the projection is made.

Also, different slides can be projected onto the same projection screen. Again, the chapter on the Chilean case by Parcerisa and Verger in this volume provides a good example: while Finland is mainly referenced by left-wing actors in Chile, the right wing also referenced Finland strategically in order to fend off the enactment of the school inclusion law. Waldow (2010) reports a similar case, where individual support for students after the Finnish model is invoked by German actors both in support of a comprehensivization of secondary schooling and in defense of the tracked system, that is, against comprehensivization (see Waldow 2010, 500–1). The projection screen "Finland" thereby becomes a site onto which *competing* images of the "good school" are projected.

Elsewhere, I have made the argument that the phenomena of "reference" on the one hand and actual educational "transfer" on the other ought to be kept analytically apart (Waldow 2017). Reference and transfer can occur together, but they can also occur independently of each other. Some of the contributions to this book show clearly the benefit of keeping reference and transfer analytically separate. This is true, for example, for the Korean case, where reference to Finland was accompanied by actual transfer from the United States (see chapter by Lee and Sung in this volume). The concept of projection clearly pertains to reference, rather than actual transfer; whether actual transfer processes accompany or follow projection or not is an open question to be answered empirically in each individual case.

## Top Scorers as Projection Screens and Projectors

The metaphor of projection may be taken to suggest that the "screen" is totally unaffected by the projections made onto it. This would be slightly misleading. Constructing images of other places is a reflexive process, that is, foreign observations of a society interact with self-perceptions and self-definitions of that society (Musiał 2002; Andersson and Hilson 2009, 222).

The picture that is presented onto the screen may be mostly determined by concerns of the "projector," but the fact that a reference society is being used as a projection screen may still affect that country in various ways. Seppänen et al. show in their chapter that Finland's high scores and the resultant international attention may not have been the "obstacle to change" that Sahlberg (2011, 119) sees in them, but that the projections by others onto the Finnish case did have an effect on various aspects of the policy process and that reforms had to be "fitted" to the PISA results. Also, Finland has tried to actively turn other countries' interest into an export strategy.

Just as low ILSA scores do not automatically lead to the scandalization of one's own education system (Steiner-Khamsi 2004), high scores do not always lead to glorification of one's own system. The achieving of high PISA scores can coexist with a sense of the education system being in crisis nevertheless. For instance, there can be a feeling that scores are being bought at too high a price or that there are pressing educational problems not captured by PISA. As the respective chapters in this volume show, both in the Korean and the Singaporean case many observers see education in a crisis despite very high PISA scores and project ideals of "good" education onto other systems, namely Finland. As Sørensen very vividly puts it in his chapter on the Singaporean case (Singapore led the league tables in all three domains in PISA 2015), PISA top scorers can suffer from "PISA envy," too.

## Projections as Narratives

ILSA results typically take the form of large sets of numerical data, often arranged in tables. Arguably, however, it is not the "naked" numbers that become relevant in education policy-making. According to the political scientist Deborah Stone (2012),

> *narrative stories* are the principal means for defining and contesting policy problems. . . . most definitions of policy problems have a narrative structure, however subtle. Problem definitions are stories with a beginning, a middle, and an end, involving some change or transformation. They have heroes and villains and innocent victims, and they pit the forces of evil against the forces of good. Stories provide explanations of how the world works. These explanations are often unspoken, widely shared, and so much taken for granted that we aren't even aware of them. (Stone 2012, 158, emphasis in original)

Arguably, Stone's contention that stories "are the principal means for defining and contesting policy problems" also applies when the latter are expressed in numerical form or with the help of numbers. Phenomena such as "governing by numbers" (Grek 2009) operate not through the numbers themselves, but because the numbers are connected to narratives: "People count things because they care about them, and they embed their counts in moral narratives about good and bad and right and wrong. These moral narratives, more than the numbers on which they seem to rest, drive politics" (Stone 2016, 169, see also Auld and Morris 2016).

One reason why reference societies are and continue to be attractive in education policy-making is because they make it possible to attach stories to the numerical results of ILSAs. Keita Takayama provided some instructive insights as to how this works in the case of Japan, when he analyzed how the "crisis-reform melodrama" (Takayama 2010, 52) constructed in the Japanese discourse around various reference societies (among them Finland) was used to legitimate and delegitimate policy agendas. Stories can contribute to presenting countries or other entities as an attractive place to borrow from, or, conversely, as a place it is not attractive or even undesirable to borrow from. Storylines can also set out presumed preconditions for continuing on a path of success or for breaking out of a certain pattern deemed unhealthy or detrimental (as described by Lee and Sung in this volume). Stories add context (even if the context is often at least partly fictitious) and a sense of reality and palpability, which in turn adds credibility and plausibility to policy agendas. Arguably, this quality of making educational agendas seem more credible and plausible is an important reason why national reference societies continue to be attractive in the field of education, even in an age where de-contextualized benchmarks and policy prescriptions are widely available and hugely successful (see especially Hattie 2009). Stories involving concrete, identifiable places—even if the way they are depicted may make them hardly recognizable to their inhabitants—seem richer in context and more evocative than mere de-contextualized benchmarks.[3]

Stories also serve to connect the present to imagined futures. The social theorist Niklas Luhmann (1976, 142–3) has noted that in modern society, "[t]he future serves as a projection screen for hopes and fears," and this can be seen to include educational hopes and fears. The narrative structure of projections is crucial for connecting the present to the expected future(s). The economic sociologist Jens Beckert (2013, 226–7) has traced how in the economic field, stories "provide causal links that show how the gap between the present state of the world and the predicted future state is actually closed, thus providing plausible reasons why one should expect the depicted outcome" (see also Beckert 2016). A similar argument can be made for the field of education. Here, too, narratives close the gap between "the present state of the world" and a "predicted future state." John Meyer stated in 1986 (i.e., at a time when United States interest in Japanese education was probably at its peak) that Americans "have shown less interest in real research on [Japanese education] than in depicting Japanese education as a mythological device to portray a desirable future" (Meyer 1986, 56). Thus, in projections, reference societies serve as real-life utopia or dystopia, that is, reference societies appear as potential (utopian or dystopian) futures for one's own society.[4]

Literally speaking, a "real-life utopia" is a paradox, since "utopia" is literally a "non-place" (see Arnswald 2010, 19), that is, a place that does not exist in real life. In a sense, this is precisely the point: in the projection, the unattainable "non-place" seemingly becomes real. Thomas Morus, whose *Utopia* gave its name to a whole genre of "political fictions" (Arnswald 2010, 4), projected his idea of an ideal social and political order onto an imaginary "non-place," the imaginary island of Utopia. Similar to Morus's imaginary island, positive reference societies serve as projection screens for ideal education systems, but they do so as a seemingly real, identifiable place, thereby arguably making the projection even more powerful.

According to Radhika Gorur (2016), ILSAs such as PISA contribute to states viewing education in a simplified, standardized way, which she terms, borrowing from James Scott (1998), "seeing like PISA" (Gorur 2016, 598). PISA becomes a "project of legibility" (Gorur 2016, 598), with the help of which the complexity of real-life education systems and situations can be reduced. Part of the attractiveness of "seeing *like* PISA" for education policy-makers and administrators thus lies in its capacity to reduce complex real-life situations to a set of numbers that can be compared and ranked. While not contradicting Gorur's argument, the chapters in this book make a different point: they investigate how looking, so to speak, "*with* PISA," numbers such as ILSA scores can be used as a starting point for projections connecting narratives to them.

## Becoming a Positive or Negative Reference Society: The Role of National Stereotypes

The chapters in this volume demonstrate very conclusively that the rise of ILSAs has not led to ILSA top scorers automatically becoming global models. Rather, ILSA successes and failures seem to be framed in particular, context-specific ways. For these framings, national stereotypes seem to play an important role, determining the way in which ILSA performance of a country is perceived elsewhere. National stereotypes are generalizations about people from one nation or ethnic group, their behavior and the character of their country and its institutions (including aspects such as education). Sometimes, several national stereotypes can be part of a larger transnational stereotype, such as "Scandinavia" or "Asia." National stereotypes can also contain racialized components. Takayama (2018) convincingly makes this point for the coverage of the PISA success of East Asian countries in Australian media, but racialized perceptions of ILSA success and failure could also easily be demonstrated in many other contexts.

How do national stereotypes influence the choice of reference societies and potential projection screens and the framing of ILSA success and failure? A concept originally developed in the field of marketing research, the "country-of-origin-effect" (Verlegh and Steenkamp 1999; Herz and Diamantopoulos 2013), may be helpful here. The country-of-origin-effect refers to the fact that the presumed origin of a product influences consumers' decisions to buy or not to buy it. Often, consumers are not even aware of this (Herz and Diamantopoulos 2013, 2017). The country-of-origin effect "links a product to an associative network of culturally shared national stereotypes with cognitive, affective and normative connotations" (Chattalas, Kramer, and Takada 2008, 58). It is important to note that the *presumed*, not the actual origin of the product creates the effect (Magnusson, Westjohn, and Zdravkovic 2011). Companies can exploit this by giving their products foreign names that are supposed to trigger certain cultural stereotypes making the product appear more desirable, for example, by giving designer furniture an Italian name, even if the furniture is neither designed nor produced in Italy. This strategy is called "foreign branding" (Leclerc, Schmitt, and Dubé 1994, 263). The country-of-origin-effect and foreign branding are based on the assumption that knowledge about the presumed origin of a product provides the consumer with a shortcut to an informed decision concerning the purchase or non-purchase of a product (see Anholt 2007). Assumptions about the character of the presumed origin of the product substitute for knowledge about the product.

Arguably, country-of-origin effects and foreign branding can also be observed in the construction of reference societies and the choice of attractive projection screens in education. The mere fact that an educational reform is marketed as "Finnish" may suffice to make it attractive by activating certain positive connotations connected to Finland.[5] Conversely, in some contexts, if an educational reform is branded "Asian," it will appear suspicious. Knowledge about the presumed origin of a reform functions as a substitute for knowledge about the reform itself.

It is easy enough to explain why some PISA top scorers, given conducive prior stereotyped perceptions, turn into positive reference societies. High scores are seen to be an indicator of high-quality education; thus, these countries appear as models it is attractive to emulate in order to improve one's own results. It is slightly harder to explain why other top scorers turn into negative reference societies, rather than being mostly ignored as reference societies like the countries with low scores. From the perspective of social psychology, this might be explained by referring to cognitive dissonance theory (Cooper 2011; Gawronski 2012). Put very simply, cognitive dissonance theory stipulates that people strive for internal consistency. Experiences of contradictory cognitions or conditions that are difficult to reconcile lead to a state of tension or displeasure. In order to relieve this stress and resolve the dissonance, cognitions are modified. For instance, in contexts where the existing stereotypes are not conducive to promoting the East Asian PISA participants to the status of a positive reference society (one example for such a context is Germany, but skepticism against East Asian education systems is more widespread, see Takayama 2018), the perception of their high PISA scores creates tension: high scores in ILSAs are seen as an indicator of "good" education, but the negative stereotype means that these countries do not lend themselves easily as positive reference societies. The subheadline of an article in a German quality newspaper dealing with education in Shanghai illustrates this: "Shanghai has the best pupils in the world. European and American experts ask what we have done wrong; the answer is: nothing" (Bork 2011). It seems as if the challenge presented by Shanghai's PISA success cannot just be ignored or shrugged off, but needs to be repudiated actively.[6] The tension connected to the cognitive dissonance seems to arise because "they" are doing well, but "we" are not following their example, despite the fact that "we" also want to do well. Presenting education in China or other East Asian countries as buying success at too high a price and/or being grounded in "cultural" factors that cannot be easily replicated elsewhere (see Sellar and Lingard 2013, 470–1) is a way to relieve this tension. Countries that do not achieve high scores do not create cognitive dissonance; that "they" do things differently in education does not challenge "us" in the same way.

In recent years, the critique of "methodological nationalism" in social science research (Wimmer and Glick Schiller 2002) has intensified. The "assumption that the nation/state/society is the natural social and political form of the modern world" (Wimmer and Glick Schiller 2002, 301) has been rightly problematized and the blind spots and distortions caused by this assumption have been pointed out (for the field of comparative and international education see Larsen and Beech 2014; Takayama 2018). However, social science research is not the only area in which the social and political form of the nation state is taken for granted and "naturalized." The cases collected in this volume illustrate that this is also true of education policy-making and the political imaginary in general. The concepts of "reference societies" and "projection" as understood here underscore the *constructedness* of nation states as basic units of the political imaginary, potentially contributing to a further "de-naturalization" of the nation state as the basic social and political unit of the modern world.

## Externalizing Uneasiness about One's Own System

So far, projection has been understood in the sense of a slide projector projecting an image onto a surface: policy agendas, expectations of possible futures, and ideas of the "good" or the "bad" school are being projected onto reference societies. The images appearing on the projection screen thus have much more to do with the "projector" than the "screen," that is, have more to do with the country from which the reference is made than the country that is being referred to, even though the "screen" may also be affected by the projection.

The chapters in this volume demonstrate clearly that an important function of these projections lies in the legitimation and delegitimation of education policies and reform agendas. The remainder of this section will discuss a related function of projections that can be observed, for example, in the German case. This function lies in externalizing uneasiness about traits of one's own education system by projecting them onto others.

This use of the term "projection" has certain parallels to how the term is used in Freudian psychoanalysis, where projection is a defensive mechanism of the self, that is, a defense against the violation of the "preferred view of self" (Baumeister, Dale, and Sommer 1998, 1082). Projection in the psychoanalytic sense means that certain personality traits one does not like about oneself or one's own group are attributed to others or other groups (List 2014). Psychoanalytic concepts have occasionally been used in the analysis of policy-making (as an example see Fotaki 2010). It is advisable to proceed very cautiously when doing this, but the parallels between the psychoanalytic use of the concept on the one hand and some phenomena observed in connection with the use of reference societies in education are striking. Zeng and LeTendre (1999) provide an interesting example. Despite the fact that at the time of writing of their chapter, the United States actually displayed higher rates of adolescent suicide, school violence, and substance abuse than Japan, these phenomena were frequently portrayed as being problems besetting primarily Japanese society in the US discussion. Zeng and LeTendre (1999) note that

> it has become soothing to focus on the problems of Japan . . . . By scapegoating Japan, American authors reduce the negative feelings we have about our own problems. By focusing on portrayals of Japan's stressed and "damaged" youth, we draw attention away from America's own schools. (Zeng and LeTendre 1999, 120–1)

In this way, "the 'problems' of Japanese education serve as a convenient outlet for American anxieties over their own school problems" (Zeng and LeTendre 1999, 104); in other words, uneasiness about aspects of education in the United States was projected onto Japan.

# The Chapters

In the following, the rationale for the selection of the cases discussed in this volume will be explained. Then, a short summary of the individual chapters will be given.

## The Rationale for the Selection of Cases

The book comprises chapters on individual countries from a wide range of contexts. Geographically speaking, the countries represented in the book lie in Asia, Australia, North and South America, and Europe. The individual country cases can be subdivided into two groups:

1. The first group of countries (Australia, Chile, Germany, Norway, United States) can be described as lying in the "PISA middle ground" with respect to their results, that is, their PISA scores lie close to, slightly below or slightly above the average results of PISA participants as a whole. These countries were chosen in order to see if and how in these countries PISA top scorers are chosen as projection screens, how the projections are connected to local conditions and how projections become connected to discussions in the respective countries.
2. The second group of countries and regions comprises PISA top scorers (Finland, Shanghai, Singapore, South Korea). Questions of interest here not only include how these countries deal with projections from outside,

how observers in these countries make sense of their success (and possibly try to use it as a resource), but also which projections they may make in turn. Due to the extraordinary echo the results of Shanghai in PISA 2009 produced in many countries (see Sellar and Lingard 2013), there are two chapters on Shanghai, one dealing with policy-makers' reactions (by Reyes and Tan), the other with academics' reactions (by Schulte).

## Looking from Below: Projections onto PISA Top Scorers

Lluís Parcerisa and Antoni Verger look at how the PISA results were processed and used by policy-makers in the context of education reforms in *Chile*. Among other things, they investigate the increasing influence of Finland and how actors from different political camps project radically different "slides" onto this reference society. They also discuss why some neighboring countries are conspicuously absent as reference societies in the Chilean discourse.

In their chapter, Bob Lingard and Sam Sellar look at policy-makers' projections onto East Asian education systems in the *Australian* context. Various political actors connect different projections to the East Asian PISA top scorers, placing them in the context of a supposed Australian educational "decline." They analyze the role of Asian proximity to and economic dependence on Asia for the particular shape and character of the projections and also explore the contested nature of new reference societies in the Australian educational landscape.

In his chapter on *Germany*, Florian Waldow analyzes how two complementary reference societies used as projection screens are constructed in the German quality press. These are on the one hand Finland as a positive and on the other hand the East Asian PISA top scorers as negative reference societies. He shows how the constructions of reference societies are grounded in stereotypical assumptions about these reference societies.

In her chapter, Kirsten Sivesind tracks how Finland was used as a positive reference in *Norwegian* education policy-making. She also gives an overview of the different Nordic countries' participation in ILSAs.

In her chapter, Nancy Green Saraisky analyzes the construction and use of reference societies in *US* media in the wake of PISA. She finds that Finland and Shanghai/China are the most prominent reference societies in the US media discussion. Different projections onto Finland and Shanghai/China are made, the case of Shanghai/China in particular being used to scandalize the US system of education. A unifying feature of references to the Finnish case on the one hand and the case of Shanghai/China on the other is that references to neither case lead to calls for actual policy borrowing.

## Coping with Success: Projections by PISA Top Scorers

The chapter on *Finland* by Piia Seppänen, Risto Rinne, Jaako Kaukko, and Sonja Kosunen shows how the PISA results were gradually "discovered" as a tool for agenda-setting and resource mobilization in Finnish education policy-making over the course of the various PISA rounds. The massive interest in Finnish education from other countries meant that policy discussions had to be "fitted" to the good PISA results. The authors also examine how Finnish politicians tried to turn the good PISA results into an exportable good.

In their chapter, Vicente Chua Reyes and Charlene Tan look at the responses of Chinese education officials to *Shanghai's* PISA success. Using concepts from Kleinian psychoanalysis, they explore "self-projections" constructing a self-image that is positive and negative at the same time, glorifying Shanghai's high scores while at the same time scandalizing (at least to a certain extent) the price paid for them, namely the effort put in by pupils in the shape of long working hours and homework.

The chapter by Barbara Schulte complements the preceding chapter on *Shanghai* by looking at academics' and educational newspapers' responses to Shanghai's PISA performance. The chapter develops a typology of responses and discusses the potential motives and agendas behind the responses and relates them to wider "policy regimes." The author shows how Shanghai's good results are perceived as a danger for the balance of education governance between different parts of the country and looks at the various stages of reflection and projection many of the responses to PISA discussed in the chapter have gone through, including the "double hermeneutic move" in which responses reflect on outside projections onto the Chinese case.

In his chapter, which deals with the *Singaporean* case, Søren Christensen discusses how league leaders are "transubstantiated" to "icons of educational excellence." He shows how these images have come to play a role for education reform in Singapore as an external endorsement of reform efforts. The self-projection by policy-makers does not take up the familiar "Asian" tropes of "drill" and "exam hell"; rather, policy-makers project these tropes onto parents' expectations, exhorting them to move away from them.

Finally, in their chapter on the *South Korean* case, Yoonmi Lee and Youl-Kwan Sung investigate the use of Finland as a projection screen for legitimizing certain policy agendas in South Korea. They show how references to Finnish education are tightly connected to struggles with Korean education and interpretations of the reasons for Korea's high scores. They also show that while Finland is popular as a projection screen, actual transfer mostly takes place from other systems, such as the United States.

In her conclusion to the volume, Gita Steiner-Khamsi reflects in a more general way on "what policy-makers do with PISA," bringing together some of the main lines of argumentation presented in this volume and placing them in the larger field of education policy studies.

Taken together, the different chapters in this volume show how differently ILSAs and the data they produce resonate with preexisting perceptions and discourses in different places and how this leads to different projections onto ILSA top scorers. They also show that projection is not confined to low performers. Actors in systems performing well in ILSAs such as PISA often do not simply bask in their success. Rather, they frequently also display, in Sørensen's graphic term (in this volume), "PISA envy" and project ideals of the "good" and the "bad" school onto other systems.

## Notes

1 According to Merton and Rossi (1968, 288), "reference group theory aims to systematize the determinants and consequences of those processes of evaluation and self-appraisal in which the individual takes the values or standards of other individuals and groups as a comparative frame of reference." Bendix transferred this notion from the individual and group level to the level of whole societies.

2 The political scientist David Wilsford (1985, 370) mentions in a footnote that reference societies could potentially also act as "negative models," but does not elaborate this point in detail, nor does he give any empirical examples.

3 In a famous experiment, psychologists Amos Tversky and Daniel Kahneman (1983) showed that adding context to a scenario made respondents choose this scenario as more likely to be true than another scenario that logically was at least as likely as the first but contained less context information.

4 The connection between reference societies and expected futures for one's own society is illustrated by a famous assertion made by the American journalist Lincoln Steffens after returning from a trip to the early Soviet Union and later quoted and repeated many times: "I have seen the future, and it works!" (quoted according to Kaplan 1974, 250).

5 It may be of interest to note here that in a now largely obsolete meaning, "projection" also denotes the central operation of alchemy, that is, the transmutation of base metals such as lead into gold or silver (*Oxford English Dictionary* 2017, entry "projection," meaning 1.)a). Arguably, hoping that an education reform will "turn to gold" by associating it with a PISA league leader such as Finland constitutes a modern form of political alchemy.

6 The article was published about a month after the publication of the results of PISA 2009, the PISA round in which Shanghai participated for the first time and immediately led the league tables in all three tested domains.

# References

Addey, C. (2018), "The Assessment Culture of International Organizations: 'From Philosophical Doubt to Statistical Certainty' through the Appearance and Growth of International Large-Scale Assessments," in C. Alarcón and M. Lawn (eds.), *Assessment Cultures: Historical Perspectives*, 379–408, Frankfurt a. M.: Peter Lang.

Addey, C., and Sellar, S. (2017), "The Rise of International Large-Scale Assessments and Rationales for Participation," *Compare*, 47(3), 434–43.

Andersson, J., and Hilson, M. (2009), "Images of Sweden and the Nordic Countries," *Scandinavian Journal of History*, 34(3), 219–28, doi: 10.1080/03468750903134681.

Anholt, S. (2007), *Competitive Identity: The New Brand Management for Nations, Cities and Regions*, Houndmills: Palgrave Macmillan.

Arbeitsgruppe Internationale Vergleichsstudie (2003), *Vertiefender Vergleich der Schulsysteme ausgewählter PISA-Teilnehmerstaaten: Kanada, England, Finnland, Frankreich, Niederlande, Schweden*, [In-Depth Comparison between School Systems of Selected PISA Participating States: Canada, England, Finland, France, the Netherlands, Sweden], Berlin: BMBF.

Arnswald, U. (2010), "Einleitung: Zum Utopie-Begriff und seiner Bedeutung in der Politischen Philosophie" [Introduction: On the Concept of Utopia and Its Meaning in Political Philosophy], in U. Arnswald and H.-P. Schütt (eds.), *Thomas Morus' Utopia und das Genre der Utopie in der Politischen Philosophie*, 1–35, Karlsruhe: KIT Scientific Publishing.

Auld, E., and Morris, P. (2016), "PISA, Policy and Persuasion: Translating Complex Conditions into Education 'Best Practice,'" *Comparative Education*, 52(2), 202–29, doi: 10.1080/03050068.2016.1143278.

Baird, J.-A., Johnson, S., Hopfenbeck, T. N., Isaacs, T., Sprague, T., Stobart, G., and Yu, G. (2016), "On the Supranational Spell of PISA in Policy," *Educational Research*, 58(2), 121–38, doi: 10.1080/00131881.2016.1165410.

Barber, M., and Mourshed, M. (2007), *How the World's Best-Performing School Systems Come Out on Top*, New York: McKinsey.

Baumeister, R. F., Dale, K., and Sommer, K. L. (1998), "Freudian Defense Mechanisms and Empirical Findings in Modern Social Psychology: Reaction Formation, Projection, Displacement, Undoing, Isolation, Sublimation, and Denial," *Journal of Personality*, 66(6), 1081–124, doi: 10.1111/1467–6494.00043.

Beckert, J. (2013), "Imagined Futures: Fictional Expectations in the Economy," *Theory and Society*, 42(3), 219–40, doi: 10.1007/s11186-013-9191-2.

Beckert, J. (2016), *Imagined Futures*, Cambridge: Harvard University Press.

Bendix, R. (1967), "Tradition and Modernity Reconsidered," *Comparative Studies in Society and History*, 9(3), 292–346, doi:10.1017/S0010417500004540.

Bendix, R. (1978), *Kings or People: Power and the Mandate to Rule*, Berkeley: University of California Press.

Bieber, T., Martens, K., Niemann, D., and Teltemann, J. (2014), "Towards a Global Model in Education? International Student Literacy Assessments and Their Impact on Policies and Institutions," in M. Hamilton, B. Maddox, and C. Addey (eds.), *Literacy as Numbers: Researching the Politics and Practices of International Literacy Assessment*, Cambridge: Cambridge University Press.

Bork, H. (2011), "Der Chinakracher" [The Chinese Firecracker], *Süddeutsche Zeitung*, January, 8.

Butts, R. F. (1973), "New Futures for Comparative Education," *Comparative Education Review*, 17(3), 289–94, doi: 10.2307/1186966.

Chattalas, M., Kramer, T., and Takada, H. (2008), "The Impact of National Stereotypes on the Country of Origin Effect: A Conceptual Framework," *International Marketing Review*, 25(1), 54–74.

Cooper, J. (2011), "Cognitive Dissonance Theory," *Handbook of Theories of Social Psychology*, 1, 377–98.

Fotaki, M. (2010), "Why Do Public Policies Fail So Often? Exploring Health Policy-Making as an Imaginary and Symbolic Construction," *Organization*, 17(6), 703–20, doi: 10.1177/1350508410366321.

Gatermann, R. (2002), "Bulmahn empfiehlt finnisches Vorbild für die Ganztagsschule: Bildungsministerin auf Lernreise in Skandinavien" [Bulmahn Recommends the Finnish Example for the All-Day School: The German Minister of Education on a Study Trip to Scandinavia], *Die Welt*, Mai, 23.

Gawronski, B. (2012), "Back to the Future of Dissonance Theory: Cognitive Consistency as a Core Motive," *Social Cognition*, 30(6), 652–68, doi: 10.1521/soco.2012.30.6.652.

Gorur, R. (2016), "Seeing Like PISA: A Cautionary Tale about the Performativity of International Assessments," *European Educational Research Journal*, 15(5), 598–616, doi:10.1177/1474904116658299.

Grek, S. (2009), "Governing by Numbers: The PISA 'Effect' in Europe," *Journal of Education Policy*, 24(1), 23–37.

Hamilton, M., Maddox, B., and Addey, C. (2015), *Literacy as Numbers: Researching the Politics and Practices of International Literary Assessment*, Cambridge: Cambridge University Press.

Hattie, J. (2009), *Visible Learning: A Synthesis of over 800 Meta-Analyses Relating to Achievement*, London: Routledge.

Herz, M. F., and Diamantopoulos, A. (2013), "Activation of Country Stereotypes: Automaticity, Consonance, and Impact," *Journal of the Academy of Marketing Science*, 41(4), 400–17, doi: 10.1007/s11747-012-0318-1.

Herz, M. F., and Diamantopoulos, A. (2017), "I Use It but Will Tell You That I Don't: Consumers' Country-of-Origin Cue Usage Denial," *Journal of International Marketing*, 25(2), 52–71, doi: 10.1509/jim.16.0051.

Hyman, H. H. (1942), "The Psychology of Status," *Archives of Psychology* (269), 5–38, 80–6.

Kamens, D. H., and McNeely, C. L. (2010), "Globalization and the Growth of International Educational Testing and National Assessment," *Comparative Education Review*, 54(1), 5–25, doi:10.1086/648471.

Kaplan, J. (1974), *Lincoln Steffens: A Biography*, New York: Simon and Schuster.

Larsen, M. A., and Beech, J. (2014), "Spatial Theorizing in Comparative and International Education Research," *Comparative Education Review*, 58(2), 191–214.

Leclerc, F., Schmitt, B. H., and Dubé, L. (1994), "Foreign Branding and Its Effects on Product Perceptions and Attitudes," *Journal of Marketing Research*, 31(2), 263–70.

Lingard, B., and Rawolle, S. (2011), "New Scalar Politics: Implications for Education Policy," *Comparative Education*, 47(4), 489–502.

List, E. (2014), *Psychoanalyse: Geschichte, Theorien, Anwendungen* [Psychoanalysis: History, Theories, Applications], 2nd ed., *UTB. Psychologie, Medizin*, Wien: facultas.

Luhmann, N. (1976), "The Future Cannot Begin: Temporal Structures in Modern Society," *Social Research*, 43(1), 130–52.

Magnusson, P., Westjohn S. A., and Zdravkovic, S. (2011), "'What? I Thought Samsung Was Japanese': Accurate or Not, Perceived Country of Origin Matters," *International Marketing Review*, 28(5), 454–72.

Martens, K., and Niemann, D. (2013), "When Do Numbers Count? The Differential Impact of the PISA Rating and Ranking on Education Policy in Germany and the US," *German Politics*, 22(3), 314–32, doi: 10.1080/09644008.2013.794455.

Matthies, A.-L. (2002), "Finnisches Bildungswesen und Familienpolitik: Ein 'leuchtendes' Beispiel?" [The Finnish Education System and Family Policy: A "Glowing" Example?], *Aus Politik und Zeitgeschichte* (B41), 38–45.

Merton, R. K., and Rossi, A. S. (1968), "Contributions to the Theory of Reference Group Behavior," in R. K. Merton (ed.), *Social Theory and Social Structure*, 279–334, New York: Free Press.

Meyer, H.-D., and Benavot, A. (eds.) (2013), *PISA, Power, and Policy: The Emergence of Global Educational Governance*, Didcot: Symposium.

Meyer, J. W. (1986), "The Politics of Educational Crises in the United States," in William K. Cummings, E. R. Beauchamp, S. Ichikawa, V. N. Kobayashi, and M. Ushiogi (eds.), *Educational Policies in Crisis: Japanese and American Perspectives*, 44–58, New York: Praeger.

Musiał, K. (2002), *Roots of the Scandinavian Model: Images of Progress in the Era of Modernisation*, Baden-Baden: Nomos.

OECD (2011), *Strong Performers and Successful Reformers in Education: Lessons from PISA for the United States, Programme for International Student Assessment*, Paris: Organisation for Economic Co-operation and Development.

Oxford English Dictionary (2017), "Projection," in *Oxford English Dictionary Online*, Oxford: Oxford University Press.

Pizmony-Levy, O. (2013), "Testing for All: The Emergence and Development of International Assessment of Student Achievement, 1958–2012," unpublished PhD dissertation, Indiana University.

Sahlberg, P. (2011), "PISA in Finland: An Education Miracle or an Obstacle to Change?" *CEPS Journal: Center for Educational Policy Studies Journal, 1*(3), 119–40.

Schriewer, J. (1990), "The Method of Comparison and the Need for Externalization: Methodological Criteria and Sociological Concepts," in J. Schriewer and B. Holmes (eds.), *Theories and Methods in Comparative Education*, 2nd ed., 25–83, Frankfurt a. M.: Peter Lang.

Scott, J. C. (1998), *Seeing Like a State: How Certain Schemes to Improve the Human Condition Have Failed*, New Haven: Yale University Press.

Sellar, S., and Lingard, B. (2013), "Looking East: Shanghai, PISA 2009 and the Reconstitution of Reference Societies in the Global Education Policy Field," *Comparative Education, 49*(4), 464–85.

Sellar, S., and Lingard, B. (2014), "The OECD and the Expansion of PISA: New Global Modes of Governance in Education," *British Educational Research Journal, 40*(6), 917–36.

Smithers, A. (2004), *England's Education: What Can Be Learned by Comparing Countries?*, Liverpool: University of Liverpool.

Steiner-Khamsi, G. (2003), "The Politics of League Tables," *Journal of Social Science Education*, 1, http://www.jsse.org/index.php/jsse/article/view/470 (accessed January 31, 2018).

Steiner-Khamsi, G. (2004), "Blazing a Trail for Policy Theory and Practice," in G. Steiner-Khamsi (ed.), *The Global Politics of Educational Borrowing and Lending*, 201–20, New York: Teachers College Press.

Steiner-Khamsi, G. (2017), "Focusing on the Local to Understand Why the Global Resonates and How Governments Appropriate ILSAs for National Agenda Setting," *Compare, 47*(3), 443–6.

Stone, D. A. (2012), *Policy Paradox: The Art of Political Decision Making*, 3rd ed., New York: Norton.

Stone, D. A. (2016), "Quantitative Analysis as Narrative," in M. Bevir and R. A. W. Rhodes (ed.), *Routledge Handbook of Interpretive Political Science*, 157–70, Milton Park: Routledge.

Takayama, K. (2010), "Politics of Externalization in Reflexive Times: Reinventing Japanese Education Reform Discourses through 'Finnish PISA Success,'" *Comparative Education Review, 54*(1), 51–75, doi:10.1086/644838.

Takayama, K. (2018), "The Constitution of East Asia as a Counter Reference Society through PISA: A Postcolonial/Decolonial Intervention," *Globalisation, Societies and Education*, doi: 10.1080/14767724.2018.1532282.

Tversky, A., and Kahneman, D. (1983), "Extensional versus Intuitive Reasoning: The Conjunction Fallacy in Probability Judgment," *Psychological Review*, *90*(4), 293.

Verlegh, P. W. J., and Steenkamp, J.-B. E. M. (1999), "A Review and Meta-Analysis of Country-of-Origin Research," *Journal of Economic Psychology*, *20*(5), 521–46, doi: 10.1016/s0167-4870(99)00023-9.

Waldow, F. (2010), "Der Traum vom 'skandinavisch schlau Werden' " [The Dream of "Becoming Smart the Scandinavian Way"], *Zeitschrift für Pädagogik*, *56*(4), 497–511.

Waldow, F. (2016), "Das Ausland als Gegenargument: Fünf Thesen zur Bedeutung nationaler Stereotype und negativer Referenzgesellschaften" [Foreign Countries as a Counterargument: Five Propositions Regarding the Significance of National Stereotypes and Negative Reference Societies], *Zeitschrift für Pädagogik*, *62*(3), 403–21.

Waldow, F. (2017), "Projecting Images of the 'Good' and the 'Bad School': Top Scorers in Educational Large-Scale Assessments as Reference Societies," *Compare*, *47*(5), 647–64.

Wilsford, D. (1985), "The Conjuncture of Ideas and Interests: A Note on Explanations of the French Revolution," *Comparative Political Studies*, *18*(3), 357–72.

Wimmer, A., and Glick Schiller, N. (2002), "Methodological Nationalism and Beyond: Nationstate Building, Migration and the Social Sciences," *Global Networks: A Journal of Transnational Affairs*, *2*(4), 301–34.

Wiseman, A. W. (2010), "The Uses of Evidence for Educational Policymaking: Global Contexts and International Trends," *Review of Research in Education*, *34*(1), 1–24.

You, Y., and Morris, P. (2016), "Imagining School Autonomy in High-Performing Education Systems: East Asia as a Source of Policy Referencing in England," *Compare: A Journal of Comparative and International Education*, *46*(6), 882–905, doi: 10.1080/03057925.2015.1080115.

Zeng, K., and LeTendre, G. (1999), " 'The Dark Side of . . . ': Suicide, Violence and Drug Use in Japanese Schools," in G. LeTendre (ed.), *Competitor or Ally? Japan's Role in American Educational Debates*, 103–21, New York: Falmer.

Zymek, B. (1975), *Das Ausland als Argument in der pädagogischen Reformdiskussion: Schulpolitische Selbstrechtfertigung, Auslandspropaganda, internationale Verständigung und Ansätze zu einer vergleichenden Erziehungswissenschaft in der internationalen Berichterstattung deutscher pädagogischer Zeitschriften, 1871–1952.* [Foreign Countries as an Argument in the Discussion of Educational Reform: Self-Justification in School Policy, Foreign Propaganda, International Understanding and Approaches to a Comparative Education Science in International Reporting of German Pedagogic Journals, 1871–1952.] Ratingen: Henn.

Part One

# Looking from Below: Interpreting National Projections into International League Leaders

# 2

# PISA Projections in Chile: The Selective Use of League Leaders in the Enactment of Recent Education Reforms

Lluís Parcerisa and Antoni Verger

## Introduction

In the past few decades, international large-scale assessments (ILSAs) have promoted profound debates on educational reform. In countries as diverse as Germany (Ertl 2006), Japan (Takayama 2008), Spain (Bonal and Tarabini 2013; Engel 2015), and Chile (Cox and Meckes 2016), obtaining "negative"—or "lower-than-expected"—results in ILSAs, such as the Programme for International Student Assessment (PISA), has generated important disputes in the education field and, in some cases, has even triggered profound educational reform processes.

According to Steiner-Khamsi (2003, 2), ILSAs' results can be used by local policy-makers and other stakeholders to "scandalize" or "glorify" their own education system and polices, as well as to try to emulate education systems from other countries. Consequently, the discourses of "scandalization" and "glorification" can lead to processes of policy borrowing or policy lending, respectively. Similarly, Breakspear (2012, 2) states that the "external shocks" produced by the ILSAs results can favor the opening of "windows of political opportunities" (cf. Kingdon 1995) that can be used by local policy entrepreneurs and other education stakeholders to legitimize policy change in education. In this sense, ILSAs' results can be mobilized and used strategically by policy-makers and other key actors (media, think tanks, social movements, etc.) to advance their particular reform agendas (Grek 2009; Gorur 2017). Overall, the reception of results in ILSAs can be mediated by a broad range of factors and local contingencies. Specifically, factors of a semiotic, historical, political, economic, and administrative nature can affect and shape the local responses to ILSA results. Thus, we need to analyze carefully the national policy contexts in order to understand the varied responses that ILSAs trigger.

The main aim of this chapter is to examine the reception and translation of ILSA results and, particularly, the ILSA projections (see Steiner-Khamsi 2016; Waldow 2017) articulated in the context of recent education reforms in Chile. These reforms were initiated as a response to a strong period of social mobilization and unrest in the Chilean education field led by the students' movement. This movement, which emerged with force in 2006 and was strongly backed by public opinion, protested against educational inequalities and profit in education and demanded the right to free and inclusive education at all levels. The ILSA results permeated Chile right in the middle of the intense education reform debates that were promoted by these strong social protests and demands.

In this chapter, we analyze which ILSA league leaders have been selected and by whom in the context of the heated educational debates held in Chile in the last decade, and how the main Chilean political forces explain and give meaning to the educational success of such league leaders. With these objectives in mind, the chapter is organized in four main sections. The first section provides a general picture of the context of the education reform in Chile. The second section analyzes the main reasons and factors that explain the growing influence of ILSAs in the Chilean education policy arena. The third section focuses on PISA projections in Chile; here, we explore the increasing influence of Finland, as a reference society, as well as the main convergences and divergences that emerge when Finland is used as an educational model in the Chilean political sphere. Finally, the chapter explores the reasons why some countries—including "good performers" in the Latin American region—are absent from the Chilean education policy scape, and why other countries are in contrast conceived as reference societies.

Methodologically, the research combines semi-structured interviews with policy-makers and key education stakeholders (Verd and Lozares 2016) with document content analysis (Bowen 2009; Mayring 2000). The interviews have focused on the main hot topics of the educational debate in Chile; namely, students' selection/exclusion on behalf of schools, education gratuity, and the abolition of for-profit motives in education, in two different reform periods (2006–10 and 2014–18). In total, twenty-one semi-structured interviews were conducted in the period that lasted from March 17 to June 25 of 2016. The sample of documents includes the Final Report of the Presidential Advisory Council (which includes the Presidential message, the main debates that were held within the advisory council, as well as the places of consensus and disagreement between actors), the History of the General Law of Education (History of the Law 20.370 2009), and the History of the Law of School Inclusion (History of the Law 20.845 2015). The last two documents include the Presidential message that justifies each law, as well as all the transcriptions of the debates derived from the process of enactment of the laws, including parliamentary minutes, and the reports produced by different parliamentary commissions, such as the Education Commission or the Finance Commission. To analyze all these data, the research followed an iterative process that combines both content and thematic analysis (Bowen 2009), which was carried out with the software Atlas.ti. Specifically, we conducted a descriptive analysis based on word frequency, which allowed us to identify the main trends regarding the use of reference societies in the political arena. Furthermore, we applied a bottom-up coding strategy (Corbin and Strauss 1990), and grouped the codes thematically within code families in order to see what were the main topics used in association to which reference societies.

## Context of the Reform: The End of Students' Selection, Co-payment and Profit in the Chilean Educational System

Since the end of the 1970s, the Chilean educational system has been involved in a constant process of reform. With the military coup of Pinochet, deep market-oriented educational reforms were adopted. These reforms went against the equity-oriented education policies of the previous democratic government of Salvador Allende (Pinedo Henríquez 2011; Burton 2012). The military government led by Pinochet, also known as *Junta Militar* (1973–90), transferred state power and resources in education to the market (Bellei 2016) and applied strong cuts to public education (Mizala 2007). The educational policies adopted by the *Junta Militar* focused on the radical decentralization of education at the municipal level, the creation of standardized tests at the national level—the PER test (*Programa de Evaluación del Rendimiento Escolar*), later on called SIMCE (*Sistema de Medición de la Calidad de la Educación*)—and, more importantly, the implementation of a voucher system to promote school choice and competition among schools. Policies that undermined teachers' working conditions and professional status were also implemented in that period. In the last year of the dictatorship, Pinochet enacted the Constitutional Education Law (LOCE) as a way to consolidate, with an organic law, the market approach to educational governance.

Through these three elements (municipalization, standardized tests, and the voucher scheme), the *Junta Militar*, which was directly influenced by the pro-market and monetarist ideas of the economists of the University of Chicago led by Milton Friedman, wanted to create a free market environment in education. Promoters of market-oriented reforms believed that these policies would increase the quality and efficiency of the education system by means of further school competition (Mizala 2007; Falabella 2015). Bellei and Vanni (2015, 3) summarize the main arguments of market advocates in these words:

> families should have the greatest possible freedom to choose their children's schools; the schools, too, ought to compete openly to obtain the greatest number of students; schools that are unable to attract families would become financially unviable and either close or react by improving the quality of their service and so becoming competitive in the school market. This virtuous competitive dynamic would, in the long run, produce an improvement in educational quality and increase the efficiency of school management.

In the first democratic period (1990–2005), educational reforms were directed toward increasing public and private resources in education. To this purpose, the government approved a co-payment system in publicly funded private schools, promoted the full school day, implemented school improvement programs, and introduced curricular reforms (Cornejo and Reyes 2008). Despite the strong tensions within the governing coalition between supporters of a strong state in education and those advocating a subsidiary role of the state (Mizala 2007), during the first democratic period there were no major changes in the core logic of the Chilean education system and the market logic prevailed (Falabella 2015).

In the early 2000s, as a result of the mediocre average students' performance in the national standardized test (SIMCE) and in ILSAs, mainly PISA and Trends in International Mathematics and Science Study (TIMSS), many stakeholders, including decision-makers, started questioning the quality of the Chilean education system.[1] In the first decade of the 2000s, the evidence derived from national and international large-scale assessments became increasingly influential in the Chilean political debate. The results obtained in both national and international tests were used to "scandalize" and underline the problems of the educational system, as well as the necessity to promote more meaningful reforms that end up crystallizing in classroom practices (Bellei and Vanni 2015). In the end, in response to the "shock" produced by bad tests' results and the hegemonic interpretations around the reasons why these results were low, the government began deploying devices of new public management and accountability in the educational sector (Falabella 2015).

The educational policies applied since the dictatorship, but also during the first democratic period, contributed to generate one of the most unequal and segregated educational systems in the world (OECD 2004). The theory of change defended by the advocates of pro-market reforms omitted the existence of "market failures" including asymmetries of information between different social groups, school vertical segmentation (as opposed to the expected horizontal segmentation), and schools selecting the most academically able students, among other discriminatory practices (Verger, Bonal, and Zancajo 2016).

## The Students' Movement and the Promotion of Several Educational Reforms

The social movement led by secondary students in 2006 and by university students in 2011 challenged market theories in education, and placed education at the center of the political agenda. The ideas included in the Organization for Economic Co-operation and Development (OECD) review of Chilean education (2004), which warned about the high level of segmentation within the Chilean education system and about the negative effects of education marketization, resonated strongly among students and teachers' organizations, and legitimated social mobilization (interview Teacher Union 9). The mission that conducted this OECD review was led by the Stanford University professor Martin Carnoy, and the resulting report was widely circulated in Chile. The students' movement and teachers' organizations incorporated some of the main ideas, data, and recommendations included in this report:

> Chile has given an inappropriate weight to the education market, which later led to another OECD report which pointed out that quasi-markets in education did not work . . . that's when it was said Chile has built the most segmented school system in the world. (Interview Teacher Union 9)

The students' movement brought to the table the need to adopt, instead of more compensatory and accountability measures, structural changes that would advance toward the de-commodification of education and a stronger public education system. Among other issues, students were able to place on the agenda issues such as the end of discrimination (e.g., students being selected/discriminated by schools), the repeal of the LOCE law approved by Pinochet, the right to free education and, related to the latter, the end of profit in education (interview key informant 6; interview Teacher Union 9; interview Students' movement activist 11). In one word, the students demanded free, inclusive, quality public education for all (Bellei and Cabalín 2013).

Bachelet's government established a Presidential Advisory Council, which included a large number of political and social actors as a way to channel the demands deriving from the intense social mobilizations in a more institutional way (Burton 2012). Within the Advisory Council, there were three existing "epistemic coalitions" (left, center-left, and right) (Cox 2012), each of which attempted to impose its vision of the causes of the educational crisis and its preferred solutions. Despite disagreements regarding the role of the State and the market in education, a certain consensus was reached regarding the need to carry out curricular reform, overcome the LOCE, and create a better system of accountability to ensure quality education (Larroulet and Montt 2010; Cox 2012). Although to a lesser extent, the center-left and the right-wing coalitions also agreed on the idea of maintaining a mixed-supply education system (with both public and private providers); they also agreed on the need to forbid the selection of students in basic education (Cox 2012). However, the representatives of the leftist coalition did not feel represented by the final agreements reached within the Advisory Council and withdrew from the final report (Bloque Social 2006; Vera 2011).

The government selected some of the proposals from the Presidential Advisory Council final report and, partially on the basis of these proposals, drafted the General Education Law (LGE, for its acronym in Spanish), as well as a Superintendency project. The LGE draft banned profit in education and school selection until the eighth school year. The right-wing party strongly opposed these two measures and presented an alternative project. Due to the veto capacity of the right-wing party, both the governing coalition and the conservatives had to sit down to negotiate in a very small technical-political committee. As a result of these negotiations, a new political pact that would crystallize in the Agreement for the Quality of Education was forged (Larroulet and Montt 2010). In this agreement, the bases of the future General Law of Education and of the National System of Assurance of the Quality of the school education were laid down, in which a new public management approach and related accountability mechanisms would occupy a central place. The student movement achieved some of its objectives, such as the repeal of LOCE, or the introduction of advances—if timid—against discrimination in education (Bellei 2016). However, the more ambitious demands of the students were finally excluded from the LGE.

In 2010, the right-wing coalition led by Sebastián Piñera came to the government. The Piñera's government was strongly committed to market-oriented principles and deepened this logic through the implementation of several performance-based incentives in education. Nonetheless, despite Piñera's electoral promises of transforming the education system, in practice, the educational policies developed by his government basically represented a continuation of the policies of the previous center-left government (Bellei and Vanni 2015).

In 2011, the university students' movement led another wave of social protests against the marketization of education. University student protests facilitated the adoption of institutional changes in higher education (Bellei, Cabalín, and Orellana 2014), but had effects beyond the higher education sector. This new cycle of students' mobilization was even more intense than the 2006 one and had a wider support from different sectors of society and public opinion. In the mid-term, this mobilization would facilitate the change in the correlation of forces between political actors and impinged those claims to decommodify education with higher centrality in the political agenda.

In 2014, the center-left government led by Michele Bachelet came to power with a political program that incorporated many of the demands of the students' movement. This government proposed to move from a paradigm where education is a market good, to another paradigm where education is conceived as a social right (Bellei 2016). The first law adopted in this new period was the School Inclusion Law (History of the Law 20.845 2015), through which the government aimed to end profit and discrimination in education (e.g., co-payment and students' selection). However, the reform process sparked a real battle of ideas and strong resistance from different actors, including opposition parties, families, neoliberal think tanks, and private schools. Even the more conservative factions of the governing coalition raised some concerns with the reform. In the context of the intense parliamentary debates on education that took place in that political period, the evidence coming from PISA (and from the OECD in general) and related references to league leaders were key in mobilizing policy ideas, constructing meanings, and framing strategies through which to persuade political opponents and civil society about the benefits or the drawbacks of the reform.

## The Changing Influence of ILSAs in the Chilean Education Policy Arena

Chile is a country with a long history of students' test-based assessments, and its participation in different ILSAs is directly related to it (Cariola et al. 2011).

Indeed, Chile is one of the first developing countries, together with India and Iran, to participate in international large-scale assessments (Lockheed 2013). Chile's first participation in ILSAs was in the 1960s, when it took part in the International Association for the Evaluation of Educational Achievement (IEA) "Six Subject Study" (Cariola et al. 2011; Cox and Meckes 2016). Nevertheless, from 1973 to 1990 its participation in this initiative was truncated by the dictatorship. Since its return to democracy, Chile has participated in a wide range of ILSAs, such as ERCE (UNESCO), TIMSS (IEA) or PISA (OECD) (Cox and Meckes 2016). With the passage of time, the results of Chile in these different ILSAs have gained media attention and relevance in policy-making circles.

As happened in other developing countries (see Lockheed 2013), during the 1990s, the IEA was perceived in Chile as a relevant international organization in terms of evaluation and research in education. In fact, Chile's participation in TIMSS was seen a relevant learning experience by the Ministry of Education (Cariola et al. 2011). First, the participation in TIMSS was seen as an opportunity to gain "first-hand knowledge" on ILSAs technologies, in order to improve procedures and processes related to the national standardized test. At the same time, the participation in TIMSS was perceived as strategic in terms of the country's development, because it provided access to valuable comparative data that would allow policy-makers to take more informed decisions in order to achieve international standards and promote the country's competitiveness in the global economy. According to Cox and Meckes (2016), TIMSS had practical effects in particular education domains such as teacher education, curriculum, and assessment.

From the ILSAs perspective, the 2000s were marked by Chile' participation in the OECD/PISA. A study carried out by Breakspear (2012) shows that in a country like Chile—which was below the PISA average in reading, mathematics and science, the political impact of PISA and its influence on the decision-making process was *moderate*.[2] Nonetheless, Cox and Meckes (2016) point out that PISA 2000 and 2003 had a consistent impact on curriculum and assessment, while the 2009 and 2012 editions had a more political type of impact in nature, mainly in the context of the definition of the School Inclusion Law.

In the Chilean education debate, both PISA and TIMSS have installed the idea in the collective imaginaries of the education system being mediocre and "stagnated" (Bellei and Vanni 2015, 9; see also Cariola et al. 2011). The results of both ILSAs, but especially PISA, have been used to justify the urgency of profound education policy changes:

In Chile [PISA] has had a role because it has allowed to install the discourse on the stagnation of the results in Chile. Here is something that at least serves us much to argue why it is necessary to make deep transformations in the educational system, and above all, because PISA . . . has indicated what are the gaps and the segregation that exists in the system. It is very unavoidable that if you say, well, it is the second most segregated country in the world measured by PISA . . . So, these are issues that are important to justify the need of the [current] reform. (interview MoE 1)

In the past decade, evidence from PISA (and the OECD more broadly) has become increasingly important in the educational debate. References to PISA have more than doubled in a few years, specifically in the period that goes from the deliberations for the General Education Law (2009) to the deliberations for the School Inclusion Law (2015). In this period, references to PISA have gone from sixteen (History of the Law 20.370 2009) to thirty-six (History of the Law 20.845 2015), and consequently, PISA has become the hegemonic ILSA in the Chilean education policy. In contrast, TIMSS has lost centrality in the education policy debate, transiting from fifteen citations in the debates on the General Law of Education (2009) to only two in context of the School Inclusion Law (2015).[3]

The lower use of TIMSS data in the education policy field in Chile is related to factors of a different nature. First, it is important to mention that, in Chile, the first results of TIMSS-R in year 1999 were presented privately to a small number of experts (mainly members of the Ministry of Education and academics) and without the presence of the media. Secondly, Chile did not participate in TIMSS 2007 (although it participated in TIMSS 2011), since at that time the government prioritized participation in PISA 2006 and in other regional large-scale assessments led by UNESCO (Cariola et al. 2011). Both factors, together with the increasing global influence of PISA, undermined the influence of TIMSS in the Chilean public arena.

Lockheed (2013) considers that the growing influence of PISA in education policy worldwide could be attributed to a range of different reasons. First, Lockheed (2013) points to the fact that the PISA tests are promoted by the OECD, which is one of the most powerful and legitimate international organizations in the global governance of education. Secondly, the fact that many secondary analyses of PISA results are carried out by independent economists makes the evidence coming from these tests very attractive and handy to policy-makers. Thirdly, the OECD Secretariat has the capacity to place a much higher number of resources in the dissemination of PISA results than the representatives of other ILSAs such as TIMSS.

> In Chile in particular, PISA is perceived as a useful instrument that serves to
> assess the situation of education in the country in comparison to other countries
> of the region and to developed countries: I think that [PISA] is an important
> thermometer to see what the situation of our country is and how to have a broad
> perspective. (interview ExMoE 2)

Overall, in Chile, like in many other countries, the OECD enjoys a great
reputation among national education policy-makers and PISA is perceived as
"the global benchmark of developed countries" (Kamens 2013). Not surprisingly,
Chile is interested in improving its position in the PISA ranking as a way to
differentiate itself from other southern countries and enter into the "club" of
developed countries (interview ExMoE2; interview ExMoE 3). In addition, the
"knowledge products" of the OECD research centers, such as the Center for
Educational Research and Innovation (CERI), are very well circulated among
and appreciated by Chilean policy-makers (interview ExMoE 3).

The use of ILSAs in Chile and the selection of particular "reference societies"
in the education domain—including some of the PISA "league leaders"—
cannot be separated from the "hot topics" in the national educational debate
(see Steiner-Khamsi 2016). In particular, in the Chilean education reform,
evidence from the OECD was key in legitimizing the School Inclusion Law,
and with it, the end of profit-making in education, and the prohibition of
co-payment and students' selection. According to one senior Ministry of
Education official, the OECD provided evidence and policy-briefs to local
policy-makers, which were "very important to place the national discussion in
a comparative perspective" (interview MoE 1). Moreover, Andreas Schleicher,
Director for Education and Skills at the OECD, intervened directly in the
education reform debate by, among other things, writing two articles in the
most well-circulated Chilean newspaper where he openly supported the main
objectives and contents of the School Inclusion Law (see Schleicher 2014a;
2014b).

## PISA Projections and Reference Societies in Chile

In the "governing by numbers" era (cf. Rose 1991; Grek 2009), we are witnessing
the emergence of "new processes of externalization and policy borrowing
and the reconstitution of reference societies for national education systems"
(Lingard 2011, 369). In this line of inquiry, the concept of "PISA projections"

(cf. Waldow, Takayama, and Sung 2014; Steiner-Khamsi 2016) invites to explore the reasons that explain why some league leaders become reference societies in some educational settings (and not in others). In the following subsections we examine the emerging "reference societies" within the Chilean educational debate as well as the meanings attached to them.

## The Increasing Influence of Finland in Chilean Education Policy-Making

Chilean policy-makers have referred to a wide range of countries as reference societies during the enactment of different educational reforms. Despite the great influence of Anglo-Saxon countries in the Chilean policy space, in recent years, Finland has been very much present in the Chilean political debate on education (see Figure 2.1). The growing influence of Finland, far from being an isolated phenomenon in Chilean education, is a global trend that has been experienced in many other world locations since this Nordic country became a top performer in most relevant ILSAs (Sahlberg 2011; Kamens 2013; Takayama, Waldow, and Sung 2013).

As can be seen in Figure 2.1, in addition to Finland, other countries such as the United States, South Korea, Germany, the Netherlands, Spain, and Ireland were also cited in the debates that took place between 2006 and 2009 in the context of the definition of the General Law of Education (LGE).

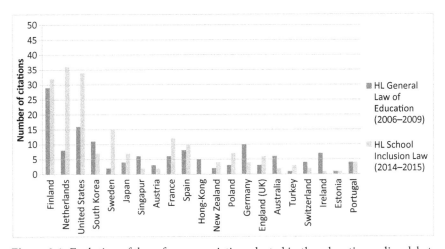

**Figure 2.1** Evolution of the reference societies selected in the education policy debate
*Source*: Authors

Later on, in the debate for the School Inclusion Law, five countries became particularly prominent. Together with Finland, the Netherlands and the United States stand out, followed by Sweden and France (see Figure 2.2). Nonetheless, the fact that the Education Commission of the House of Representatives selected France, the United States and the Netherlands as "case studies" contributed to these countries being overrepresented in the chart. Chilean policy-makers pay attention to the Netherlands because it combines a decentralized quasi-market structure (similar to the Chilean one) with high performance in ILSAs (interview FMoE 4; interview, ExMoE 2). In the case of the United States, the focus was on the "role of school districts" in relation to the allocation of students to schools:

> In the United States, some districts assign students to schools in consideration of their academic diversity, class size, and income diversity. (History of the Law 20.845 2015, 69)

On its part, France was selected as a "counter-example" of a centralized state with strong public sector and free education:

> Yes, because . . . there was an agreement with the ambassadors and because in both systems there were interesting aspects to look at. France because it was starting relevant reforms and Finland by the example it meant in the world in terms of its educational practice, and Chile looks at it. (interview MoE 1)

Finally, Sweden was chosen to reflect on the negative effects of education privatization and for-profit schools, in terms of learning outcomes and equity.

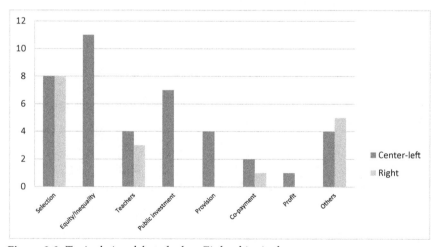

**Figure 2.2** Topics being debated when Finland is cited
*Source*: Authors

> The country that has made the least progress in this period is Sweden, where quality and equity fell, due to the opening of private-subsidized schools with ends of profit. (History of the Law 20.845 2015, 637)

Although it was not selected as a case study, Finland was highly relevant in the public discussion and captured the attention of policy-makers and experts. Some of them even did "international policy tourism" (cf. Whitty 2012, 354) to Helsinki in order to learn from the Finnish experience. Next, we analyze how the example of Finland is used, usually in a contradictory way, in relation to the hottest topics of the Chilean educational debate (namely, end of profit, student selection, and co-payment).

## Projecting Different Slides on the Same Screen: Convergences and Divergences within the Political Spectrum

Top-performing countries in ILSAs are often invoked in national and subnational education debates. Nevertheless, those countries that end up being selected as reference societies, and the use and meaning attributed to their success, can vary between countries, but also between different political factions within the same country. Therefore, in order to delve into the study of the dynamics of policy borrowing, it is important to inquire into why and how reference societies are used in the political debate to facilitate or hinder the enactment of a particular education reform model. Reference societies are constructed and settled in collective imaginaries in concrete political, cultural, and economic contexts, and, in particular, historical moments. In Chile, reference societies have evolved throughout history, so that according to some observers:

> At all ages, we have had educational models: at the end of the nineteenth century and the beginning of the twentieth, German education. Afterwards, the New School and the Education for Democracy. Today New Zealand, Finland and Korea are our models. In all of them, there is a predominance of free and pluralistic state education. (History of the Law 20.845 2015, 833–4)

In the case of Chile, since the students' mobilization of the year 2006, Finland has resonated strongly within both the policy and the civil society fields, since references to this country are connected with demands of higher quality in public schools and more equity in the education system. In general terms, the example of Finland was mostly used by center-left policy-makers and left-leaning stakeholders (64 percent), while in the case of the right-wing forces, which traditionally have felt a greater attraction toward the Anglo-Saxon countries, Finland had a smaller presence (36 percent).

Nonetheless, counterintuitively, during the debate on the School Inclusion Law, right-wing actors cited Finland more than the left. Specifically, the right-wing coalition, that only cited Finland twice in the context of the General Law of Education, cited this Nordic country nineteen times in the context of the School Inclusion Law. Meanwhile, the citations made by the center-left decreased from twenty-two to sixteen. According to Bellei (2016), the deliberations for the adoption of the School Inclusion Law were marked by a strong resistance from a broad conservative coalition, in which the main right-wing party channeled the demands of neoliberal think tanks, parents associations, and organizations of private schools providers. For the reasons we develop below, the right-wing party strategically mobilized the example of Finland as a way to challenge the pro-inclusion law.

Figure 2.2 shows the education reform hot topics that were associated to references to Finland by Chilean politicians from the two predominant political positions in the Parliament.

Regarding the first topic, *students' selection*, Finland was used by both the center-left and the right at the same level, but with very different objectives. In the case of the center-left, the comparison with Finland is used to argue that academic excellence can be combined with educational inclusion, and to show the negative effects of students' selection on quality and equity in education. The left uses the example of Finland to delegitimize the fact that schools select students based on their academic performance due to its negative effects in terms of social inequalities:

> Regarding Finland, I simply want to say that in this country students selection is applied at age 15, at age 15! We would like to be Finland, but we are not. We have a completely heterogeneous situation. And in societies as heterogeneous as ours, the recommendation is not to select, it is not to discriminate under any circumstances. I do not even want to talk about surname discrimination. (History of the Law 20.845 2015, 1479)

On their part, right-wing party representatives use the example of Finland to argue that in many top-performing countries students' selection is a common practice, and that this practice does not necessarily harm vulnerable students. Moreover, the right wing uses PISA data and the example of Finland in particular, to maintain that Chile is a country with low levels of students' selection.

[Student] selection does not harm vulnerable students. Examples: Finland, Holland and Singapore. (History of the Law 20.845 2015, 661)

The equality frame, at least in relation to the Finnish case, is exclusively articulated by the center-left. The example of Finland is specifically used by the center-left to scandalize the Chilean educational system for its high level of commodification and segregation, the enormous social and educational inequalities, and the low performance of the most disadvantaged students. The center-left is also the only actor resorting to Finland to defend the importance of public funding and state provision in education, as well as the end of profit generation in the education system.

Both right and center-left parties emphasize that teacher policy is a key issue to understand the Finnish success in PISA and that useful lessons can be extracted from this. The professional status of teachers, including how demanding the entry to the teaching profession and the training they receive is, are emphasized by the center-left. On the contrary, the right-wing coalition is more focused on the effectiveness of teachers and on the autonomy of Finnish schools to hire teachers. In fact, for the right, the Finnish policies on teachers delegitimize the inclusion reform being carried out in Chile:

This reform [the Inclusion Law] closes schools, because it doesn't ask the right questions. Why do families, whenever they can, take their children out of municipal education? . . . I hope that those who travel to Finland will see with more pragmatism that the key is to put teachers at the center of the discussion. (History of the Law 20.845 2015, 428)

Regarding the co-payment policy, the left uses the Finnish example to point out that in the top-performing countries, families' expenditure in education is much lower than in Chile. On the other side, the right-wing coalition cites Finland to legitimize the co-payment system, under the argument that this practice is present in the Finnish kindergartens:

Regarding the copayment, . . . when members of the Commission visited Finland, including the President of this body, [they asked if] parents made contributions to the kindergarten system. The answer was positive, that is to say that they can effectively do them with a differentiated tariff system. Then, each country has its own adjustments. So, Spain, Denmark and Finland have copayment systems. (History of the Law 20.845 2015, 1238)

In the Chilean case, policy-makers and stakeholders who participated in the debates for the adoption of the General Law of Education and the School

Inclusion Law used Finland as the main "reference society." Nonetheless, the content of the projected slides on Finland differed markedly since both left- and right-leaning policy-makers were very selective in identifying and presenting the explanatory variables of the Finnish success.

## Regional Absences and Emerging Projection Screens in the Chilean Education Debate

Historically, Chile has been a country with elites and governments very open to global influences and interested in learning about main trends and innovative educational ideas from foreign countries (Cox and Meckes 2016), and Northern countries in particular. As noted above, Chile has seen in the OECD an opportunity to enter into the "club of developed countries" and differentiate itself from other developing countries of the region. The fact that Chile is the top PISA performer in the Latin American region, but at the same time is still far from the average of the OCED (History of the Law 20.370 2009, 752), makes Chile to try to emulate educational systems beyond the region. Thus, not surprisingly, when we look at the reference societies selected during the analyzed political debates, the absence (or lack of use) of regional examples is noticeable (see Figure 2.3). Probably, the most striking absence is the one of Brazil, considered by the OECD itself as a "successful reformer",[4] followed by that of Cuba, which is the top performer in the large-scale assessments implemented by UNESCO in the region (Carnoy et al. 2007). In Figure 2.3, we include Finland to show how significant is the difference between the number of references between this Nordic country and the number of references to the most cited countries in the region.

Chilean policy-makers justify the low level of references to Latin American and the Caribbean (LAC) countries using "auto-stereotypes" and "hetero-stereotypes" (see Waldow et al. 2014, 315). They argue that the cultural and institutional features of Chile make their country incomparable with other countries in the region. They also point to economic differences and to different levels of social and educational development as potential impediments to learn from other Latin American countries:

> Latin America has problems of the first generation, namely access, infrastructure, basic conditions and so on, which the Chilean educational system does not have. (interview MoE 1)

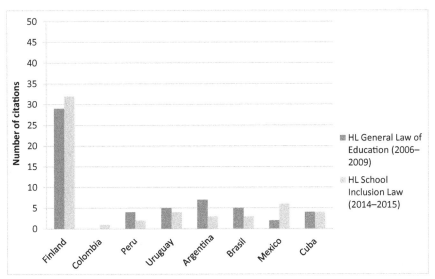

**Figure 2.3** Latin American countries as reference societies
*Source*: Authors

Notwithstanding, behind these differences, there are also—more or less—hidden relations of economic, political, and cultural competition between the countries in the region. At the geopolitical and economic level, Chile has prioritized alliances with non-LAC countries, differentiating itself from the rest of the region also in the commercial terrain. For example, Chile "joins APEC in 1994, signed free-trade agreements with Canada in 1996, Mexico in 1998, the United States in 2003, and became a member of the OECD in 2010" (Cox and Meckes 2016, 512). In addition, the fact that Chile has fewer natural resources than its neighboring countries puts pressure on Chile to develop a more intense *knowledge economy* and to look for educational references outside Latin America (interview ExMoE 2).

The presence of Asian countries in the public debate on education is small, mainly due to the "cultural differences" that make comparing these countries to Chile difficult. Only a few Asian countries such as South Korea and Japan are used sporadically as reference societies in the Chilean education debate:

Asia has cultural characteristics that make it very incomparable with other regions, and although you can look at some things, in general, they have a completely different culture. (interview MoE 1)

Finally, in the School Inclusion Law debate, the center-left resorted to two quite unusual reference societies in Chile, Turkey, and Poland, under the argument that the success of these two countries in ILSAs is due to the implementation of equity-oriented reforms:

> The OECD countries that have shown the most significant progress in the PISA tests are precisely the two countries that made a greater educational effort to end segregation: Turkey and Poland. (History of the Law 20.845 2015, 459).

To sum up, this chapter has shown that the reasons why a country becomes a reference society can be very diverse. Becoming a top-performing country in ILSAs is a necessary condition to become a "reference society." However, not all top performers become reference societies everywhere. Studying the selection and social construction of a country as a reference society requires taking into account both the characteristics of the country which is projecting the image (projector) and the processes of meaning-making and previous perceptions regarding a particular reference society (projection screen) (Waldow 2017).

Nevertheless, the mobilization of one or another "reference society" also depends on political factors (Takayama 2012). When a reference society is used as a projection screen, a set of values, ideas, and narratives are projected on what is considered good and desirable (or bad and avoidable) for the educational system of a country. Thus, policy-makers and educational stakeholders tend to highlight those characteristics of top performers that are more aligned with their priorities and policy preferences (Waldow, Takayama, and Sung 2014; see also Takayama et al. 2013). As we have seen in this chapter, despite the fact that Finland is usually mobilized by the left to frame and defend progressive ideas in education, especially in contexts where public education has been eroded by the advance of neoliberal policies and views (Takayama 2012), in the Chilean case, right-wing policy-makers used the example of Finland strategically to avoid the enactment of the School Inclusion Law.

Finally, this chapter has also shown that there is no correspondence between geographical distance and the selection of particular reference societies. On the contrary, sometimes hidden competitive relationships between countries can inhibit the selection of regional "league leaders" or "successful reformers."

## Conclusions

In the last decades, Chilean politics has been profoundly challenged by a long cycle of students' mobilizations that became particularly intense in the years 2006 and 2011. The students' movement has consistently demanded the elimination of school fees and the for-profit purpose from the education system, as well as for the prohibition of students' selection practices that caused the high levels of school segregation and exclusion. In 2006, the students' protests triggered a reform process that led to the adoption of the General Education Law, which introduced only very minor improvements in terms of equity. In contrast, the 2011 protests derived into a more ambitious educational reform channeled through, to a great extent, the School Inclusion Law, which was adopted by a center-left coalition in 2015. In the context of the deliberations behind the two mentioned laws, evidence coming from ILSAs was mobilized both for and against the adoption of the reforms.

This chapter has examined the reception and different uses of ILSAs in the context of the most recent Chilean education reforms. We have shown that PISA is the international assessment that—as has happened in many other world locations—has gained more centrality in the Chilean educational debate. The chapter has also shown that different *slides* of the international league leaders have been used to justify the political preferences of both proponents and opponents of the reforms.

ILSAs help policy-makers to identify which international "best practices" from which countries they could try to borrow and emulate. However, the selection of certain top-performing countries and the exclusion of others is mediated by cultural factors and geopolitical aspirations, but also by the perceived status of the potential "reference societies." References to Latin American "successful reformers," such as Brazil, or to "regional league leaders," such as Cuba, are conspicuously missing from the Chilean education debate. In contrast, references to both European and North-American countries are much more present in this debate. Among them, Finland stands out. Despite the fact that this Nordic country is a "league slipper" (cf. Steiner-Khamsi 2017, 7), it remains as a strong reference society in the imaginary of Chilean education policy-makers. In fact, references to Finland are mobilized by both advocates and detractors of the School Inclusion Law, although through the articulation of very different and even contradictory arguments.

International comparisons often lead to the over-simplification of international best practices and to the omission of relevant contextual characteristics (Kamens 2013). Moreover, references to top ILSA performers are usually particular and partial (Bonal and Tarabini 2013). This is due to the fact that the knowledge that national policy-makers have of external and distant societies is inevitably bounded, but also because references to these societies are intentionally simplified as the result of a strategically selective meaning-making process. Overall, in an increasingly globalized education policy field, national policy-makers and politicians are increasingly tempted to instrumentally resort to top ILSA performers as a way to promote their own education reform plans. These meaning-making dynamics and strategies are even more central in the context of highly politicized education reform processes, as those that Chile has gone through in the last decade.

# Notes

1  Although, at least in the case of the national test, this perception of low quality did not take sufficiently into account the methodological changes introduced in the SIMCE test (see Bravo 2011), neither the enactment of the curriculum reform, which was being implemented at that moment.
2  Methodologically, Breakspear applied a survey to the PISA Governing Board (PGB), which included representatives from sixty-five different countries that participated in the PISA 2009 edition.
3  Similarly, citations to the OECD have increased substantially, from thirty to seventy-one, whereas citations to the International Association for the Evaluation of Educational Achievement (IEA) have gone from one to zero.
4  Recent accountability reforms in Brazil have allowed this country to improve significantly in PISA. See: http://www.oecd.org/pisa/pisaproducts/strongperformers/.

# References

Bellei, C. (2016), "Dificultades y resistencias de una reforma para des-mercantilizar la educación" [Challenges and Resistances to a Reform to De-Commodify Education], *RASE: Revista de la Asociación de Sociología de la Educación*, 9(2), 232–47.

Bellei, C., and Cabalin, C. (2013), "Chilean Student Movements: Sustained Struggle to Transform a Market-Oriented Educational System," *Current Issues in Comparative Education*, 15(2), 108–23.

Bellei, C., and Vanni, X. (2015), "The Evolution of Educational Policy in Chile 1980–2014," in S. Schwartzman (ed.), *Education in South America*, 179–200, London: Bloomsbury.

Bellei, C., Cabalín, C., and Orellana, V. (2014), "The 2011 Chilean Student Movement against Neoliberal Educational Policies," *Studies in Higher Education*, 39(3), 426–40.

Bloque Social (2006), "La crisis educativa en Chile: diagnóstico y propuestas" [The Education Crisis in Chile: Diagnosis and Proposals], 16 December, http://opech.cl/bibliografico/calidad_equidad/Documento_Bloque_Social_Noviembre.pdf.

Bonal, X., and Tarabini, A. (2013), "The Role of PISA in Shaping Hegemonic Educational Discourses, Policies and Practices: The Case of Spain," *Research in Comparative and International Education*, 8(3), 335–41.

Bowen, G. A. (2009), "Document Analysis as a Qualitative Research Method," *Qualitative Research Journal*, 9(2) 27–40.

Bravo, J. (2011), "SIMCE: pasado, presente y futuro del sistema nacional de evaluación" [The Education Quality Measurement System: Past, Present, and Future of the National Evaluation System], *Estudios Públicos*, 123, 189–211.

Breakspear, S. (2012), "The Policy Impact of PISA: An Exploration of the Normative Effects of International Benchmarking in School System Performance," *OECD Education Working Papers*, 71, Paris: OECD, http://dx.doi.org/10.1787/5k9fdfqffr28-en.

Burton, G. (2012), "Hegemony and Frustration: Education Policy Making in Chile under the Concertación, 1990–2010," *Latin American Perspectives*, 30(10), 1–19.

Cariola, L., Covacevich, C., Gubler, J., Lagos, E., and Ortiz, M. (2011), "Chilean Participation in IEA Studies," in C. Papanastasiou, T. Plomp, and E. Papanastasiou (eds.), *IEA 1958–2008: 50 Years of Experiences and Memories*, Nicosia, Cyprus: Cultural Center of the Kykkos Monastery.

Carnoy, M., Gove, A. K., and Marshall, J. H. (2007), *Cuba's Academic Advantage: Why Students in Cuba Do Better in School*, Palo Alto: Stanford University Press.

Corbin, J., and Strauss, A. (1990), "Grounded Theory Research: Procedures, Canons and Evaluative Criteria," *Zeitschrift für Soziologie*, 19(6), 418–27.

Cornejo, R., and Reyes, L. (2008), *La cuestión docente. Chile: experiencias organizacionales y acción colectiva de profesores* [The Teacher Issue. Chile: Organizational Experiences and Collective Action of Teachers], Buenos Aires: Foro Latinoamericano de Políticas Educativas (FLAPE).

Cox, C. (2012), "Política y políticas educacionales en Chile 1990–2010" [Politics and Educational Policies in Chile 1990–2010], *Revista Uruguaya de Ciencia Política*, 21(1), 13–43.

Cox, C., and Meckes, L. (2016), "International Large-Scale Assessment Studies and Educational Policy-Making in Chile: Contexts and Dimensions of Influence," *Research Papers in Education*, 31(5), 502–15.

Engel, L. C. (2015), "Steering the National: Exploring the Education Policy Uses of PISA in Spain," *European Education*, 47(2), 100–16.

Ertl, H. (2006), "Educational Standards and the Changing Discourse on Education: The Reception and Consequences of the PISA Study in Germany," *Oxford Review of Education*, 32(5), 619–34.

Falabella, A. (2015), "El mercado escolar en Chile y el surgimiento de la Nueva Gestión Pública: El tejido de la política entre la dictadura neoliberal y los gobiernos de la centroizquierda (1979 a 2009)" [The School Market in Chile and the Emergence of the New Public Management: The Fabric of Politics Between the Neoliberal Dictatorship and the Goverments of the Center-Left (1979–2009)], *Educação & Sociedade*, 36(132), 699–722.

Gorur, R. (2017), "Towards Productive Critique of Large-Scale Comparisons in Education," *Critical Studies in Education, 58*(3), 1–15.

Grek, S. (2009), "Governing by Numbers: The PISA 'Effect' in Europe," *Journal of Education Policy* 24(1) 23–37.

History of the Law (2009), *20.370*, 12 September, Valparaíso, Chile: Biblioteca del Congreso Nacional de Chile, 2009.

History of the Law (2015), *20.845*, 8 June, Valparaíso, Chile: Biblioteca del Congreso Nacional de Chile.

Kamens, D. H. (2013), "Globalization and the Emergence of an Audit Culture: PISA and the Search for 'Best Practices' and Magic Bullets," in H. Meyer and A. Benavot (eds.), *PISA, Power, and Policy: The Emergence of Global Educational Governance*, 117–39, Oxford: Symposium Books.

Kingdon, J. W. (1995), *Agendas, Alternatives and Public Policies* (2nd ed.), New York: HarperCollins.

Larroulet, C., and Montt, P. (2010), "Políticas educativas de largo plazo y acuerdo amplio en educación: el caso chileno" [Long-Term Educational Policies and a Comprehensive Agreement in Education: The Case of Chile], in S. Martinic and G. Elacqua (eds.), *Fin de Ciclo: Cambios en la Gobernanza del Sistema Educativo*, Santiago: Facultad de Educación, Unesco y Pontificia Universidad Católica de Chile.

Lingard, B. (2011), "Policy as Numbers: Ac/Counting for Educational Research," *The Australian Educational Researcher, 38*(4), 355–82.

Lockheed, M. (2013), "Causes and Consequences of International Assessments in Developing Countries," in H. Meyer and A. Benavot (eds.), *PISA, Power, and Policy: The Emergence of Global Educational Governance*, 163–83, Oxford: Symposium.

Mayring, P. (2000), "Qualitative Content Analysis," *Forum: Qualitative Social Research, 1*(2), 1–7.

Mizala, A. (2007), *La economía política de la reforma educacional en Chile* [The Political Economy of the Educational Reform in Chile], Santiago: CIEPLAN.

OECD (2004), *Reviews of National Policies for Education.* Chile/París: OECD.

Pinedo Henríquez, C. (2011), "Educación en Chile: ¿Inclusión o exclusión?" [Education in Chile: Inclusion or Exclusion?], *Tejuelo: Didáctica de la Lengua y la Literatura. Educación*, 12, 47–79.

Rose, N. (1991), "Governing by Numbers: Figuring Out Democracy," *Accounting, Organizations and Society, 16*(7), 673–92.

Sahlberg, P. (2011), *Finnish Lessons. What Can the World Learn from Educational Change in Finland?*, New York: Teachers College Press, Columbia University.

Schleicher, A. (2014a), "No existe un sistema educativo exitoso con un sistema débil de escuelas públicas" [There Is No Successful Educational System with a Weak System of Public Schools], *El Mercurio*, July 23, http://www.elmercurio.com/blogs/2014/07/23/23736/No-existe-un-sistema-educativo-exitoso-con-un-sistema-debil-de-escuelas-publicas.aspx.

Schleicher, A. (2014b), "El precio de la segregación educacional" [The Price of Educational Segregation], *El Mercurio*, November 22, http://www.elmercurio.com/ blogs/2014/11/22/27102/El-precio-de-la-segregacion-educacional.aspx.

Steiner-Khamsi, G. (2003), "The Politics of League Tables," *Journal of Social Science Education*, 2(1), 1–6.

Steiner-Khamsi, G. (2016), "New Directions in Policy Borrowing Research," *Asia Pacific Education Review*, 17(3), 381–90.

Steiner-Khamsi, G. (2017), *Understanding Business Interests in International Large-Scale Student Assessment: A Focus on PISA and TIMSS* (GLOBED Master Lecture), Barcelona: Universitat Autònoma de Barcelona.

Takayama, K. (2008), "The Politics of International League Tables: PISA in Japan's Achievement Crisis Debate," *Comparative Education*, 44(4), 387–407.

Takayama, K. (2012), "Bringing a Political 'Bite' to Educational Transfer Studies: Cultural Politics of PISA and the OECD in Japanese Education Reform," in G. Steiner-Khamsi and F. Waldow (eds.), *World Yearbook of Education 2012: Policy Borrowing and Lending in Education*, 148–66, New York: Routledge.

Takayama, K., Waldow, F., and Sung, Y. (2013), "Finland Has It All? Examining 'Finnish PISA Success' as a Multiaccentual Sign in Australia, Germany, and South Korea," *Journal of Research in Comparative and International Education*, 8, 307–25.

Vera, S. (2011), "Cronología del Conflicto: El Movimiento Estudiantil en Chile 2011" [Chronology of the Conflict: The Student Movement in Chile 2011], in *Anuario del Conflicto Social 2011* (252–61), Barcelona: Observatorio del Conflicto Social.

Verd, J. M., and Lozares, C. (2016), *Introducción a la investigación cualitativa. Fases, métodos y técnicas* [Introduction to Qualitative Research. Phases, Methods, and Techniques], Madrid: Síntesis.

Verger, A., Bonal, X., and Zancajo, A. (2016), "What Are the Role and Impact of Public-Private Partnerships in Education? A Realist Evaluation of the Chilean Education Quasi-Market," *Comparative Education Review*, 60(2) 223–48, doi: 10.1086/685557.

Waldow, F. (2017), "Projecting Images of the 'Good' and the 'Bad School': Top Scorers in Educational Large-Scale Assessments as Reference Societies," *Compare: A Journal of Comparative and International Education*, 47(5), 1–18.

Waldow, F., Takayama, K., and Sung, Y-K. (2014), "Rethinking the Pattern of External Policy Referencing: Media Discourses over the 'Asian Tigers'' Pisa Success in Australia, Germany, and South Korea," *Comparative Education*, 50(3), 302–21.

Whitty, G. (2012), "Policy Tourism and Policy Borrowing in Education: A Trans-Atlantic Case Study," in G. Steiner-Khamsi and F. Waldow (eds.), *World Yearbook of Education 2012: Policy Borrowing and Lending in Education*, 334–70, London: Routledge.

# 3

# Schooling Reform in Australia: Legitimation through "Projections" onto Shanghai and East Asian Schooling Systems

Bob Lingard and Sam Sellar

## Introduction

This chapter examines the impact in Australia of projections onto East Asian schooling systems following Shanghai's top performance in PISA 2009 and 2012. As Waldow (2010; 2017; see also Waldow, Takayama, and Sung 2014; Takayama 2018) has argued, top performers in international large-scale assessments (ILSAs) such as PISA can become reference societies onto which other nations project their ideas about good and bad schools. Educational debate in Australia following Shanghai's top performance in PISA 2009 has involved the projection of images of good schools and students onto Shanghai and East Asian systems more broadly. These projections emerged in the context of the so-called Asian Century and a wider debate about Australia's place in, or in relation to, Asia and its economic reliance on China's growth.

Politicians and policy-makers have used these projections to support a narrative of crisis in Australian schooling and to legitimize the need for educational reform. Federal Labor governments (2007–13) and federal Conservative governments (2013-present) have used externalization and projection in different ways to legitimize existing reform agendas in education. There has been no policy learning in these cases, simply externalization (Schriewer 1990). Our focus here is on policy usages of externalization and projection. We concede that there are other ways one might analyze the media coverage and scholarship in Australia concerning the high levels of performance on PISA of East Asian schooling systems. Takayama (2017; 2018), for example, has offered a critical, postcolonial analysis situated against Australia's deep ambivalence historically about Asia. We will position our argument against his at various points in this chapter.

PISA has perhaps played a more important role in education debates in Australia compared with many other OECD nations. This is due, in part, to the role that the Australian Council for Education Research (ACER) played in developing the test and managing the assessments during the late 1990s and 2000s, as well as the important roles that Australian academics and researchers have held within the OECD's education work, which has in turn influenced the epistemic community of policy-makers in Australia. From 2006, political, policy, and media conversations about Australia's declining PISA performance were an important component of the backdrop to a substantial national reform agenda that was implemented from 2007 onwards by a federal Labor government (Baroutsis and Lingard 2017). However, public attention to PISA reached a new degree of intensity with the publication of a Grattan Institute report in early 2012 (Jensen et al. 2012), titled *Catching Up: Learning from the Best School Systems in East Asia*, which dealt with Australia's declining performance on the 2009 PISA reported in 2010. The report exhorted Australian policy-makers to learn from the schooling systems of Shanghai, Korea, Hong Kong, and Singapore, all of which had performed well on PISA. The report was accompanied by a media campaign that generated many headlines extolling the virtues of Shanghai's schools, and it was launched a few days before an influential report on school funding in Australia. Our focus in this chapter is on the representations of East Asian schooling that emerged from this time and their mobilization by the media and policy-makers to legitimize changing reform agendas linked to changes in government. As already noted, these representations were contested (Takayama 2017).

The chapter has five main sections. Next, we provide a brief overview of Australia's performance on PISA from 2000 to 2012. We then discuss the performance of Shanghai on PISA 2009 and 2012, which shifted the global gaze onto East Asian schooling, or at least the gaze of some Anglo-American nations (Sellar and Lingard 2013; Waldow 2017). The response to this performance in Australia and the distinctive view of East Asian schooling that emerged are the focus of the next two sections, and we then provide a brief summative conclusion.

## PISA in Australia

In both the 2000 and 2003 PISA, Australia performed very well and there was positive media coverage of the results, especially after the release in 2004 of the

2003 results, when there was increased media coverage and positive reporting. For example, the headline in the *Canberra Times* stated, "Australia's education system gets full marks" (O'Connor 2004). There was some decline in Australia's PISA performance from 2006 onward (Table 3.1). Additionally, Shanghai's stellar performance on PISA 2009 caused real consternation in Australian policy and political circles, following extensive media coverage. This concern was about declining performance especially in comparison with that of East Asian schooling systems in the context of the so-called Asian Century and Australia's increasing economic reliance on Asia. The policy debate from 2012 onward has focused on Australia's decline in the rankings and mean scores in the three major domains of mathematics, reading and science, although performance across Australia's state and territory education systems is by no means uniform (Gorur and Wu 2015).[1]

As can be seen from Table 3.1, between the 2000 and 2012 PISA tests, there was a 16-point drop in reading literacy and very significantly a 29-point drop in mathematical literacy. These declines had political and policy effects in the context of the top level performance of East Asian systems and arguments in Australia and elsewhere about the significance of the STEM subjects, including science and mathematics, to the quality of a nation's human capital and ipso facto the nation's future economic prosperity.

## Shanghai's Performance on PISA 2009 and 2012

On December 7, 2010, the results of PISA 2009 were released and the *New York Times* ran a front page article with the headline: "Top test scores from Shanghai stun educators." The major domain in 2009 was reading, for the first time since PISA 2000, when Finland was the top performer with a mean score of

**Table 3.1** Australian PISA Performance, 2000–12 (Major Domain in Bold)

|      | Reading | Mathematics | Science |
|------|---------|-------------|---------|
| 2000 | **528** | 533         | 528     |
| 2003 | 525     | **524**     | 525     |
| 2006 | 513     | 520         | **527** |
| 2009 | **515** | 514         | 527     |
| 2012 | 512     | **504**     | 521     |

546. Shanghai was the top ranked participant on the 2009 PISA with a score of 570 for reading literacy. Shanghai was also the top performer in the other two domains of mathematics and science. While other East Asian nations had been at the top of the rankings in previous rounds, Shanghai's top performance across all domains and its high mean scores created a sensation and contrasted sharply with Finland's performance, which had dominated attention up until this point, and with Australia's performance (Table 3.2) (Sellar and Lingard 2013).

However, Shanghai's performance is difficult to interpret for a number of reasons. Shanghai was one of twelve Chinese regions that participated in PISA 2009 and it was the top performer in this group. As Chan and Seddon (2014) have shown, the overall Chinese average of 486 in reading was below the OECD average of 493 (and below Australia's mean score) and reflects the wide spread of scores across the twelve participating regions. Normally, releasing results publicly is a condition of participation in PISA, but in 2009 China only allowed the OECD to publish the results for Shanghai and the OECD was acquiescent. This encouraged a view that Shanghai was representative of Chinese schooling more broadly, which it clearly was not. Chan and Seddon argue that "using the PISA result of a single Chinese city as if it were a country-to-country comparison is invalid" (2014, 212). Nevertheless, the OECD and others held up Shanghai as a model from which other systems could learn (OECD 2011; Tucker 2011).

Shanghai is a developed and wealthy metropolis with schools that serve a relatively elite cohort of Chinese students compared with other parts of the country. Loveless has shown that the Chinese hukou system is likely to have affected the sample of students who sat the test in Shanghai. As Loveless explains, "hukou is a household registration system that restricts rural migrants' access to urban social services, including education" (2014, 9). Without a Shanghai hukou, access to high school in Shanghai is restricted and many migrant families send their children back to the province of their hukou registration for high school or to poor quality low-fee private schools in Shanghai. As a result, "[h]ukou acts as a giant sifting machine, barring or driving out migrant children from urban

**Table 3.2** Performance in PISA 2009 (Shanghai, Finland, and Australia)

|           | Reading | Mathematics | Science |
|-----------|---------|-------------|---------|
| Shanghai  | 556     | 600         | 575     |
| Finland   | 536     | 541         | 554     |
| Australia | 515     | 514         | 527     |

schools" (Loveless 2014, 10) and Shanghai is an outlier in relation to the number of fifteen-year-olds it reports on as a percentage of the predicted number of fifteen-year-olds in that jurisdiction. This concern about sampling was also expressed in Chinese media coverage of the results (Chan and Seddon 2014).

We also must take into account a number of cultural and historical factors when interpreting Shanghai's scores. As Tan (2013) has shown, the high stakes national college entrance examination drives a deeply embedded "cultural script" for Shanghai parents who pressure children for academic achievement and high grades. In the context of the (then) one-child policy and competition for good universities and jobs, parents are active choosers of well-reputed schools and place emphasis on home tuition and homework, with the result that many "Shanghai students are . . . competitive, highly motivated, hardworking and pragmatic" (Tan 2013, 62). Some of these cultural factors are also common to other nations with cultures influenced by Confucianism, which are also top performers on PISA

The OECD (2011) and other analysts (e.g., Tucker et al. 2011, Jensen et al. 2012) have played down these administrative and cultural factors and have instead emphasized the influence of education reforms in China since the Cultural Revolution and more recently in Shanghai. As Loveless suggests, "[p]olicy relevance has become PISA's overarching objective, which has led to excessive and unfounded policy recommendations" (2014, 13). The value of PISA as an instrument for shaping global education policy discourses and as an evidence-base for policy-making across national contexts depends on performance being attributable primarily to policy, and this has created a tendency to promote policy explanations and the agency of schools over and above other factors such as socio-economic context contributing to PISA results

Secondary analyses of PISA results by Feniger and Lefstein (2014) and Jerrim (2015)[2] have also shown that Chinese immigrants who have undertaken all of their education in Australian schools perform similarly to students in Shanghai. These findings highlight the dangers of over-attributing PISA performance to school practices or systemic policies when, as Jerrim observes, "the attitudes and beliefs East Asian parents instill in their children make an important contribution to their high levels of academic achievement" (2015, 329). Jerrim argues that "policymakers should make it clear that there are many influences upon a country's PISA performance, and that climbing significantly up these rankings is unlikely to be achieved by the efforts of schools alone" (2015, 329). However, this has not been the case in Australia. There was no acknowledgment of these matters in the Australian projections onto Shanghai that we deal with in this chapter. Rather, Shanghai's performance was largely taken at face value.

## Australia's Mediated Response to Shanghai's PISA Performance

We argue that Australia experienced a PISA shock in 2010 following the release of the 2009 PISA results and the high quality performance of a number of East Asian schooling systems (four of the top five performing systems were in East Asia—Shanghai, Hong Kong, South Korea, and Singapore). The performance of Shanghai was particularly significant. Interestingly, though, this PISA shock was delayed and only came to full fruition after the publication of a report, *Catching Up: Learning from the Best School Systems in East Asia* (Jensen et al., 2012), produced by the Grattan Institute, an Australian think tank based in Melbourne (see Sellar and Lingard 2013; Baroutsis and Lingard 2017). This report evoked and provoked extensive media coverage in early 2012, and it also played into, and helped constitute, a narrative of decline in Australian schooling. The Grattan Institute report was written in language conducive to media take-up (Medvetz 2012). In February 2012, a headline in the national newspaper *the Australian*, derived from the report, noted, "Lessons from Asia show the way forward for our schools" (Ferrari 2012). The *Financial Review*, the other national newspaper in Australia, also ran with a story from the Grattan Report, with the headline, "Asian education goes to the top of the class" (Walker 2012). A related *Sydney Morning Herald* story ran with the headline, "Shanghai surprise reveals a great learning culture" (Harrison 2012). In responding to this extensive negative media coverage, the then Prime Minister, Julia Gillard, expressed deep concern about Australia's declining performance on PISA, particularly when set against the comparative performance of the East Asian systems and the emerging Asian Century. She noted specifically,

> Four of the top five performing school systems in the world are in our region and they are getting better and better . . . On average, kids at 15 in those nations are six months ahead of Australian kids at 15 and they are a year in front of the OECD mean . . . If we are talking about today's children—tomorrow's workers—I want them to be workers in a high-wage economy where we are still leading the world. I don't want them to be workers in an economy where we are kind of the runt of the litter in our region and we've slipped behind the standards and the high-skill, high-wage jobs are elsewhere in our region. (Franklin 2012, 1)

It is important to note here that the Grattan Institute report was an outcome of its own research, but following a roundtable hosted by the Institute on September 27–28, 2011. Importantly, this roundtable was attended by the then Prime Minister, Julia Gillard, the then federal Education Minister, Peter Garrett, Andreas Schleicher from the OECD, and a range of educational leaders and researchers from Korea, Singapore, Shanghai, Hong Kong, and the United States. All Directors-General from Australian schooling systems also attended. The title of the roundtable was *Learning from the Best—a Grattan Institute Roundtable on High-Performing Systems in East Asia,* and it was sponsored by a range of government bodies and private groups.

We might see this roundtable and the report that followed as formal establishment of these East Asian schooling systems as references for Australia. The Grattan report, as with the argument proffered by Waldow (2017), also projected desirable traits for Australian schools onto these systems. Thus, the report noted how the gap between policy and implementation in these systems had been overcome, while in Australia there was still a disconnect between policy and classrooms. It was also argued that increased funding was not the solution for improving Australia's performance; a refrain taken up in earnest by Conservative governments in Australia after the 2013 election. After documenting the outstanding performance of four schooling systems (Korea, Hong Kong, Shanghai, and Singapore), the report also documented improvement in their scores on international tests achieved in a short period of time. There was also rejection of the argument that the performance of those systems could be explained by the influence of Confucian culture. Rather, throughout the report, referencing these systems, great stress is placed on high quality teacher education, education for school principals, mentors for all teachers focused on improvement, recognition of teachers as researchers, regular use of classroom observations for improvement, and promotion of effective teachers as master teachers responsible for improving teaching and learning outcomes. The report rejected outright accounts of schooling in the four systems under the spotlight as teacher-directed, noncreative, and focused on rote learning.

The projections onto the four East Asian schooling systems in the Grattan report can be contrasted with the criticisms of these systems presented in some media coverage and in some more scholarly Australian responses. It is these more negative references that Takayama (2017) focuses on in his account of Australian responses to the performance of East Asian systems on PISA from 2009 onward. He quotes research by two Australian academics, Dinham (2013) and Yelland (2012), which is extremely critical of East Asian approaches and rejects their relevance to Australia. He also analyses media coverage critical of the "Tiger Mother" phenomenon in Shanghai and which is offered as an explanation for Shanghai's 2009 performance on PISA. Takayama situates these critiques in the context of deep historical ambivalence in Australia about Asia and Australia's relation to it.

Our argument here is that there is clearly contestation within any given nation about new reference societies and new reference systems. In the case here, we would argue it was the Grattan report and its involvement of leading policy-makers that had more effect in this respect than the accounts canvassed by Takayama in his postcolonial critique. This is not to deny that Australia has an ongoing ambivalent attitude toward Asia, manifest at this very moment in concerns about Chinese involvement in Australian politics and in respect of Chinese students taking higher degrees in Australian universities.

One explicit policy outcome of this Australian PISA shock was the Gillard government legislating for Australia to be ranked in the top five on PISA by 2025. In the prime minister's statement above, we can see the significance of Asian schooling systems as reference systems for Australia. This is a vastly different situation from that in Germany, where Waldow (2017) has shown how these East Asian schooling systems have been rejected as valid reference systems for Germany. We note then the significance of a nation's geopolitical and economic positioning to the choice of reference systems. Around this time, the Australian government had commissioned a White Paper, *Australia and the Asian Century* (Australian Government 2012), which provides another context for the impact of Australia's declining comparative PISA performance and of the Grattan Institute report. We can also see the concept of a global education race implied in the prime minister's observations, and as well a human capital framing of schooling policy. This is why Julia Gillard wanted to be the "Education Prime Minister"; education policy was now central to economic policy and the future of the nation. In the effects of extensive media coverage of Australia's declining comparative performance with Asian schooling systems, and as articulated in the Grattan Institute report, we can see what has been called "catalyst data" at work (Lingard and Sellar 2013); that is, school system performance data that has real policy effects.

The report from a Labor government commissioned review of federal government funding of all Australian schools, conducted by the eminent business man, David Gonski, was released three days after the Grattan Institute report and provides an important additional context for the focus on East Asian schooling in education policy debates at the time. The Gonski review of school funding commissioned a 2011 report by the consultancy group, Nous Group (2011), which also made much of Australia's declining PISA performance when compared with East Asian systems. The report, *Schooling Challenges and Opportunities: A Report for the Review of Funding for Schooling Panel* helped strengthen the acceptance of the narrative of decline in influential policy circles. Interestingly, it also supported the necessity of more funding for schools and a more redistributive approach to funding.

Labor governments, following the 2010 release of the 2009 PISA results and subsequent to the extensive media coverage of the Grattan Institute report, used such comparative data to further legitimate their so-called Education Revolution that had been implemented after their first election victory in 2007. Paradoxically perhaps, much of that agenda, particularly the introduction of national census testing of Australian students in all schools at Years 3, 5, 7 and 9, the National Assessment Program—Literacy and Numeracy (NAPLAN), and accountability structured around test scores for schools and systems, had been borrowed from reforms in New York and we know the United States performs poorly on PISA. Labor had also introduced a national curriculum and national standards for teachers and school leaders and gained agreement to a new statement of goals for all Australian schools.

The Labor commissioned Gonski review of school funding was concerned to develop a needs-based, redistributive funding approach for all schools; government, Catholic, and independent. The Labor government committed to this increased needs-based funding for all schools but was defeated at the 2013 election before the Gonski funding proposal could be fully implemented. Labor also had a number of national policies that redistributed money into schools serving poor communities and schools with the poorest results on NAPLAN. The accountability for this extra funding was meeting state targets for improved NAPLAN test scores and improved NAPLAN test results at schools receiving additional targeted funding, much of which had perverse effects on the quality of teaching and learning in schools (Lingard and Sellar 2013).

When the Conservative federal government, led by arch conservative Tony Abbott, came to power in 2013, they used the narrative of PISA decline as a justification for their reform agenda in schooling. Interestingly, while they tend to be more federalist in approach than the more centralist Labor party, the Conservatives accepted Labor's national agenda and have largely left it in place, except for the funding element. They also argued that Labor's additional funding had not led to improved tests scores and thus that additional funding was not the issue. This echoed the claims of the Grattan Institute report. They also ended all of Labor's national policies that had a clear equity and redistributive funding focus. This was an argument strongly prosecuted by Prime Minister Abbott and his Education Minister, Christopher Pyne. Instead, they focused their schooling policy discourse around teacher quality, more autonomy for schools, and a strong curriculum, arguing that these were more significant for improvement than increased funding; a stance clearly aligned with their argument of the necessity of so-called budget-repair. Despite committing at the 2013 election to match Labor's long-term funding increases for all schools, the Abbott government backed away from this commitment. When the less conservative Malcolm Turnbull took over the leadership from Abbott and became prime minister, he eventually committed to a weakened version of Gonski funding. However, their framing meta-policy, *Students First*, was still structured around teacher quality, school autonomy and a strong curriculum. Under these conservative governments, declining PISA performance had almost transmogrified into a broader narrative of general school decline. East Asian systems remained important reference societies and with Singapore topping PISA 2015, as reported in 2016, this continued as did projections onto East Asian school systems.

## Theorizing Australian Projections onto East Asian Schooling Systems

In an earlier paper, we argued that Shanghai's stellar performance on PISA 2009 shifted the global gaze of policy-makers in education from Finland to Shanghai and more broadly to East Asian schooling systems (Sellar and Lingard 2013). Waldow (2017) has rightly criticized our argument, suggesting that more is required than simply good PISA results for new reference societies to be constituted and we agree. As we have shown above, there are certain specific features of Australia's geopolitical positioning on the edge of Asia and its projected economic future in Asia, which have ensured the constitution of new reference systems for Australia. Australia has looked East, as it were, and constituted new reference societies in Asia. We would accept that it is more accurate to argue that Shanghai's stellar performance on PISA 2009 momentarily shifted the gaze of some Anglo-American policy-makers to Shanghai and East Asian schooling systems (Sellar and Lingard 2013).

   Citing Bendix (1978), Waldow (2017) defines a reference society as a country toward which intellectual leaders and informed publics in other countries have a positive or negative reaction. Waldow clearly outlines four relations between reference societies and policy transfer. First, reference to another society can occur with transfer in the case of policy borrowing. Second, policy transfer can also occur without reference to other countries. The third and fourth relations involve the dynamic of projection, which Waldow argues can be understood in an optical sense of an image being projected onto a screen, but also in a psychoanalytical sense. Positive reference can be made to other societies without anything being transferred, in which case the reference may simply serve to legitimize practices that observers hold to be important, rather than actual practices present in the reference society. Finally, negative reference can be made to other societies to delegitimize certain practices, but again, these may or may be projected onto the reference society. As Waldow argues, these negative projections may involve externalization of characteristics of the projecting society about which there is anxiety (opening up the potential for a psychoanalytical reading).

As mentioned above, in a critical postcolonial analysis of the projection onto East Asian schooling systems by Australian media and scholars, Takayama (2017) has proffered a vastly different analysis to the one we provide here. We are largely looking at positive projections. Takayama argues, using different media coverage and particular scholarly analyses, that these projections onto East Asian systems have been largely negative, stressing rote learning, lack of creativity and the Tiger Mother phenomenon. Interestingly, though, and utilizing the psychoanalytical aspect of Waldow's concept of projection, Takayama argues that these characteristics layered over East Asian schooling systems, are also those emerging in Australian schooling, resulting from the imposition of national testing and accountability linked to test results.

The reaction in Australia to the performance of Shanghai and other East Asian participants in PISA 2009 and 2012 cuts across Waldow's typology in interesting ways. First, policy documents and media coverage in Australia have tended to refer explicitly to Asia in general and implicitly to East Asia. Where attention has focused specifically on Shanghai, this Chinese region is often used as a synecdoche for East Asia. So, the references made in recent Australian education debates have not been so much to a nation, but rather to sub- and supra-national regions. Second, these references have been broadly positive in the policy documents and media coverage we have discussed here. Waldow argues that "[w]hether countries are viewed as positive or negative reference societies is largely due to stereotyped prior perceptions of countries, determining how success in LSAs is framed" (2017, 21). Australia's geographical proximity to Asia and its close economic and cultural ties, as well as a history of recent efforts to strengthen diplomatic and trade ties to Asia dating back to the early 1990s, provide a framing in which Asia is seen as a largely positive reference for Australia. For example, the *Australia in the Asian Century White Paper* (Australian Government 2012) makes the following argument:

> Recent improvements in the performance of schools in the Asian region, and beyond, should be a source of learning for Australia. Australia has its own unique schooling system and not every approach would work here. But our schools can, and should, adapt the lessons of school systems in our region to drive improvements here at home, and to share our own successes with them. (Jensen et al. 2012, 166)

This is an explicit argument for policy borrowing from Asian school systems and the Grattan Institute report, which is cited here, is designed to facilitate such borrowing.

However, the context of the Gonski review inflected these positive references. References to Shanghai focused on success despite large class sizes and downplayed the role of funding. These were issues being debated in Australia at the time and we would argue that references to Shanghai and East Asia thus involved gestures toward policy borrowing and positive projections that played up policies and practices that were seen to be important by key intellectual leaders in the context of the school funding debate in Australia at the time. There was neither actual transfer of policies from Shanghai nor disregard for actual policies there (the first and third relations between reference and transfer in Waldow's typology above), but rather selective positive attention to actual policies in order to delegitimize other positions within Australian policy debates. And as Takayama (2017) demonstrates, there were also negative references to the successful East Asian systems in the Australian context. Thus, we would argue new reference systems and projections onto them are contested spaces.

## Conclusion

In this chapter, we have demonstrated how Shanghai's performance on PISA 2009, as well as the top performances of other East Asian schooling systems, notably, Korea, Hong Kong, and Singapore, set against Australia's declining PISA performance since 2006, turned Australian policy-makers' gaze toward East Asia. Indeed, we have argued that East Asian schooling systems have become new reference systems for some Anglo-American school systems and East Asia a new reference region for Australia. This resulted from extensive media coverage of these matters. More important here, though, was the significant intervention of the Grattan Institute report that we have paid much attention to. This report, and related media coverage, had substantial policy effects, largely because of the involvement of the most powerful and influential policy-makers in the related roundtable organized by the Grattan Institute. The report projected positive images onto the East Asian systems in question; projections of desirable practices for Australian systems and schools that would putatively help to close the policy-practice gap in the Australian education policy context.

Our argument has also demonstrated that, as Waldow (2017) has suggested, high-level performance on PISA is not enough to reconstitute reference societies and reference systems. In line with Waldow's thesis, we have shown that Australia's increasing economic reliance on Asia and concern about its position within Asia in the context of the Asian Century have been central contextual factors in the constitution of these new reference systems and positive projections. Yet, drawing on Takayama (2017), we have also argued that these new reference systems and positive projections have been contested by other more critical accounts. We accept Takayama's argument that there is a deep historical legacy of ambivalence in Australia concerning Australia's position in and relations with Asia. This historical ambivalence provides the space for contestation over these new reference systems and their different usages under different political regimes, for example, under federal Labor governments (2007–13) and under federal Conservative governments (2013-present).

# Notes

1  Most of the media coverage reports Australia's comparative mean scores on the three tests. This hides substantial differences in performance between the states and territories that constitute Australian federalism. In part, the poor comparative performance of the Northern Territory and Tasmania masks the better performance of say the Australian Capital Territory. The aggregation to the Australian mean scores fuels the discourse of decline.

2  We note that Takayama (2017) suggests that Jerrim's analysis essentializes Chinese students and culture, while Feniger and Lefstein are more wary of these risks of reasoning with PISA.

# References

Australian Government (2012), *Australia in the Asian Century: White Paper*, Canberra: Australian Government Printing Service.

Baroutsis, A., and Lingard, B. (2017), "Counting and Comparing School Performance: An Analysis of Media Coverage of PISA in Australia, 2000–2014," *Journal of Education Policy*, 32(4), 432–49.

Bendix, R. (1978), *Kings or People: Power and the Mandate to Rule*, Berkeley: University of California Press.

Chan, P. W. K., and Seddon, T. (2014), "Governing Education in China: PISA, Comparison and Educational Regions," in T. Fenwick, E. Mangez, and J. Ozga (eds.), *Governing Knowledge: 2014 World Yearbook of Education*, 200–17, London: Routledge.

Dinham, S. (2013), "The Quality Teaching Movement in Australia Encounters Difficult Terrain: A Personal Perspective," *Australian Journal of Education*, 57(2), 91–106.

Feniger, Y., and Lefstein, A. (2014), "How Not to Reason with PISA Data: An Ironic Investigation," *Journal of Education Policy*, 29(6), 845–55.

Ferrari, J. (2012), "Lessons from Asia Show Way Forward for Schools," *The Australian*, 1, February 17.

Franklin, M. (2012), "We Risk Losing Education Race, PM Warns," *The Australian*, 1, January 24.

Gorur, R., and Wu, M. (2015), "Leaning Too Far? PISA, Policy and Australia's 'Top Five' Ambitions," *Discourse: Studies in the Cultural Politics of Education*, 36(5): 647–64.

Harrison, D. (2012), "Shanghai Surprise Reveals a Great Learning Culture," *Sydney Morning Herald*, 13, February 20.

Jensen, B., Hunter, A., Sonneman, J., and Burns, T. (2012), *Catching Up: Learning from the Best School Systems in East Asia*, Melbourne: Grattan Institute.

Jerrim, J. (2015), "Why Do East Asian Children Perform So Well in PISA? An Investigation of Western-Born Children of East Asian Descent," *Oxford Review of Education*, 41(3), 310–33.

Lingard, B., and Sellar, S. (2013), " 'Catalyst Data': Perverse Systemic Effects of Audit and Accountability in Australian Schooling," *Journal of Education Policy*, 28(5), 634–56.

Loveless, T. (2014), *The 2014 Brown Center Report on American Education: How Well Are American Students Learning? With Sections on the PISA-Shanghai Controversy, Homework, and the Common Core*, Washington, DC: Brookings Institution.

Medvetz, T. (2012), "Murky Power: 'Think Tank' as Boundary Organisations," *Research in the Sociology of Organisations*, 34, 113–33.

Nous Group (2011), *Schooling Challenges and Opportunities: A Report for the Review of Funding for Schooling Panel*, Melbourne: Nous Group.

O'Connor, C. (2004), "Australia's Education System Gets Full Marks," *Canberra Times*, 11, December 13.

OECD (2011), *Strong Performers and Successful Reformers in Education: Lessons from PISA for the United States*, Paris: OECD.

Schriewer, J. (1990), "The Method of Comparison and the Need for Externalization: Methodological Criteria and Sociological Concepts," in J. Schriewer and B. Holmes (eds.), *Theories and Methods in Comparative Education*, 25–83, Frankfurt a. M.: Peter Lang.

Sellar, S., and Lingard, B. (2013), "Looking East: Shanghai, PISA 2009 and the Reconstitution of Reference Societies in the Global Education Policy Field," *Comparative Education*, 40(6), 917–36.

Takayama, K. (2017), "Imagining East Asian Education Otherwise: Neither Caricature, nor Scandalization." *Asia Pacific Journal of Education*, 37(2), 262–74.

Takayama, K. (2018), "The Constitution of East Asia as a Counter Reference Society through PISA: A Postcolonial/Decolonial Intervention," *Globalisation, Societies and Education*, doi: 10.1080/14767724.2018.1532282.

Tan, C. (2013), *Learning from Shanghai: Lessons on Achieving Educational Success*, Dordrecht: Springer.

Tucker, M. (2011) (ed.), *Surpassing Shanghai: An Agenda for American Education Built on the World's Leading Systems*, Cambridge: Harvard Education Press.

Waldow, F. (2010), "Der Traum vom 'skandinavisch schlau werden'. Drei Thesen zur Rolle Finnlands als Projektionsfläche in der gegenwärtigen Bildungsdebatte" [The Dream of "Becoming Smart the Scandinavian Way": Three Hypotheses Regarding the Role of Finland as a Projection Surface in the Current Debate on Education], *Zeitschrift für Pädagogik*, 56(4), 497–511.

Waldow, F. (2017), "Projecting Images of the 'Good' and the 'Bad School': Top Scorers in Educational Large-Scale Assessments as Reference Societies," *Compare: A Journal of Comparative and International Education*, doi: 10.1080/03057925.2x016.1262245.

Waldow, F., Takayama, K., and Sung, Y-K. (2014), "Rethinking the Pattern of External Policy Referencing: Media Discourses over the 'Asian Tigers'' PISA Success in Australia, Germany and South Korea," *Comparative Education*, 3, 302–21.

Walker, T. (2012), "Asian Education Goes to the Top of the Class," *Financial Review*, 62, February 18.

Yelland, N. (2012), "Learning by Rote: Why Australia Should Not Follow the Asian Model of Education," *The Conversation*. July 9, http://theconversation.com/learning-by-rote-why-australia-should-not-follow-the-asian-model-of-education-5698 (accessed December 21, 2017).

# 4

# "Pedagogical Paradise" and "Exam Hell": PISA Top Scorers as Projection Screens in German Print Media

Florian Waldow

## Introduction: Reference Societies after the German "PISA Shock"

This chapter investigates how Finland was constructed as a positive reference society and the East Asian PISA top scorers as a negative reference society in the German quality press in the wake of PISA. It looks at how these reference societies were used as projection screens for conceptions of the "good" and the "bad" school and discusses which functions they fulfilled in the media debate on education policy-making in Germany.[1]

The impact of the first round of PISA results in Germany has been described as "Tsunami-like" (Gruber 2006, 195; cf. also Tillmann et al. 2008). After the publication of the results of PISA 2000 in early December 2001, PISA dominated the news headlines for weeks. Martens and Niemann (2013) demonstrate that media coverage of PISA in Germany was much more intensive than in most other participating countries. They see one important reason for this in the fact that expectations on the one hand and results on the other differed particularly strongly in Germany, that is, many German observers had expected German pupils to perform much better in PISA than they actually did. The suddenness of the so-called PISA shock was probably aggravated by the fact that Germany had largely abstained from participating in ILSAs in the 1908s and 1990s, that is, prior to TIMSS, the results of which were published in 1997 (cf. Baumert et al. 1997). The public was therefore not prepared for the image PISA gave of the relative standing of German education.

The PISA shock led to a massive scandalization (Steiner-Khamsi 2003) of the German education system. The following four areas received the most attention: (1) the average literacy levels of German pupils were below the OECD average in all three domains and mediocre compared to those of other OECD countries; (2) the proportion of German pupils that left school without even basic competences in reading, mathematics and natural science was high compared to other OECD countries; (3) the difference between the lowest achievers and the highest achievers was particularly large in Germany; and (4) PISA showed enormous differences in achievement and educational opportunities between different social groups and between those of and not of immigration background. In addition, in an extension of the original study design (called PISA-E), enormous differences of achievement between the German federal states were highlighted (in Germany, responsibility for education lies largely in the hands of the sixteen federal states). The publication of the results of PISA-E in June 2002 (Baumert and Deutsches PISA-Konsortium 2002) created another media stir that was even bigger than that caused by the publication of the international study (Tillmann et al. 2008, 72) and led to a massive scandalization of the federal states performing particularly badly, such as Bremen (cf. Tillmann et al. 2008).

Some of the problems highlighted by PISA, such as the wide achievement gap between different social groups and the high number of pupils leaving school without basic competences, were known to specialists prior to the publication of the study. However, it was only through PISA that a wider audience became aware of them (van Ackeren 2002). Since the first round of PISA, the German results have improved moderately in some respects (cf. OECD 2016) and the media storm around PISA has abated somewhat, but PISA and what should follow from it are still important topics in the media and policy discussions.

In the wake of the PISA-shock, the perceived shortcomings of the German education system were discussed very much in relation to OECD averages and the results of other countries participating in the study. The German reaction to PISA is therefore a textbook case of a scandalization, where "the weaknesses of one's own educational system" are highlighted "as a result of comparison" (Steiner-Khamsi 2003). In the course of this scandalization, a number of reference societies played an important role as a projection screen for conceptions of the good and the bad school. Among these, Finland and some of the East Asian PISA top scorers are particularly important with regard to K–12 education in Germany. There are other reference societies with regard to other sectors of the education system, such as the United States in the field of higher education, which, however, will not be discussed here.

# Data and Methods

The following section will set out the empirical basis of this chapter as well as the method used to analyze the data.

## Data

The analysis presented here is based on all the articles mentioning education in Finland on the one hand and education in Shanghai, South Korea, and Japan on the other that appeared in *Süddeutsche Zeitung* and *Frankfurter Allgemeine Zeitung* (including *Frankfurter Allgemeine Sonntagszeitung*) between January 1, 2001 and December 31, 2014 (Table 4.1).[2] *Süddeutsche Zeitung* (in the following *SZ*) and *Frankfurter Allgemeine Zeitung* (in the following *FAZ*) are the two leading quality newspapers in Germany, with circulations between 300,000 and 400,000 (the most recent data can be found at Informationsgemeinschaft zur Feststellung der Verbreitung von Werbeträgern e.V. 2018). In terms of their political orientation, the *SZ* can be described as center-left (Hachmeister 2012) and the *FAZ* as center-right (Burkhardt 2012). By focusing on quality papers, the analysis only captures one segment of the media debate, albeit a particularly important one in the context of the policy process (Eilders 2000; cf. also Jarren and Vogel 2011). An interesting extension of the study presented here would be the analysis of other mass media such as television or the tabloid press or social media such as blogs and posts on social networks.

All articles from the two newspapers referring to education in Finland or the East Asian PISA-participants named above were included in the sample, except for articles merely mentioning PISA-scores or just naming the country's education system without providing any additional information or argument. This means that the sample comprises a quite diverse array of article genres, ranging from short notices based on news agency material to articles with a non-educational focus mentioning education only in passing to long in-depth reports with an exclusively educational focus to op-ed pieces. Since the East Asian PISA top scorers are often lumped together in the articles analyzed under the label "Asia/Asian education systems" (see discussion below), Table 4.1 lists the references to these education systems under the label "Asia." To avoid misunderstandings, it should be stressed already here that the lumping together of the three countries reflects a feature of the discourse that is strongly homogenizing and obscures a considerable degree of diversity between the education systems referred to under this label.

**Table 4.1** Articles Mentioning Education in Finland and "Asia" (Shanghai, Japan, South Korea) in Süddeutsche Zeitung and Frankfurter Allgemeine Zeitung from 2001 to 2014

| | 2001 | 2002 | 2003 | 2004 | 2005 | 2006 | 2007 | 2008 | 2009 | 2010 | 2011 | 2012 | 2013 | 2014 |
|---|---|---|---|---|---|---|---|---|---|---|---|---|---|---|
| Finland SZ | 7 | 53 | 30 | 16 | 14 | 7 | 23 | 11 | 13 | 6 | 8 | 3 | 12 | 9 |
| Finland FAZ | 5 | 46 | 17 | 8 | 15 | 4 | 23 | 8 | 13 | 2 | 4 | 4 | 4 | 4 |
| "Asia" SZ | 1 | 1 | 1 | 1 | 1 | 0 | 3 | 0 | 0 | 3 | 13 | 6 | 9 | 13 |
| "Asia" FAZ | 1 | 9 | 2 | 5 | 1 | 1 | 1 | 1 | 0 | 2 | 11 | 11 | 9 | 11 |

## Frame Analysis

The media do not just depict social reality, but in a very real sense *produce* it: "What we know about the world we live in we know through mass media" (Luhmann 2009 [1996], 9).[3] In this production process, the media utilize so-called frames, which reduce complexity in the perception and processing of social reality. Media frames and their role in the political process have been studied extensively by scholars of communication studies and political scientists (Callaghan and Schnell 2001; Matthes and Kohring 2008; Potthoff 2012; Brüggemann 2014). Frames can be analyzed in a wide variety of different ways and for different purposes (see Scheufele and Tewksbury 2007 and Matthes and Kohring 2008 for an overview), and definitions of what constitutes a frame as well as recommendations how frames should be investigated abound (cf. Potthoff 2012). The approach to frame analysis employed here is grounded in a hermeneutic-interpretative sociology of knowledge and can be seen to be a variant of discourse analysis (Keller 2005, 2011). In this view, frames are "interpretative schemes" (Keller 2005) or "patterns of making sense of the world," which are "rooted in culture and articulated by the individual" (Brüggemann 2014, 62–3, 61). They can be seen as part of the " 'interpretative repertoire' . . . by which a discourse tends to achieve its symbolic structuring of the world" (Keller 2005 with reference to Potter and Wetherell 1995).

The media draw the frames they use from the "*frame repository* in a given society" (Brüggemann 2014, 68, emphasis in the original). The frames the media use resonate with the frames of their audience, and media frames and the frames of their audiences influence each other. Therefore, an analysis of the frames used by the media makes it possible to draw—tentative—conclusions about the patterns of interpreting the world prevalent among a wider population (cf. Volkmann 2004; Van Gorp 2007).

Frames used by the media also play an important role in the policy-making process in a more narrow sense, although how important this role is depends on the specific situation and on the conditions under which media and policy-makers operate (cf. Walgrave and Van Aelst 2006). The media can pre-structure the debate, for example, by agenda setting, adding or denying salience to a topic. To a lesser extent, the media may also peform the function of informing policy-makers (Callaghan and Schnell 2001; Van Aelst and Walgrave 2016; Sevenans 2017). Conversely, policy-makers often try to consciously influence the way the media present a certain topic (cf. Rawolle 2010).

**Table 4.2** Positive, Negative, and Neutral/Ambivalent Framing of Education in Finland and "Asia" (Shanghai, Japan, South Korea) in Articles (Süddeutsche Zeitung and Frankfurter Allgemeine Zeitung)

|  | Finland (%) | "Asia" (Shanghai, Japan, South Korea) (%) |
|---|---|---|
| positive | 273  (74.0) | 19  (16.2) |
| negative | 8  (2.2) | 77  (65.8) |
| ambivalent/neutral | 88  (23.8) | 21  (17.9) |
| Total | 369  (100.0) | 117  (100.0) |

The frame analysis presented in this chapter focuses on the frames *shared* by a large majority of contributors to the media discussion. In other words, frame analysis is used here to identify "the bounds of acceptable discourse" (Entman 1993, 55). Differences how Finnish and "Asian" ILSA success is framed in the *SZ* on the one hand and the *FAZ* on the other will be discussed, but a more thorough analysis of different perceptions and positions to be found *within* the "bounds of acceptable discourse" is not the focus of this chapter.

As a first step of the analysis, the articles were coded according to whether they frame education in the respective reference societies in (1) a primarily *positive* way, (2) a primarily *negative* way, or (3) in a *neutral or ambivalent* way. The results of this analysis are presented in Table 4.2. The articles were then subjected to a close reading in order to identify shared frames and recurrent themes. In a final step, the frames identified for the Finnish case on the one hand and the "Asian" case on the other were compared.

# Reference Societies in Germany after PISA

In the following section, I will first discuss the timing of the references to Finland and the East Asian PISA top scorers in the media. Then, I will proceed to discuss how Finland is used as a positive and "Asia" as a negative reference society in the two newspapers studied.

## Finland and "Asia" in the Media: Timing of the References

Seen over the entire period studied here, there are about five times as many articles referring to education in Finland than education in "Asia" (Table 4.1).

Interestingly, the number of articles on Finnish education did not peak after the publication of the results of the international PISA study in winter 2001/2002, but in summer 2002 in conjunction with the release of the results of PISA-E, that is, the extension of the original PISA study comparing the results of the different federal states in Germany. Thus, the international reference society Finland became particularly salient in conjunction with a discussion of differences *within* Germany; comparison between different nations and subsequent scandalization was intertwined with comparison within Germany and the subsequent scandalization of individual German federal states.

Until 2011, the number of articles per year mentioning education in Finland always outnumbered the number of articles mentioning the countries and regions grouped together under the label of "Asia," sometimes by a factor of ten. This was the case despite the fact that Japan and Korea participated already in the first round of PISA and did extremely well (see below). From 2011, the total number of articles mentioning "Asia" was higher than the number of articles mentioning Finland. One explanation for this is the interest generated by the results of Shanghai. Shanghai first participated in PISA 2009, immediately moving to the top of the league tables in all three literacy domains. The results of PISA 2009 were released in December 2010, triggering more articles on "Asia" in 2011. The fact that China is a major trading partner and economic competitor and that the Shanghainese PISA results can be connected to a "falling behind in relation to China"-narrative in Germany (cf. Richter, Gebauer, Heberer, and Hafez 2010) probably contributed to the intensified attention given to education in "Asia".

## Finland as a Positive Reference Society

In the wake of PISA 2000, Finland became the number one positive reference society for educational policy-making in Germany, which is clearly reflected in the media debate (Waldow 2010; Takayama, Waldow, and Sung 2013). The Finnish results serve as a quantitative and qualitative benchmark that is put in relation to German results. A quote such as "Finland reaches an average result that exceeds that of Bavaria by 25 points, that of Baden-Württemberg by 36 and Saxony by 39 points" (Frankfurter Allgemeine Zeitung 2005) again shows how scandalization through comparison with other countries is intertwined with scandalization of federal states within Germany. The Finnish success in education is often discussed in conjunction with other fields that are seen as related to education, such as economic competitiveness or the general well-being of children.

The framing of education in Finland is overwhelmingly positive. Almost three quarters of all articles in the sample frame Finnish education in a positive way, and only about two percent in a negative way (see Table 4.2). The traits that are often ascribed to Finnish education in Germany are that education is "progressive" in the sense that it is child-centered and pupils learn because of a favorable learning environment and intrinsic motivation, not because of external pressure through examinations, and so forth (cf. Taffertshofer and Herrmann 2007, in *SZ*). Teachers enjoy high status, and entrance to the teaching profession is highly selective; according to Heike Schmoll (2002a) in *FAZ*, Finland is the country "where only the best become teachers" (Schmoll 2002a, 10). Other aspects that are mentioned are the high degree of support available (e.g., for pupils with special needs), a classroom climate that is conducive to learning and the high degree of school autonomy.

Although both newspapers portray Finnish education in an overwhelmingly positive light, there are also certain differences in how success is framed. This becomes most clear with regard to comprehensivization of education, which has been a recurrent bone of contention in German education policy-making since the nineteenth century (cf. Oelkers 2006). *SZ* is generally favorable to comprehensivization, and the Finnish results can be easily attached to this narrative. For instance, according to *SZ* journalist Jeanne Rubner (2002b), Finland proves that it is possible to combine equality and excellence in a comprehensive system. Authors writing in *FAZ* acknowledge that the Finnish comprehensive system is producing good results, but contest whether this is transferable to Germany due to contextual and cultural factors (cf. e.g., Schmoll 2002b; the title of the article is "The Finns Know Where the Principle of Equality Has Its Limits"). Some of the factors mentioned in this context that are claimed to be not easily reproducible in Germany are "Finnish reading culture" (Schmoll 2002c) and the low number of immigrants in Finland. Also, Heike Schmoll of *FAZ* claims that what looks like a unified comprehensive system in Finland really is internally quite diverse and that the "ostensible uniformity of Finnish school is an optical illusion" (Schmoll 2004, 4). Therefore, according to Schmoll (2004), the Finnish example cannot be invoked as support for comprehensivization of the German system. The *SZ*, by contrast, also mentions the "reading culture that is second to none" (Maidt-Zinke 2013) and the low number of immigrants in Finland, but does not place this in the context of an anti-comprehensivization argument.

Finland's positive image builds on earlier perceptions of the Scandinavian countries, which have been referenced positively in Germany for a long time.[4]

Romanticizing views about "The North" go back at least as far as the romantic period (Henningsen 1993), with various shifts in which Nordic country was seen as the most prominent embodiment of the "North" or "Scandinavia" (Musiał 2002). From about the end of the Second World War, Scandinavia, especially Sweden, was seen as a model in educational matters by observers in many countries, especially in West Germany (Ruth 1984; cf. Nilsson 1987; cf. also Andersson and Hilson 2009). Berthold Franke (2008) has argued that one reason why Sweden was (and is) so popular especially in Germany is that there is a "collective projection" among Germans that Sweden is a version of what Germany might have been if history had unfolded differently, especially if there had been no Nazi era (Franke 2008, 261). Sweden is thus used as a projection screen for an imaginary alternative utopian future of Germany.

Arguably, in the wake of PISA Finland increasingly took over the role as the prime representative of "Scandinavia," building on the earlier prominence of Sweden. After the first few PISA-rounds, Sweden and Finland were still often named in one breath as "PISA top scorers" (cf. Kobarg and Prenzel 2009), a pairing that gradually disappeared following the decline of the Swedish scores. The relative decline in the Finnish PISA results in recent PISA-rounds only led to a partial revision of the positive picture presented in the *SZ* and *FAZ*. When the results of PISA 2012 were published, Heike Schmoll (2013, 2) claimed that the slogan "Learning from Scandinavia means learning to win" is a thing of the past,[5] while one year later Ralph Bollmann (2014) in the same newspaper still praises Finland as the "PISA-winner."

In the German media discourse analyzed here, the Finnish education system appears to be highly child-centered and based on intrinsically motivating children to learn. At the same time, it seems to produce excellent results across the board, with little variation between pupils and schools. The system appears to be largely free of internal contradictions and tensions usually besetting real-life education systems. For example, Blankart and Koester (2003) celebrate on the one hand competition between Finnish schools and on the other the low between-school variation in Finland, although arguably the latter exists *despite* the former, being a relic from a time when the school system was tightly centrally controlled and there was no competition (Takayama, Waldow, and Sung 2013, 312–13). The utopian character of the image projected onto the projection screen Finland also becomes obvious through the language used, for example, in article titles such as "Paradise in the North" (Taffertshofer and Herrmann 2007), "paradise" being the ultimate utopia. The subtitle to this article gives the reasons why Finland is an educational paradise: "more teachers, no pressure to get good grades, no repetition of grades," taking up various topics that were hotly debated in Germany at the time the article appeared. "No pressure to get good grades" in addition seems to suggest that schools in Finland somehow escape the negative effects produced by education systems' social allocation function.

Against this overwhelmingly positive backdrop, the treatment of comprehensivization by *SZ* and *FAZ* shows how broadly similar "slides" can be connected to differing reform narratives by different actors. In the progressive narrative, the Finnish case demonstrates that comprehensive education works and can go along with good results. In the conservative narrative, comprehensive schooling and good results may coexist, but are not transferable to other contexts such as Germany for "cultural" reasons (a point that will be returned to in the conclusion).

Finally, it should be added that while the picture of Finland presented in the two newspapers is overwhelmingly positive, there is also a small number of articles pointing to internal contradictions and tensions in the Finnish education system (e.g., Zekri 2002). Also, some journalists seem to be well aware of the selective and projective use of foreign reference societies, including Finland, in the German debate, for example, Jürgen Kaube (2002, 64) from *FAZ*: "those who love the tracked school system refer to Bavaria. Those who love comprehensive schooling point to Finland or Sweden."

## "Asia" as a Negative Reference Society

The mirror image to the Finnish case is provided by the East Asian participants scoring highly in PISA, often grouped together and discussed under the summary and homogenizing label "Asia." Being a continent rather than a nation state, Asia is of course not a reference society in the narrow sense of the word. However, in the discourse analyzed here, the construct of "Asia" is used in an analogous way to a reference society (cf. also Takayama 2018). The countries and regions mainly discussed under this label are the Chinese regions participating in PISA (especially Shanghai), South Korea, (to a lesser extent) Japan, and (to an even lesser extent) Singapore and Taiwan. Shanghai is sometimes more or less implicitly taken as *pars pro toto* for the whole of China, which in the light of Shanghai's unusual character in the context of China as a whole is problematic (see the discussion in the chapter by Lingard and Sellar in this volume). Other East Asian countries such as Thailand and Indonesia participated in various PISA-rounds,[6] but they are not relevant as reference societies in the media debate on education policy-making in Germany.

In contrast to the generally very positive image of Finland, "Asia" is mostly portrayed in a negative light (see Table 4.2): almost two thirds of the articles on "Asia" frame education in these countries and regions negatively, and only about 16 percent provide a positive framing (the corresponding figures for Finland are two percent negative and 74 percent positive).

The narrative connected to the East Asian PISA top scorers is very uniform. The traits that are usually ascribed to "Asian" education are that education systems in these countries are characterized by severe drill, rote learning, grueling examinations (often referred to as "examination hell" (Frankfurter Allgemeine Zeitung 2008), no time for play and a great deal of "shadow education" (e.g., private tutoring) and cram schools which are not part of compulsory mass schooling such as the Japanese *juku* (an article that takes up all of these traits is Bork 2011). The strain this places on pupils creates a "youth without sleep" (Kolb 2007), and many pupils get ill or even kill themselves. Empirical research on education in "Asia" that paints a more nuanced picture (see e.g., Schubert 2005; Park 2013; Takayama 2013; Takayama and Sung 2014) tends not to find its way into the newspapers analyzed here to any greater extent.

Against this overwhelmingly negative picture, only some individual aspects of education in East Asian countries are sometimes singled out as positive, such as the low achievement gap between pupils from different backgrounds in Korea (Hanimann 2003). The high respect learning enjoys in East Asia sometimes arouses envy, although some articles add that this respect can easily turn into an obsession, thereby turning what at first glance appears like a positive reference into its opposite and again contributing to the negative framing of PISA results.

Just as in the Finnish case, the way in which education in the East Asian PISA top scorers is framed has a long history. Already in the early 1990s, that is, long before the first round of PISA, the (rare) articles on education in these countries painted a fairly negative picture consistent with the frames prevalent in the period studied here (cf. Aznarez 1993, with the illustrative article title: "When Discipline Crowds out Creativity"; or Schneppen 1999, with the article title: "At an Age of Two Years, the First Steps into Examination Hell"). The publication of the TIMSS results in 1997 (Baumert et al. 1997), in which Singapore, Japan, Korea, and Hong Kong were among the top scorers, created a certain fascination for Japanese "problem-centered" mathematics teaching, but this was not sufficient to turn Japan into a more stable positive reference society in the German educational debate.

After the publication of the results of the first round of PISA, references to East Asian systems of education slowly became more frequent, although it is remarkable that references to these systems only started outnumbering references to Finland in 2011 despite the fact that already in the first round of PISA, Japan, and Korea had higher scores in scientific and mathematical literacy than Finland. This, however, did not lead to them becoming a media sensation at the time. Only when Shanghai led the league tables in all three domains in PISA 2009 did references to the East Asian systems of education start outnumbering references to Finland. As was mentioned in the introduction to this chapter, this may have to do with the fact that China is a main trading partner and economic competitor of Germany and that there is a widespread fear articulated in the media that the rise of China may go hand in hand with the decline of Germany (Richter et al. 2010, 15–16).

Especially striking in comparison to the Finnish case is how unanimous *SZ* and *FAZ* are in their negative depiction of "Asian education" and their negative framing of PISA success in these systems. As was discussed above, there are differences in how the center-left *SZ* and the center-right *FAZ* depict education in Finland and how they insert their projections into the debate on education policy-making in Germany. This could be seen for example, in how the two newspapers discuss the issue of comprehensivization. In the case of "Asia," it is hard to find such differences. If Finland is an educational utopia for most of the authors writing in the two newspapers (even though for some observers one that it is impossible to emulate outside Finland), almost all observers seem to agree that "Asia" is an educational dystopia. Observers of different political persuasions seems to be employing the same "slide" and to be agreeing that nothing can be learnt from these education systems. Grzanna (2014) expresses the mainstream view prevalent in *SZ* and *FAZ* when he claims in *SZ* that the "result of the PISA study is deceptive and must by no means encourage us to emulate China." If articles mention the possibility that Germany might learn anything from education in East Asian countries at all, they do this in an extremely tentative way (Süddeutsche Zeitung 2014a).

Still, the East Asian PISA successes seem to present a challenge that cannot simply be ignored, especially since the rising world power China entered the game (in the shape of Shanghai) and performed so well in PISA 2009. This challenge seemingly needs to be addressed, that is, it needs to be explained why Germany should not borrow from the East Asian systems (cf. Bork 2011 and the discussion in the introduction to this volume).

Germany is far from being the only place where negative images of education in East Asian countries can be found (cf. Takayama 2018), but when compared to the education policy-making discourse in countries such as the UK or the United

States, the fact that observers both in the center-left *SZ* and the center-right *FAZ* almost unanimously share a negative perspective on "Asian" education appears as rather extreme. For instance, in the UK, the picture of "Asian" education is far from unanimously positive, but there are some efforts to borrow reforms from East Asian systems (cf. Sellar and Lingard 2013; You and Morris 2016; You 2017). In their chapter in this volume, Lingard and Sellar show how widespread the recommendation to learn from East Asia is in Australian education policy-making. In the United States, too, the picture is much more varied than in Germany. References to education in East Asian countries have been a recurrent feature in the US education policy-making debate for many years, with the stances taken toward "Asian" education differing over time and between different groups of observers and ranging from admiration to abhorrence (Cummings 1989; Cummings and Altbach 1997; White 1999; LeTendre 1999, see also the chapter by Green Saraisky in this volume). The particularly negative German reaction suggests that the "Asian" PISA success may strike a particular chord in the German context.

In the introduction to this volume, the proposition was put forward that projections may serve to externalize unease about aspects of one's own education system to other systems. In this context, it is striking that some of the main aspects that are criticized in the German discussion concerning education in "Asia" are aspects that are also heavily criticized in relation to education in Germany. Two examples may suffice to illustrate this point:

1. The first example is the debate on "overburdening" of pupils, which goes back to the nineteenth century and has resurfaced periodically since then. According to the proponents of the "overburdening"-thesis, schooling, especially academic-track secondary schooling, overtaxes the mental and bodily strength of pupils, leading to mental and bodily illness and deformation (cf. Whittaker 2013). In the wake of the shortening of the German *Gymnasium* (selective academic-track secondary school) from nine to eight years in most federal states, the "overburdening" argument has surfaced again (cf. Kühn et al. 2013). Some arguments put forward against the eight-year *Gymnasium* bear a striking resemblance to depictions of schooling in "Asia" in the German media.
2. The second example concerns feeling ill at ease with the social allocation function the education system performs for society as a whole (cf. Fend 2008) by allocating life chances to pupils via the awarding of educational certificates (cf. Yair 2007). Through its tracked structure, German

secondary schooling makes the fact that the education system opens and closes doors for pupils particularly apparent. Many studies have shown that many educators as well as parents are ill at ease with the education system's allocative function and consider its effects on teaching and learning detrimental and corrupting (Terhart 2006; Streckeisen, Hänzi, and Hungerbühler 2007; Falkenberg 2017). Possibly, the criticism of the supposed "exam hell" of "Asian" schooling echoes this uneasiness with the selectivity of the German school system.

Thus, German observers may feel particularly uncomfortable with certain aspects of the image of "Asian" education because they feel they are uncomfortably close to conditions in the German education system. When damning the supposedly "Asian" cram school and "exam hell," the German media may be projecting and thereby externalizing uneasiness about aspects of their own system. Just as criticizing adolescent suicides and substance abuse in Japanese schools may have served to deflect attention from the same (much more prevalent) shortcomings in the United States (see introduction to this volume and Zeng and LeTendre 1999), German media may be revealing at least as much about the German system than about education in "Asia" when writing about the latter.

## Conclusion

The chapter has shown that the ILSA-successes of Finland on the one hand and the East Asian PISA top scorers Shanghai, Japan, and South Korea on the other are framed in two radically different ways in the German quality newspapers analyzed here. The Finnish success is framed in an extremely positive way as being founded on child-centeredness, intrinsic motivation of pupils, high status of the teaching profession, and so on, while the high scores of Shanghai, Japan, and South Korea are presented as being bought at too high a price by inhuman drill. These framings are at least partially grounded in heterostereotypes about the two contexts that go back a long time. The chapter has also demonstrated that the projections made onto the projection screens of Finland and "Asia" have more to do with topics that are considered important or controversial in Germany than with the realities in the respective reference societies.

Sellar and Lingard (2013, 470–1) argue that the "value of PISA as an instrument for shaping global education policy discourses . . . depends on performance being attributable to policy as well as cultural factors, not simply the latter" (see also the discussion in the chapter by Lingard and Sellar in this volume). This argument resonates well with the findings presented here: explanations of the "Asian" PISA success often center on supposedly "cultural" values. Therefore, "Asian" recipes for success in LSAs cannot be easily borrowed, even if this was desired. In a similar way, conservative voices try to make the case that the Finnish success is not borrowable for "cultural" reasons.

Images of positive and negative reference societies can interact with each other, stabilizing and reinforcing each other. A "heaven-and-hell"-logics seems to be at work here. Possibly, "educational heaven" becomes more attractive and "educational hell" more repulsive if there is a respective counterpart serving as a kind of mirror image. Arguably, presenting a model to emulate is more effective if there is a very unattractive counter-model to compare the desirable one with. Some articles in the sample employ a rhetoric that displays this dichotomization clearly: Finland appears as an educational "paradise" (Taffertshofer and Herrmann 2007) to which people undertake "pilgrimages" (Rubner 2002a). The "Asian" systems present the mirror image of an "examination hell" (Frankfurter Allgemeine Zeitung 2008) populated by a "youth without sleep" (Kolb 2007) where children have to "run the gauntlet from examination to examination" (Bork 2011, 3). Metaphors referring to Finland invoke redemption, metaphors referring to "Asia" damnation and torture.

This chapter has focused on the "bounds of acceptable discourse," that is, on commonalities in the "frame repository" (cf. Brüggemann 2014, 68) available to writers contributing to *SZ* and *FAZ*. This approach may lead to the impression that the available frame repository is more unified than it actually is. While the frame repositories available in a given society constrain the ways in which reference societies can be depicted, the repository can contain partly conflicting frames. In addition, a more detailed analysis, also taking into account other media than the two discussed newspapers or groups of actors outside the media such as policy-makers, would probably have made even clearer how the same reference society can be integrated in quite different, sometimes opposing, political agendas (cf. Waldow 2010).

By now, there is ample research showing that PISA (and ILSAs more generally) have had a massive impact on how education is perceived and talked about, what types of education are considered relevant and what should be taught (cf. Addey and Sellar 2017). ILSAs may have contributed to a certain standardization of ways of conceiving of education and education reform agendas. However, ILSAs have not led to a complete uniformization of the discourse everywhere. The chapters in this volume demonstrate that reactions to PISA and ILSAs in general are not uniform across different contexts and that the narratives attached to results and the framing of success and failure differ, sometimes radically. In different contexts, different countries lend themselves as "projection screens" and different slides are projected onto them. Arguably, PISA has acquired such a ubiquitous presence in education policy-making precisely because so many different narratives can be attached to it.

Whether this diversity will persist or whether the projections connected to PISA and ILSAs in general will become more uniform in the future is an open question, however. Even if heterostereotypes tend to be quite stable, they are not completely immutable. For the German case, it will be particularly interesting to monitor how the framing of "Asian" education develops over time. While "Asia" was still overwhelmingly rejected as potential source of "educational borrowing" in Germany at the end of the period studied here, there may be (as of yet very weak) signs that this could be changing. For example, in an article reporting on the UK's scheme of "importing" Shanghai mathematics teachers and sending British teachers to Shanghai on study visits, the *SZ* in 2014 very tentatively asks whether this might also become a model for Germany (Süddeutsche Zeitung 2014a).[7] Especially if East Asian countries and regions continue to dominate the top positions of LSA ranking tables or even increase their dominance and if countries perceived as "culturally similar" to Germany (such as the UK) adopt a positive stance towards education in East Asian countries, the negative framing may be reversed or at least become weaker. Conversely, if Finland continues to slip in the league tables, its sparkle as an educational utopia may fade, not just in Germany.

# Notes

1   This chapter builds partially on the argument and material presented in Waldow (2017).

2   I would like to thank Franziska Primus for invaluable help with compiling the database and coding the articles.

3   Rereading the quote at the time of writing of this chapter (2018), that is, more than twenty years after Luhmann's text first was written, Luhmann's assumption that the mass media "produce" our (shared) reality seems more problematic than it probably appeared at the time of writing, that is, before the rise of social media. According to an often-heard argument (cf. Sunstein 2017) one problem connected to this rise is that it has led to an increased fragmentation of shared realities.

4   Geographically, Finland is not part of Scandinavia, but nevertheless it is often
    included in this group of countries due to perceived cultural and political
    similarities.

5   In PISA 2012, Finland reached twelveth place in mathematical literacy, 5th place
    in scientific literacy and 6th place in reading literacy (OECD 2014). With the
    formulation quoted in the main text, Schmoll (2013) alludes to a GDR propaganda
    poster from the 1950s. The original slogan was "Learning from the people of the
    Soviet Union means learning to win" (cf. Haus der Geschichte der Bundesrepublik
    Deutschland no year). One may wonder whether by making this connection,
    Schmoll, writing for the conservative *FAZ*, is subtly accusing the advocates of a
    "Scandinavian" approach in educational matters of bearing a certain similarity to
    Soviet propagandists.

6   Full information on which countries took part in which round of PISA can be
    obtained from OECD (n.d.).

7   However, only two days later, page one of the same newspaper featured a squib
    poking fun at this scheme (Süddeutsche Zeitung 2014b).

# References

Addey, C., and Sellar, S. (2017), "The Rise of International Large-Scale Assessments and
    Rationales for Participation," *Compare*, *47*(3), 434–43.

Andersson, J., and Hilson, M. (2009), "Images of Sweden and the Nordic Countries,"
    *Scandinavian Journal of History*, *34*(3), 219–28, doi: 10.1080/03468750903134681.

Aznarez, J. (1993), "Wenn die Disziplin die Kreativität verdrängt" [When Discipline
    Suppresses Creativity], *Süddeutsche Zeitung*, July 24, 8.

Baumert, J., and Deutsches PISA-Konsortium (2002), *PISA 2000: Die Länder der
    Bundesrepublik Deutschland im Vergleich* [PISA 2000: A Comparison of the German
    Bundesländer], Opladen: Leske + Budrich.

Baumert, J., Lehmann, R., Lehrke, M., Schmitz, B., Clausen, M., Hosenfeld, I., Köller,
    O., and Neubrand, J. (1997), *TIMSS—Mathematisch-naturwissenschaftlicher
    Unterricht im internationalen Vergleich: Deskriptive Befunde* [TIMSS—Mathematic-
    Scientific Education in an International Comparison: Descriptive Results],
    Opladen: Leske + Budrich.

Blankart, C. B., and Koester, G. (2003), "Schulen im Wettbewerb" [Schools in
    Competition], *Frankfurter Allgemeine Zeitung* 207, September 6, 13.

Bollmann, R. (2014), "Lobt die Lehrer!" [Praise the Teachers], *Frankfurter Allgemeine
    Zeitung*, 15 June, 18.

Bork, H. (2011), "Der Chinakracher" [The Chinese Firecracker], *Süddeutsche Zeitung*,
    January 8, 15.

Brüggemann, M. (2014), "Between Frame Setting and Frame Sending: How Journalists Contribute to News Frames," *Communication Theory*, 24(1), 61–82.

Burkhardt, K. (2012), "Frankfurter Allgemeine Zeitung," Institut für Medien- und Kommunikationspolitik, Last Modified May 4, 2012, https://www.mediadb.eu/de/forum/zeitungsportraets/faz.html (accessed March 14, 2018).

Callaghan, K., and Schnell, F. (2001), "Assessing the Democratic Debate: How the News Media Frame Elite Policy Discourse," *Political Communication*, 18(2), 183–213, doi: 10.1080/105846001750322970.

Cummings, W. K. (1989), "The American Perception of Japanese Education," *Comparative Education*, 25(3), 293–302, doi: 10.2307/3099203.

Cummings, W. K., and Altbach P. G. (1997), *The Challenge of Eastern Asian Education: Implications for America, SUNY Series, Frontiers in Education*, Albany: State University of New York Press.

Eilders, C. (2000), "Media as Political Actors? Issue Focusing and Selective Emphasis in the German Quality Press," *German Politics*, 9(3), 181–206, doi: 10.1080/09644000008404613.

Entman, RM. (1993), "Framing: Toward Clarification of a Fractured Paradigm," *Journal of Communication*, 43(4), 51–58, doi: 10.1111/j.1460–2466.1993.tb01304.x.

Falkenberg, K. (2017), "Gerechte Noten? Eine Grounded Theory-Studie zu Gerechtigkeitsüberzeugungen von Lehrkräften in Bezug auf schulische Leistungsbeurteilung im deutsch-schwedischen Vergleich" [Fair Assessment? A Grounded Theory Study on Swedish and German Teachers' Justice Beliefs Regarding Assessment], [unpublished dissertation], Humboldt-Universität zu Berlin.

Fend, H. (2008), *Neue Theorie der Schule: Einführung in das Verstehen von Bildungssystemen* [New Theory of School: Introduction into the Comprehension of Education Systems], 2nd ed., Wiesbaden: VS Verlag für Sozialwissenschaften.

Franke, B. (2008), "Das Bullerbü-Syndrom: Warum die Deutschen Schweden lieben" [The Bullerby Syndrom: Why Germans Love Sweden], *Merkur*, 62(3), 256–61.

Frankfurter Allgemeine Zeitung (2005), "Erhebliche Leistungsfortschritte" [Significant Performance Progress], *Frankfurter Allgemeine Zeitung*, July 15, 1.

Frankfurter Allgemeine Zeitung (2008), "Vor der Schule lernen wir" [We Study before School], *Frankfurter Allgemeine Zeitung*, December 2, 40.

Gruber, K-H. (2006), "The German 'PISA-Shock': Some Aspects of the Extraordinary Impact of the OECD's PISA Study on the German Education System," in H. Ertl (ed.), *Cross-National Attraction in Education: Accounts from England and Germany*, 195–208, Oxford: Symposium.

Grzanna, M. (2014), "In der Billigfalle" [In the Low-Cost Trap], *Süddeutsche Zeitung*, April 11, 25.

Hachmeister, L. (2012), "Süddeutsche Zeitung," Institut für Medien- und Kommunikationspolitik, last modified May 4, 2012, https://www.mediadb.eu/de/forum/zeitungsportraets/sueddeutsche-zeitung.html (accessed March 14, 2018).

Hanimann, J. (2003), "PISA zum Zweiten: Auch in Asien liest man besser" [Second Round of PISA: Students in Asia Read Better, as Well], *Frankfurter Allgemeine Zeitung*, July 2, 42.

Haus der Geschichte der Bundesrepublik Deutschland (n.d.) "Plakat 'Von den Sowjetmenschen lernen . . . ' " [Poster: "Learning from the Soviets . . . "], https://www.hdg.de/lemo/bestand/objekt/plakat-sowjetmenschen-siegen.htm (accessed March 13, 2018).

Henningsen, B. (1993), "Der Norden: Eine Erfindung: Das europäische Projekt einer regionalen Identität: Antrittsvorlesung 28. Mai 1993" [The North: An Invention: The European Project of a Regional Identity: Inaugural Lecture on May 28, 1993], Humboldt-Universität zu Berlin http://edoc.hu-berlin.de/humboldt-vl/henningsen-bernd/PDF/Henningsen.pdf (accessed March 13, 2018).

Informationsgemeinschaft zur Feststellung der Verbreitung von Werbeträgern e.V. (2018), "Downloadcenter," http://www.ivw.eu/downloadcenter (accessed March 13, 2018).

Jarren, Otfried, and Martina Vogel (2011), " 'Leitmedien' als Qualitätsmedien: Theoretisches Konzept und Indikatoren" ["Leading Media" as Quality Media: Theoretical Concepts and Indicators], in *Krise der Leuchttürme öffentlicher Kommunikation: Vergangenheit und Zukunft der Qualitätsmedien*, R. Blum, H. Bonfadelli, K. Imhof, and O. Jarren (eds.), 17–29, Wiesbaden: VS Verlag für Sozialwissenschaften.

Kaube, J. (2002), "Ein Jahr nach PISA" [One Year after PISA], *Frankfurter Allgemeine Sonntagszeitung*, December 8, 64.

Keller, R. (2005), "Analysing Discourse: An Approach from the Sociology of Knowledge," *Forum Qualitative Social Research*, 6(3), http://www.qualitative-research.net/index.php/fqs/article/view/19/42 (accessed March 13, 2018).

Keller, R. (2011), *Diskursforschung: Eine Einführung für SozialwissenschaftlerInnen* [Discourse Analysis: An Introduction for Social Scientists], 4th ed., Wiesbaden: VS Verlag für Sozialwissenschaften.

Kobarg, M., and Prenzel, M. (2009), "Stichwort: Der Mythos der nordischen Bildungssysteme" [Keyword: The Myth of the Nordic Educational Systems], *Zeitschrift für Erziehungswissenschaft*, 12(4), 597–615, doi: 10.1007/s11618-009-0098-7.

Kolb, M. (2007), "Jugend ohne Schlaf: Südkoreas Schüler sind sehr leistungsstark, doch in dem Land wächst die Kritik an der unentwegten Paukerei" [Youth without Sleep: South Korean Students Are Very Hard-Working, but Criticism towards the Constant Drill Is Rising in the Country], *Süddeutsche Zeitung*, December 3, 16.

Kühn, S. M., van Ackeren, I., Bellenberg, G., Reintjes, C., and im Brahm, G. (2013), "Wie viele Schuljahre bis zum Abitur? Eine multiperspektivische Standortbestimmung im Kontext der aktuellen Schulzeitdebatte" [How Many Years until Abitur in German Upper Secondary Schooling?—Taking Stock in the Context of Current School Duration Debates], *Zeitschrift für Erziehungswissenschaft*, 16(1), 115–36, doi: 10.1007/s11618-013-0339-7.

LeTendre, G. K. (ed.) (1999), *Competitor or Ally? Japan's Role in American Educational Debates*, 1407, London: Routledge.

Luhmann, N. ([1996] 2009), *Die Realität der Massenmedien* [The Reality of Mass Media], 3rd ed., Wiesbaden: VS-Verlag für Sozialwissenschaften.

Maidt-Zinke, K. (2013), "Weltmeister im Lesen" [World Champions in Reading], *Süddeutsche Zeitung*, November 4, 12.

Martens, K., and Niemann, D. (2013), "When Do Numbers Count? The Differential Impact of the PISA Rating and Ranking on Education Policy in Germany and the US," *German Politics*, *22*(3), 314–32, doi: 10.1080/09644008.2013.794455.

Matthes, J., and Kohring, M. (2008), "The Content Analysis of Media Frames: Toward Improving Reliability and Validity," *Journal of Communication*, *58*(2), 258–79.

Musiał, K. (2002), *Roots of the Scandinavian Model: Images of Progress in the Era of Modernisation*, Baden-Baden: Nomos.

Nilsson, I. (1987), *En spjutspets mot framtiden: En analys av de svenska enhets- och grundskolereformerna i utländsk vetenskaplig litteratur 1950–1980* [A Spearhead into the Future: An Analysis of the Swedish Comprehensive School Reforms in Foreign Scientific Literature 1950–1980], Lund: Universitet.

OECD (n.d.), "PISA Participants," https://www.oecd.org/pisa/aboutpisa/pisaparticipants.htm.

OECD (2016), *Country Note Germany*, Paris: Organisation for Economic Co-operation and Development.

OECD (2014), *PISA 2012 Results in Focus: What 15-Year-Olds Know and What They Can Do With What They Know*, Paris: Organisation for Economic Co-operation and Development.

Oelkers, J. (2006), *Gesamtschule in Deutschland: Eine historische Analyse und ein Ausweg aus dem Dilemma* [The Comprehensive School in Germany: A Historic Analysis and a Way Out of the Dilemma], Weinheim: Beltz.

Park, H. (2013), *Re-evaluating Education in Japan and Korea: Demystifying Stereotypes*, London: Routledge.

Potter, J., and Wetherell, M. (1995), "Soziale Repräsentationen, Diskursanalyse und Rassismus" [Social Representations, Discourse Analysis, and Racism], in U. Flick (ed.), *Psychologie des Sozialen: Repräsentationen in Wissen und Sprache*, 177–99, Reinbek: Rowohlt.

Potthoff, M. (2012), *Medien-Frames und ihre Entstehung* [Media Frames and Their Emergence], Wiesbaden: VS Verlag für Sozialwissenschaften.

Rawolle, S. (2010), "Understanding the Mediatisation of Educational Policy as Practice," *Critical Studies in Education*, *51*(1), 21–39, doi: 10.1080/17508480903450208.

Richter, C., Gebauer, S., Heberer, T., and Hafez, K. (2010), *Die China-Berichterstattung in den deutschen Medien* [The Reporting on China in German Media], Berlin: Heinrich-Böll-Stiftung.

Rubner, J. (2002a), "Diesmal besteht Hoffnung" [This Time, There Is Hope], *Süddeutsche Zeitung*, May 27, 4.

Rubner, J. (2002b), "Ein Schock, der auch Gutes bewirkte" [A Shock That Also Resulted in Something Good], *Süddeutsche Zeitung*, December 31, 9.

Ruth, A. (1984), "The Second New Nation: The Mythology of Modern Sweden," *Daedalus, 113*(2), 53–96.

Scheufele, D.A., and Tewksbury, D. (2007), "Framing, Agenda Setting, and Priming: The Evolution of Three Media Effects Models," *Journal of Communication, 57*(1), 9–20, doi: 10.1111/j.0021-9916.2007.00326.x.

Schmoll, H. (2002a), "Das Land, in dem die Besten Lehrer werden" [The Country in Which the Best Become Teachers], *Frankfurter Allgemeine Sonntagszeitung*, February 24, 10.

Schmoll, H. (2002b), "Die Finnen wissen, wo das Gleichheitsprinzip seine Grenzen hat" [The Finns Know the Limits of the Principle of Equality], *Frankfurter Allgemeine Zeitung*, February 9, 3.

Schmoll, H. (2002c), "Finnische Lesekultur" [Finnish Reading Culture], *Frankfurter Allgemeine Zeitung*, February 14, 12.

Schmoll, H. (2004), "Die Einheitsschule bis Klasse 7 hilft leistungsschwachen Kindern nicht" [The Comprehensive School until 7th Grade Does Not Help Low-Performing Students], *Frankfurter Allgemeine Zeitung*, December 10, 4.

Schmoll, H. (2013), "PISA mal Daumen" [The PISA Rule-of-Thumb], *Frankfurter Allgemeine Zeitung*, December 4, 2.

Schneppen, A. (1999), "Mit zwei Jahren die ersten Schritte in die Prüfungshölle" [The First Steps into the Examination Hell at the Age of Two], *Frankfurter Allgemeine Zeitung*, December 9, 14.

Schubert, V. (2005), *Pädagogik als vergleichende Kulturwissenschaft: Erziehung und Bildung in Japan* [Pedagogics as a Comparative Cultural Science: Education in Japan], Wiesbaden: VS Verlag für Sozialwissenschaften.

Sellar, S., and Lingard, B. (2013), "Looking East: Shanghai, PISA 2009 and the Reconstitution of Reference Societies in the Global Education Policy Field," *Comparative Education, 49*(4), 464–85.

Sevenans, J. (2017), "The Media's Informational Function in Political Agenda-Setting Processes," *The International Journal of Press/Politics, 22*(2), 223–43, doi: 10.1177/1940161217695142.

Steiner-Khamsi, G. (2003), "The Politics of League Tables," *Journal of Social Science Education, 1*, doi: 10.4119/UNIBI/jsse-v2-i1-470.

Streckeisen, U., Hänzi, D., and Hungerbühler, A. (2007), *Fördern und Auslesen: Deutungsmuster von Lehrpersonen zu einem beruflichen Dilemma* [To Promote and Select: Teachers' Interpretations of a Professional Dilemma], Wiesbaden: VS Verlag für Sozialwissenschaften.

Süddeutsche Zeitung (2014a), "Briten importieren Mathe-Lehrer aus China" [The British Import Maths Teachers from China], *Süddeutsche Zeitung*, March 12.

Süddeutsche Zeitung (2014b), "Das Streiflicht" [The Streak of Light], *Süddeutsche Zeitung*, March 14, 1.

Sunstein, C. R. (2017), *#Republic: Divided Democracy in the Age of Social Media*, Princeton: Princeton University Press.

Taffertshofer, B., and Herrmann, G. (2007), "Mehr Lehrer, kein Notendruck, kein Sitzenbleiben: Das Paradies im Norden: Warum Finnlands Schulen Weltspitze sind—und was Bayern daraus lernen kann" [More Teachers, No Grade Pressure, No Repetition of Classes: The Paradise in the North: Why Finlands Schools Are World Leaders—and What Bavaria Can Learn from That], *Süddeutsche Zeitung*, June 16, 46.

Takayama, K. (2013), "Not Just Tiger Mums and Rote Learning: It's Time for a Balanced View of Asian Education," *The Conversation: Academic Rigour, Journalistic Flair*, December 5, http://theconversation.com/not-just-tiger-mums-and-rote-learning-its-time-for-a-balanced-view-of-asian-education-21154.

Takayama, K. (2018), "The Constitution of East Asia as a Counter Reference Society through PISA: A Postcolonial/Decolonial Intervention," *Globalisation, Societies and Education*, doi: 10.1080/14767724.2018.1532282.

Takayama, K., and Sung, Y.-K. (2014), "Re-Evaluating Education in Japan and Korea: Demystifying Stereotypes," *Asia Pacific Journal of Education*, 34(2), 249–52, doi: 10.1080/02188791.2014.888698.

Takayama, K., Waldow, F., and Sung, Y-K. (2013), "Finland Has It All? Examining the Media Accentuation of 'Finnish Education' in Australia, Germany, and South Korea," *Research in Comparative and International Education*, 8(3), 307–25.

Terhart, E. (2006), "Giving Marks: Constructing Differences: Explorations in the Micro-Politics of Selection in Schools," in H. Drerup and W. Fölling (eds.), *Gleichheit und Gerechtigkeit: Pädagogische Revisionen*, 114–25, Dresden: TUDpress.

Tillmann, K.-J., Dedering, K., Kneuper, D., Kuhlmann, C., and Nessel, I. (2008), *PISA als bildungspolitisches Ereignis: Fallstudien in vier Bundesländern* [PISA as an Event in Education Policy: Case Studies in Four German Bundesländer], Wiesbaden: VS Verlag für Sozialwissenschaften.

van Ackeren, I. (2002), "Von FIMS und FISS bis TIMSS und PISA: Schulleistungen in Deutschland im historischen und internationalen Vergleich" [From FIMS and FISS to TIMSS and PISA: A Historic and International Comparison of School Performance in Germany], *Die Deutsche Schule*, 94(2), 157–75.

van Aelst, P., and Walgrave, S. (2016), "Political Agenda Setting by the Mass Media: Ten Years of Research, 2005–2015," in N. Zahariadis (ed.), *Handbook of Public Policy Agenda Setting*, 157–79, Cheltenham: Edward Elgar.

van Gorp, B. (2007), "The Constructionist Approach to Framing: Bringing Culture Back In," *Journal of Communication*, 57(1), 60–78, doi: 10.1111/j.0021-9916.2007.00329.x.

Volkmann, U. (2004), "Die journalistische Konstruktion gerechter Ungleichheiten" [The Journalist Construction of Fair Inequalities], in S. Liebig, H. Lengfeld and S. Mau (eds.), *Verteilungsprobleme und Gerechtigkeit in modernen Gesellschaften*, 297–328, Frankfurt a. M.: Campus.

Waldow, F. (2010), "Der Traum vom 'skandinavisch schlau Werden' " [The Dream of "Becoming Smart the Scandinavian Way"], *Zeitschrift für Pädagogik*, 56(4), 497–511.

Waldow, F. (2017), "Projecting Images of the 'Good' and the 'Bad School': Top Scorers in Educational Large-Scale Assessments as Reference Societies," *Compare*, 47(5), 647–64.

Walgrave, S, and Van Aelst, P. (2006), "The Contingency of the Mass Media's Political Agenda Setting Power: Toward a Preliminary Theory," *Journal of Communication*, 56(1), 88–109, doi: 10.1111/j.1460-2466.2006.00005.x.

White, M. (1999), "Introduction," in G. K. LeTendre (ed.), *Competitor or Ally? Japan's Role in American Educational Debates*, xi-xxii, New York: Falmer.

Whittaker, G. (2013), *Überbürdung—Subversion—Ermächtigung: Die Schule und die literarische Moderne 1880–1918, Literatur- und Mediengeschichte der Moderne* [Overtaxing—Subversion—Empowerment: The School and Literary Modernism 1880–1918, History of Modern Literature and Media], Göttingen: V&R unipress.

Yair, G. (2007), "Meritocracy, " in G. Ritzer (ed.), *The Blackwell Encyclopedia of Sociology*, 2954–8, Oxford: Blackwell.

You, Y. (2017), "Comparing School Accountability in England and Its East Asian Sources of 'Borrowing,' " *Comparative Education*, doi: http://dx.doi.org/10.1080/0305 0068.2017.1294652.

You, Y., and Morris, P. (2016), "Imagining School Autonomy in High-Performing Education Systems: East Asia as a Source of Policy Referencing in England," *Compare: A Journal of Comparative and International Education*, 46(6), 882–905, doi: 10.1080/03057925.2015.1080115.

Zekri, S. (2002), "Tango Finnale" [Tango the Finnish Way], *Süddeutsche Zeitung*, January 26, 13.

Zeng, K., and LeTendre, G. (1999), " 'The Dark Side of . . . ': Suicide, Violence and Drug Use in Japanese Schools," in G. K. LeTendre (ed.), *Competitor or Ally? Japan's Role in American Educational Debates*, 103–21, New York: Falmer.

# 5

# Nordic Reference Societies in School Reforms in Norway: An Examination of Finland and the Use of International Large-Scale Assessments

Kirsten Sivesind

## Introduction

When international large-scale assessments (ILSAs) were first enlisted in education reform, Sweden attracted considerable attention as the leading Nordic country in the rankings (Telhaug, Aasen, and Mediås 2004). However, after the first round of the Program for International Student Assessment (PISA) in December 2001, Finland outperformed Sweden and thus replaced it as the focus of international attention. While this might imply that Finland is now regarded as the standard bearer of excellence in education, public recognition of both Finland and Sweden's education systems, as well as the three other Nordic countries in Europe—Norway, Denmark, and Iceland—has varied ever since. To trace the impact of ILSAs and system comparisons, this chapter presents an overview of Nordic participation and variations in how the results were interpreted in terms of Norwegian policy documents. What I find is that Finland is seen by Norwegian policy-makers as a country from which to learn.

To develop insights into the policy borrowing process and the amount of attention paid to Finland, I begin by outlining how participation in ILSAs has varied across the Nordic region during the past fifty years. By describing the frequency of participation in IEA (see www.iea.nl) and OECD (see www.oecd.org/about) testing programs in different policy realms, I show which type of ILSAs were most frequently conducted in each Nordic country.

In the second part of the chapter I analyze twenty-two Norwegian governmental papers written between 1995 and 2016 to examine the use of ILSAs, and how the results were received. My aim was to identify how they fit into the broader picture of what counts as relevant evidence within school reform, and how policy-makers perceive Finland as a country for emulation. Questions include: To what extent are Norwegian policy-makers and experts using ILSAs to call for policy borrowing from Finland? Is foreign knowledge used to evaluate, assess, and justify school reform by referencing best practices? If so, in which realms are international data and findings considered relevant?

## Policy Borrowing by Governance and Evidence

Though educational systems all over the world look elsewhere for "best practices" and "success stories" from which to learn (Steiner-Khamsi 2014), what these constitute is contested. Knowledge providers such as the International Association for the Evaluation of Educational Achievement (IEA) and the Organization for Economic Co-Operation and Development (OECD) tend to suggest their own assessments as a tool for setting policy. Moreover, policy-makers are under increased pressure to borrow "lessons from elsewhere" and may base their recommendations on systems that are similar to their own (Steiner-Khamsi 2003).

Some researchers see this phenomenon as confirming a global mode of governance at the cost of state sovereignty and national educational structures (Meyer and Benavot 2013). Researchers also view ILSAs as creating regional education spaces beyond the control of national governments (Lawn and Lingard 2002). This perspective helps one understand how ILSAs serve as a form of soft governance (Grek 2009, 2010) which determines how "skills" and "competences" are internationalized (see also Nordin and Sundberg 2016; Wahlström 2016). At the same time, researchers argue that the direction of influence between the local and the global is not prescribed by global cultures or practices, but reliant on how written texts modify policy transfer (Karseth and Sivesind 2010; Sivesind et al. 2016), and depend on transnational discourses and the construction of policy among actors (Grek et al. 2009). Thus, Steiner-Khamsi (2014) calls for regional and local studies and argues that a country's performance will only be transferred from one country to another if it fits a domestic policy agenda and is interpreted and translated within specific contexts.

This perspective is supported by earlier work on externalization by Schriewer (2003) and current research by Takayama (2010), Waldow (2012), Pizmony-Levy (2017), and Baek et al. (2017). A possible way to assess the transfer is examining how ILSAs evidence are used, separated from, or accompanied by alternative knowledge sources . . . in policy documents.[1] Moreover, the use of ILSAs and the projection of success must be considered within a specific context. As Waldow (in this volume, chapter 1) proclaims in the introduction to this book, the milieu of projection, along with conception of the education system being projected, can be more powerful in reforming education than the projection screen. The documents I cite in this chapter does not show how school authorities and others run their education system to create outstanding quality but, rather how Finnish achievement is projected and ILSAs are used for reforming education in one Nordic country.

## Methods and Analytical Approach

I begin with an overview of the types and contents of ILSAs conducted within Nordic countries based primarily on information from IEA and OECD webpages. Only ILSAs for basic education (i.e., primary and lower secondary) and teacher education are included. The overview is presented in Table 5.1.[2]

The second part of the study draws on a qualitative content analysis including a structured comparison of themes and variables (Sivesind 1999). This includes twenty-two policy papers related to school reform in Norway with a selection of document sections that serve as units for analysis. Eight green papers and fourteen white papers written between 1995 and 2016 were analyzed. Green papers are produced by a commission of experts appointed by the parliament with a formal mandate to provide analysis and advice related to specific issues for the government. White papers are written within the ministries as a government-issued document laying out problems and justifying solutions, which are then decided upon by the parliament. This data reflects both political and policy-oriented issues based on how experts and officials refer to national and international evidence for reform.

I first searched the documents to determine how they positioned Finland as a reference system and whether other countries were mentioned. Only documents relevant to national school reform (grades 1–10), teacher education and related innovations were included. I condensed this into a four-page matrix with each row identifying the name of the document downloaded, a keyword that helped

**Table 5.1** Year, Number of Participating Education Systems and Distribution of Participating Countries

| ILSAs | Year | Systems | Denmark | Finland | Iceland | Norway | Sweden |
|---|---|---|---|---|---|---|---|
| **IEA: Studies in mathematics, natural sciences, ICT and digital skills** | | | | | | | |
| FIMS | 1964 | 12 | | ✓ | | | ✓ |
| FISS | 1971 | 19 | | ✓ | | | ✓ |
| SIMS | 1982 | 20 | | ✓ | | | ✓ |
| SISS | 1984 | 24 | | ✓ | | | ✓ |
| TIMSS | 1995 | 45 | ✓ | | ✓ | ✓ | ✓ |
| SITES | 1998–99 | 27 | ✓ | ✓ | ✓ | ✓ | |
| TIMSS Adv. | 1995 | 7 | | | | ✓ | |
| TIMSS | 1999 | 38 | | ✓ | | ✓ | |
| SITES | 2001 | 24 | ✓ | ✓ | ✓ | ✓ | |
| TIMSS | 2003 | 49 | ✓ | | | ✓ | ✓ |
| SITES | 2006 | 21 | | ✓ | | ✓ | |
| TIMSS | 2007 | 59 | ✓ | | | ✓ | ✓ |
| TIMSS Adv. | 2008 | 6 | | | | ✓ | |
| TIMSS | 2011 | 63 | ✓ | ✓ | | ✓ | ✓ |
| TEDS-M | 2008 | 17 | | | | ✓ | |
| ICILS | 2013 | 21 | ✓ | | | ✓ | |
| TIMSS | 2015 | 64 | ✓ | ✓ | | ✓ | ✓ |
| TIMSS Adv. | 2015 | 9 | | | | ✓ | |
| *Subtotal* | | | 8 | 10 | 3 | 14 | 9 |

## IEA: Reading literacy and democratic participation 1971–2015

| Study | Year | Number | | | | | |
|---|---|---|---|---|---|---|---|
| ICCS[4] | 1971 | 9 | ✓ | ✓ | | | ✓ |
| RLS | 1991 | 32 | ✓ | ✓ | | ✓ | ✓ |
| ICCS (CIVED) | 1999 | 29 | ✓ | ✓ | ✓ | ✓ | ✓ |
| PIRLS | 2001 | 35 | | ✓ | | ✓ | ✓ |
| PIRLS | 2006 | 40 | ✓ | ✓ | | ✓ | ✓ |
| ICCS | 2009 | 38 | ✓ | | ✓ | ✓ | ✓ |
| PIRLS | 2011 | 49 | | ✓ | | ✓ | ✓ |
| PIRLS | 2016 | 50 | ✓ | ✓ | | ✓ | ✓ |
| ICCS | 2016 | 24 | ✓ | | ✓ | | ✓ |
| *Subtotal* | | | *7* | *7* | *3* | *8* | *9* |
| **OECD international assessment studies** | | | | | | | |
| PISA | 2000 | 43 | ✓ | ✓ | ✓ | ✓ | ✓ |
| PISA | 2003 | 41 | ✓ | ✓ | ✓ | ✓ | ✓ |
| PISA | 2006 | 57 | ✓ | ✓ | ✓ | ✓ | ✓ |
| TALIS | 2008 | 24 | ✓ | | | ✓ | |
| PISA | 2009 | 65 (75*) | ✓ | ✓ | ✓ | ✓ | ✓ |
| PISA | 2012 | 65 | ✓ | ✓ | ✓ | ✓ | ✓ |
| PIAAC | 2008–13 | 23 | ✓ | ✓ | ✓ | ✓ | ✓ |
| TALIS | 2013 | 38 | ✓ | ✓ | ✓ | ✓ | ✓ |
| PISA | 2015 | 72 | ✓ | ✓ | ✓ | ✓ | ✓ |
| PISA | 2018 | 80 | ✓ | ✓ | ✓ | ✓ | ✓ |
| *Subtotal* | | | *10* | *9* | *9* | *10* | *9* |
| ***TOTAL*** | | | *25* | *26* | *15* | *32* | *25* |

* Includes education systems that participated in 2010

to categorize it, a short description of the theme, a code classifying how Finland was used as an example, whether the section referred to an ILSA or other specific documents, as well as how many countries' education systems were referenced along with Finland.[3]

The keywords were assigned to five thematic groups (Table 5.2): school conditions, curriculum, quality and development of basic education, student achievement and improvement, and professional development. Every unit was categorized according to whether Finland was cited positively, negatively, or neutrally, and then how PISA and other ILSAs were used to project Finland as a model for emulation. Before examining how policy-makers and experts in Norway responded to Finland's success, I will provide a brief description of Nordic participation in ILSAs.

## Nordic Participation in ILSAs

### A Comparison across Time and ILSAs

Nordic countries do not all share the same assessment history with ILSAs. Differences exist both in terms of periods of involvement and the types of studies conducted. As Table 5.1 shows, Finland and Sweden pioneered participation in the first studies organized by the IEA, starting with the First International Mathematics Study (FIMS) in 1964. They also participated in one of the first studies in science, the Six Subject Survey (1970–1), known as the First International Science Study (FISS). In an attempt to measure educational achievement over time, these studies were followed by the Second International Mathematics Study (SIMS), 1980–2.

Norway entered into the field of comparative studies in 1983–4 by conducting the Second International Science Study (SISS), while the first pan-Nordic participation in ILSAs, including Denmark and Iceland, occurred in 1991 with the Reading Literacy Study (RLS). Four of the Nordic countries were also involved in the start-up of the four-year cycle of assessments in mathematics and science in 1995 with the Third International Mathematics and Science Study (TIMSS), now known as the Trends in International Mathematics and Science Study. The study involved Denmark, Norway, Sweden and Iceland, followed by Finland, which participated in 1999. In a later IEA study, the Teacher Education and Development Studies in Mathematics (TEDS-M 2008), Norway was the only Nordic country. The overview in Table 5.1 for the IEA studies shows that Sweden

**Table 5.2** References to ILSAs and Projections of Finland

| Thematic areas | Period | Projections of Finland | References to ILSAs | Nordic countries | Other European countries | Non-European countries |
|---|---|---|---|---|---|---|
| **CONDITIONS** | | | | | | |
| School structure | 1997–2012 | Neutral 5 | | 20 | 7 | 2 |
| Time allocation | 2003 | Neutral 1 | | 3 | 2 | |
| Student–teacher ratio | 2003 | Neutral 1 | | 3 | 1 | |
| Guidance and counseling | 2003 | Neutral 1 Negative 1 | | 4 | | |
| Special education | 2003–2007 | Neutral 2 Positive 3 | PIRLS | 7 | 7 | |
| School–home collaboration | 2011 | Neutral 1 | | 4 | | |
| Private schooling | 2014 | Neutral 1 | | 2 | | |
| Safe school environment | 2015 | Neutral 1 | | | | 1 |
| **CURRICULUM** | | | | | | |
| General principles | 2003–2015 | Neutral 11 Positive 1 | | 28 | 10 | 2 |
| Religion and world view | 1995–2000 | Neutral 3 | | 11 | 11 | |
| Foreign language | 2003 | Neutral 1 | | 3 | | |
| ICT | 2003–2007 | Neutral 1 Negative 1 | SITES 2006 | 5 | | |
| Mother language | 2014 | Neutral 4 | | 11 | 2 | |
| Mathematics | 2014 | Neutral 3 | | 5 | 2 | |
| Natural sciences | 2014 | Neutral 1 | | 2 | 2 | |

Table 5.2  (Continued)

| Thematic areas | Period | Projections of Finland | References to ILSAs | Nordic countries | Other European countries | Non-European countries |
|---|---|---|---|---|---|---|
| **QUALITY DEVELOPMENT** | | | | | | |
| Quality assurance | 2002–2014 | Neutral 2 | | 6 | 2 | |
| Student assessment | 2003–2015 | Neutral 10 Positive 1 | | 21 | 5 | 1 |
| Learning strategies | 2015 | Neutral 1 | | 1 | | 1 |
| Competences and twenty-first-century skills | 2003–2015 | Neutral 2 | | 4 | 14 | 8 |
| International collaboration | 2003 | Neutral 1 | | | | |
| **STUDENT ACHIEVEMENT AND IMPROVEMENT** | | | | | | |
| General | 2001–2016 | Neutral 1 Positive 11 Negative 3 | PISA 11 TIMSS 1 CIVIC 1 ILSA 1 | 24 | 7 | 5 |
| Reading | 1996–2012 | Neutral 1 Positive 4 Negative 1 | PIRLS 3 PISA 3 RLS 1 | 14 | 20 | 13 |
| Mathematics and natural science | 2012–2014 | Positive 1 Negative 1 | | 3 | | |
| Adult literacy | 2012 | Neutral | PIAAC | 3 | 1 | |
| **PROFESSIONAL DEVELOPMENT** | | | | | | |
| School leadership education | 2007–2016 | Neutral 2 | | 5 | | |
| Teacher training | 2001–2008 | Neutral 3 | | 5 | 1 | |
| Centre of excellence | | Neutral 1 | | 2 | 1 | |

and Finland were the first countries involved in ILSAs, however (whether for political or economic reasons), every Nordic country has since participated (Edelstein 1987; Telhaug et al. 2004).

## References to ILSAs and Projections of Finland

In this section I describe findings and interpretations from the document analysis through an overview of how ILSAs are used as evidence, and how Finland is projected as a model for emulation. The results are summarized under five subheadings: (1) Conditions for organizing education; (2) Curriculum policies; (3) Quality and development of basic education; (4) Learning assessment as a key instrument for student achievement and improvement; and (5) Professional development.

### Policy Domains and References to ILSAs

As Steiner-Khamsi (2013, 27) has argued, not all types of comparisons necessarily lead to policy borrowing. This is especially the case if systems are similar in terms of both input parameters and outcomes on ILSAs. However, in the case of historical and organizational conditions that are important dimensions of school reform, several dimensions are context-dependent. Only those dimensions that are generic, either in terms of outcomes or in terms of systems or standards, are possibly subject to change by ILSAs.

### Conditions for Schooling

Of the seventeen times policy-makers and experts referred to Finland in terms of school structure, time allocation, student-teacher ratio, school-home collaboration, special education, private schooling, safe schools, and guidance counseling, only one ILSA was mentioned (see Table 5.2). Comparisons of school structure are the most valuable because they are the most internationalized theme.

### Curriculum Policies

Nordic countries are known for their comprehensive school reforms and national curricula (Midtsundstad and Hopmann 2010). Curricula outline how teaching and learning is organized, and are also decisive in structuring subject matter (Scholl 2012). Since curriculum development addresses the formation of subject matter knowledge for different school subjects, themes associated with knowledge areas are also part of this category. These include religion and word view, languages, ICT, mathematics, and the natural sciences (see Table 5.2). As the table shows, Finland was used as a neutral reference in eleven instances and as a positive one with respect to issues related to the national curriculum. The documents selected for this study reflect two large school reforms, the first initiated in 2004 and the second in 2015.

## Quality and Development of Basic Education

Quality assurance and support for student learning are more generic than conditions and curricula. Nevertheless I found several references to Finland in regards to student assessment. The Green Paper (NOU 2014) *Student Learning in the Future School—A Knowledge Review* depicts similarities between Norway, Scotland, Poland, and Finland in the way competences and skills across subjects are measured. The paper refers positively to the Finnish national exam that evaluates learning to learn as an example of assessments that include social and emotional competences. This approach is associated with deep learning and twenty-first-century skills and is used to promote pedagogy and learning.

This leads to a larger project called the Asia-Europe Meeting (ASEM), which was included in an earlier Green Paper (NOU 2003). This network project was characterized as an informal dialogue of cooperation between ten Asian and fifteen EU countries (see Table 5.2), which have collaborated on political, economic, and cultural issues. Three reports came out of this initiative in the autumn of 2002, including one on Basic Learning, which initiated a discussion about competences. A similar reference to this project was included in a later Green Paper (NOU 2015b), *The School of the Future—Renewal of Subjects and Competences*, which prepared for a new Norwegian reform that is currently underway.

## Learning Assessment as a Key Instrument for Improving the Quality of Education

Learning assessment is a core theme in Norwegian policy documents where ILSAs are used as the main knowledge source. The most-referenced study is PISA, and Finland is most often highlighted as an example to learn from, particularly with respect to reading, mathematics, and science. Norway is profiled as an outstanding example when it comes to the assessment of civics (see Table 5.2). In White Paper No. 33 (2002–3), *About the Allocation of Resources within Basic Education* (Ministry of Education and Research 2003), Norway is the top-ranked country in adult education. The drop-out rate of Norwegian students at the secondary level is also lower than that of other OECD countries.

However, in terms of knowledge and skills in other areas, Norwegian students perform average in reading comprehension, mathematics, and science, and Finnish students excel at everything else. The documents presents Norway as facing a gap between high and low achievers, especially in reading. They refer to the PISA survey, which indicates that teachers are neither highly demanding of students, nor are they using strategies to promote independent learning.

In White Paper No. 39 (2002–3), *Not for Pleasure Alone* (Ministry of Education and Research 2003), girls score better than boys in all countries included in the PISA survey. The differences in Norway are relatively large compared with other countries; however, gender differences are greatest in Finland. The documents also refer to the PIRLS survey also showing a relatively large literacy gap in Norway, while Sweden and the Netherlands have the smallest.

## Professional Development

In this paper, I also examine professional development because national policies align teacher education reform with school reform for basic education. A common view of teachers in Finland is that they are outstanding (Reinikainen, 2012) and Table 5.2 shows how Norwegian government papers from 2001 to 2016 address the issue.

## Projections of the Finnish Education System

The bar diagram in Figure 5.1 demonstrates that curriculum, quality and development, and student achievement are three main areas where policy-makers and experts look to Finland as a country from which to learn. However, as the overview in Table 5.2 shows, ILSA are first and foremost used as evidence within the student achievement and improvement area. Moreover, sixteen of the twenty-four times ILSAs were used as evidence of student achievement, Finland was projected in a positive way (see Figure 5.1). For the other thematic groups, ILSAs are typically not considered relevant.

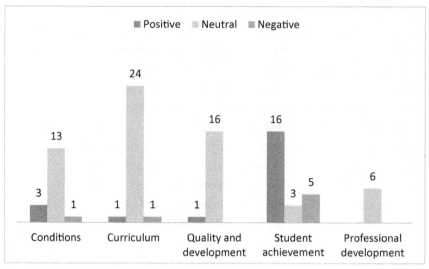

**Figure 5.1** Overview of how the education system in Finland is projected as a model for emulation

## Discussion

All of the above raises two questions: Is foreign knowledge of best practices used to evaluate, assess, and justify school reform? If so, in what realms are international data and findings considered relevant, and how are ILSAs used to project best practices? Finland has received enormous attention for its outstanding results within the Nordic region, especially since 2001 when they were first published (Takayama et al., 2013). This raises additional questions: How do policy-makers and experts project the Finnish education system as a standard for emulation? To what extent and for what purposes are Norwegian policy-makers and experts using ILSAs to call for policy borrowing from Finland? My study offers three insights, which will be summarized in this final part of the chapter.

### Reference Systems in Norway

Finland is mentioned frequently (a hundred times in total) within the analyzed white and green papers published from 1996 onward. However, the sections that mention Finland also reference the education systems of other countries, particularly Sweden. There is no doubt that the Swedish education system gained the best reputation within the Nordic region during the second half of the twentieth century. Due to a stronger economy and a political system that permitted private investment in education research, the Swedish system was long considered the most advanced and served as a model for Norway, Finland, Denmark, and Iceland. By the 1980s and 1990s researchers claimed that Swedish education reforms were ten to twenty years ahead of Norway's (Gundem 1990, 125–6). Today, this narrative has changed somewhat due to the mixed results on the PISA study.

Finland also performed very well before PISA. In the IEA's 1991 Reading Literacy Study, Finland showed the highest country performance on overall reading. According to Elley (1992) this result was unexpected given the country's social and economic circumstances. Still, researchers suggested various explanations for the good results, such as wealth, linguistic homogeneity, literacy, student-centered assessment and even the regularity of Finnish orthography (cf. Shiel and Cosgrove 2002, 691). Though Sweden also performed well, its results were not as impressive.

Nonetheless, PISA measurements are only one of several OECD sources that inform recommendations for member countries in the education sector. Other sources and international assessment studies also influence policies within and across countries. The first part of this chapter shows that both the IEA and the OECD have gained increasing importance as knowledge producers during the last decades in nearly all Nordic countries. Although compared to Finland, Norway is a late-comer in the IEA, it is currently the most active country. Despite their significance in international policy contexts, the success of a transfer is not determined by transnational actors, but rather on externalization processes, that is, how policy is borrowed and projected by the state.

## Participation in ILSAs

Until now researchers have paid little attention to variations in regional participation in ILSAs. This varies across the Nordic region, with Iceland being the most absent (see Table 5.1). These differences could be explained by political decisions as well as interest among researchers. Unlike Norway, Denmark, and Iceland, Finland, and Sweden share a de-politicized system in which reform decisions are not necessarily authorized by the government (Telhaug, Mediås, and Aasen 2006). Scientific purposes better explain their engagement in comparative studies because both countries pioneered research in comparative education (Lawn 2014). Table 5.1 shows that engagement varied, with PISA being the *only* ILSA to attract pan-Nordic participation. This may be because PISA has grown into a global project attracting nearly every country with a developed education system. Being marketed as a non-curriculum-based study that tests students' generic knowledge and skills independent of geographic location or national education system is certainly among the key reasons for PISA's success.

## The Projection of Finland

The document analysis, reported in this chapter demonstrates how ILSA results are used in policy contexts. However, the analysis also shows that policy borrowing processes are highly selective by nature with respect to not only how countries are compared to one another, but also how ILSAs are used to steer policy within individual locations.

Table 5.2 and Figure 5.1 show how often Finland is referenced in comparison with other countries around the world, as well as the number of references to ILSAs within these units. This examination demonstrates that ILSAs are described in terms of normative statements legitimizing the best and, occasionally, the worst systems. This approach to norm-setting is typical of the type of evaluative state that Norway has become, one that prefers to define the average by creating scales for what can be measured as good or bad (Skedsmo 2011). This differs from earlier norm-setting policies, which directed professionals to focus on the appropriateness of their pedagogies, using equality as a guide for how to organize education.

The numbers in Table 5.2 confirm that policy borrowing typically happens through the method of comparison, which can take different forms, such as evaluating different countries' systems or outcomes (Steiner-Khamsi 2013). As the table shows, comparisons are used in policy processes not merely to illustrate the typical traits or other qualities of successful education systems, but also to support evaluations of what have proven to be the *best* and, occasionally, *worst* practices. Thus, in the current study, Finland's success is used as both a normative standard for comparing other systems and a justification for a deeper examination of other systems' conditions for schooling. Moreover, as a reference country, Finland may serve as a point for contrast, rather than as a measure of good or bad qualities.

In other words, though ILSAs are used for evaluative and steering purposes to facilitate policy transfer across countries, contextual conditions will eventually decide how information is interpreted and translated. For this reason, the Finnish education system also reflects other kinds of evidence from policy realms other than learning assessment as key instrument for improvements to education quality.

This is especially true for dimensions of education that are not easily assessed or standardized by quantitative measures. Conditions, curricula, and the qualification and professionalization of teachers and principals are among those dimensions that demand contrasting types of comparisons that cannot benefit from evidence-based measurements. The success of policy borrowing depends not only on how ILSAs are translated into a particular context, but also on the context itself, which is historically embedded in cultures and structures and is not easily transformed by ILSA knowledge.

## Notes

1   This work was supported by the UTNAM Policy Transfer in Education (Sivesind and Steiner-Khamsi), University of Oslo ES578742/271314 and continues within the FINNUT research project Policy Knowledge and Lesson Drawing in Nordic School Reform in an Era of International Comparison (2018–23).

2   I would like to thank Torgeir Onstad, researcher emeritus, Institute for Teacher Education and School Research, University of Oslo, and Rolf Vegard Olsen, Center for Educational Measurement, University of Oslo, for helpful comments on Table 5.1.

3   The master's degree students Venke Sortland and Rehab Kazem Kamel Ahmed assisted in data systematization and copy editing. Categorizations were conducted with their collaboration to ensure reliability.

4   Six Subject Survey.

## References

Baek, C., Hörmann, B., Karseth, B., Pizmony-Levy, O., Sivesind, K., and Steiner-Khamsi, G. (2017), "Policy Learning in Norwegian School Reform: A Social Network Analysis of the 2020 Incremental Reform," *Nordic Journal of Studies in Educational Policy*, doi: 10.1080/20020317.2017.1412747.

Edelstein, W. (1987), "The Rise and Fall of the Social Science Curriculum Project in Iceland, 1974–1984: Reflections on Reason and Power in Educational Progress," *Journal of Curriculum Studies*, 19(1), 1–23, doi:10.1080/0022027870190102.

Elley, W. B. (1992), *How in the World Do Students Read? IEA Study of Reading Literacy*, https://files.eric.ed.gov/fulltext/ED360613.pdf (accessed March 27, 2018).

Grek, S. (2009), "Governing by Numbers: The PISA 'Effect' in Europe," *Journal of European Policy, 1*, 23–37.

Grek, S. (2010), "International Organisations and the Shared Construction of Policy 'Problems': Problematisation and Change in Education Governance in Europe," *European Educational Research Journal, 9*(3), 396–406. doi:10.2304/eerj.2010.9.3.396.

Grek, S., Lawn, M., Lingard, B., Ozga, J., Rinne, R., Segerholm, C., and Simola, H. (2009), "National Policy Brokering and the Construction of the European Education Space in England, Sweden, Finland and Scotland," *Comparative Education, 45*(1), 5–21, doi:10.1080/03050060802661378.

Gundem, B. B. (1990), "Making of a School Subject: The Influence of Research and Practice," *Scandinavian Journal of Educational Research, 34*(2), 123–41, http://timssandpirls.bc.edu/timss2015/international-results/timss-2015/about-timss-2015/ (accessed March 27, 2018).

Karseth, B., and Sivesind, K. (2010), "Conceptualizing Curriculum Knowledge: Within and beyond the National Context," *European Journal of Education*, March (45), 103–20.

Lawn, M. (2014), "Nordic Connections: Comparative Education, Zilliacus and Husén, 1930–1960," in A. Nordin and D. Sundberg (eds.), *Transnational Policy Flows in European Education: The Making and Governing of Knowledge in the Education Policy Field*, 21–45, Oxford: Symposium Books.

Lawn, M., and Lingard, B. (2002), "Constructing a European Policy Space in Educational Governance: The Role of Transnational Policy Actors," *European Educational Research Journal, 1*(2), 290–307.

Meyer, H.-D., and Benavot, A. (2013), *PISA, Power, and Policy: The Emergence of Global Educational Governance*, Oxford: Symposium Books.

Midtsundstad, J. H., and Hopmann, S. T. (2010), "Diversity United: The Scandinavian Traditions of Lesson Planning," *Bildung und Erziehung, 63*(4), 431–50.

Ministry of Education and Research (1998), "About Parental Participation within Basic Education," *Report No. 14 to the Storting [Parliament] 1997–1998*, Oslo: Norwegian Government Service Centre.

Ministry of Education and Research (2001), "Evaluation of the School Subject Christianity with Religion and Ethics," *Report No. 32 to the Storting [Parliament] 2000–2001*, Oslo: Norwegian Government Service Centre.

Ministry of Education and Research (2002), "The Quality Reform: On Teacher Education: Diverse, Demanding, Relevant," *Report No. 16 to the Storting [Parliament] 2001–2002*, Oslo: Norwegian Government Service Centre.

Ministry of Education and Research (2003), "Not for Pleasure Alone," *Report No. 39 to the Storting [Parliament] 2002–2003*, Oslo: Norwegian Government Service Centre.

Ministry of Education and Research (2003), "About the Allocation of Resources within Basic Education," *Report No. 33 to the Storting [Parliament] 2002–2003*, Oslo: Norwegian Government Service Centre.

Ministry of Education and Research (2004), "Culture for Learning," *Report No. 30 to the Storting [Parliament] 2003–2004*, Oslo: Norwegian Government Service Centre.

Ministry of Education and Research (2007), "No One Left Behind . . . Early Intervention for Lifelong Learning," *Report No. 16 to the Storting [Parliament] 2006–2007*, Oslo: Norwegian Government Service Centre.

Ministry of Education and Research (2008), "Quality in Schooling," *Report No. 14 to the Storting [Parliament] 1997–1998*, Oslo: Norwegian Government Service Centre.

Ministry of Education and Research (2009), "The Teacher: Role and Education," *Report No. 11 to the Storting [Parliament] 2007–2008*, Oslo: Norwegian Government Service Centre.

Ministry of Education and Research (2013), "On the Right Track," *Report No. 20 to the Storting [Parliament] 2012–2013*, Oslo: Norwegian Government Service Centre.

Ministry of Education and Research (2015), "Changes within the Private School Legislation (New Name of the Law, New Approval Basis, etc.)," *Proposition 84 L to the Storting [Parliament] 2014–2015*, Oslo: Norwegian Government Service Centre.

Ministry of Education and Research (2016), "Subjects—In-Depth Learning—Understanding: A Renewal of the Knowledge Promotion Reform," *Report No. 28 to the Storting [Parliament] 2015–2016*, Oslo: Norwegian Government Service Centre.

Ministry of Education and Research (2017), "Eager to Learn—Early Intervention and School Quality, "*Report No. 21 to the Storting [Parliament] 2016–2017*, Oslo: Norwegian Government Service Centre.

Nordin, A., and Sundberg, D. (2016), "Travelling Concepts in National-Curriculum Policy Making: The Example of Competencies," *European Educational Research Journal*, 15(3), 314–28, http://journals.sagepub.com/doi/pdf/10.1177/1474904116641697 (accessed March 27, 2018).

NOU = Norges Offentlige Utredninger [engl.: Official Norwegian Reports] (1995), "New Legislation on Education 'And Otherwise You Can Do as You Want,'" *Report No. 18.*

NOU = Norges Offentlige Utredninger [engl.: Official Norwegian Reports] (1995), "Identity and Dialogue," *Report No. 9.*

NOU = Norges Offentlige Utredninger [engl.: Official Norwegian Reports] (1996), "Teacher Education—Between Requirements and Ideals," *Report No. 22.*

NOU = Norges Offentlige Utredninger [engl.: Official Norwegian Reports] (2002), "Prime Quality from the First Grade: A Suggestion of a Framework for a National Quality System in Norwegian Basic Education," *Report No. 10.*

NOU = Norges Offentlige Utredninger [engl.: Official Norwegian Reports] (2003), "In the First Row. By the Commission for Quality," *Report No. 16.*

NOU = Norges Offentlige Utredninger [engl.: Official Norwegian Reports] (2014), "Student Learning in the Future School—A Knowledge Review," *Report No. 7.*

NOU = Norges Offentlige Utredninger [engl.: Official Norwegian Reports] (2015), "To Belong To—Tools for a Safe Psychosocial School Environment," *Report No. 2.*

NOU = Norges Offentlige Utredninger [engl.: Official Norwegian Reports] (2015b), "The School of the Future—Renewal of Subjects and Competences," *Report No. 8.*

NOU = Norges Offentlige Utredninger [engl.: Official Norwegian Reports] (2016), "More to Get-Better Learning for Students with Great Learning Potential," *Report No. 14.*

Pizmony-Levy, O. (2017), "Big Comparisons, Little Knowledge: Public Engagement with PISA in the United States and Israel," in A. W. Wiseman and C. Stevens Taylor (eds.), *The Impact of the OECD on Education Worldwide*, 125–56, Bingley: Emerald.

Reinikainen, P. (2012), "Amazing PISA Results in Finnish Comprehensive Schools," in H. Niemi, A. Toom, and A. Kallioniemi (eds.), *Miracle of Education. The Principles and Practices of Teaching and Learning in Finnish Schools*, 3–38, Rotterdam: Sense.

Scholl, D. (2012), "Are the Traditional Curricula Dispensable? A Feature Pattern to Compare Different Types of Curriculum and a Critical View of Educational Standards and Essential Curricula in German," *European Educational Research Journal*, 11(3), 328–41.

Schriewer, J. (2003), "Globalisation in Education: Process and Discours," *Policy Futures in Education*, 1(2), 271, doi:10.2304/pfie.2003.1.2.6.

Shiel, G., and Cosgrove, J. (2002), "International Perspectives on Literacy: International Assessments of Reading Literacy," *The Reading Teacher*, 55(7), 690–2.

Sivesind, K. H. (1999), "Structured, Qualitative Comparison," *Quality and Quantity*, 33(4), 361–80.

Sivesind, K., Afsar, A., and Bachmann, K. (2016), "Transnational Policy Transfer over Three Curriculum Reforms in Finland: The Construction of Conditional and Purposive Programs (1994–2016)," *European Educational Research Journal*, 6(3), 345–65.

Skedsmo, G. (2011), "Formulation and Realisation of Evaluation Policy: Inconsistencies and Problematic Issues," *Educational Assessment, Evaluation and Accountability*, 23(1), 5–20.

Steiner-Khamsi, G. (2003), "The Politics of League Tables," *Journal of Social Science Education*, 2(1), http://www.jsse.org/jsse/index.php/jsse/article/view/470/386.

Steiner-Khamsi, G. (2013), "What Is Wrong with the 'What-Went-Right' Approach in Educational Policy?" *European Educational Research Journal*, 12(1), 20–33.

Steiner-Khamsi, G. (2014), "Cross-National Policy Borrowing: Understanding Reception and Translation," *Asia Pacific Journal of Education*, 34(2), 153–67, doi:10.1080/02188791.2013.875649.

Takayama, K. (2010), "Politics of Externalization in Reflexive Times: Reinventing Japanese Education Reform Discourses through 'Finnish PISA Success,'" *Comparative Education Review*, 54(1), 51–75, doi:10.1086/644838.

Takayama, K., Waldow, F., and Sung, Y.-K. (2013), "Finland Has It All? Examining the Media Accentuation of 'Finnish Education' in Australia, Germany and South Korea: Research," *Comparative and International Education*, 8(3), 307–25.

Telhaug, A. O., Aasen, P., and Mediås, O. A. (2004), "From Collectivism to Individualism? Education as Nation Building in a Scandinavian Perspective," *Scandinavian Journal of Educational Research*, 48(2), 141–58.

Telhaug, A. O., Asbjørn Mediås, O., and Aasen, P. (2006), "The Nordic Model in Education: Education as Part of the Political System in the Last 50 Years," *Scandinavian Journal of Educational Research*, 50(3), 245–83, doi:10.1080/00313830600743274.

Wahlström, N. (2016), "A Third Wave of European Education Policy: Transnational and National Conceptions of Knowledge in Swedish Curricula," *European Educational Research Journal*, 6(3), 298–313.

Wahlström, N., and Sundberg, D. (2017), *Transnational Curriculum Standards and Classroom Practices: The New Meaning of Teaching*, New York: Routledge.

Waldow, F. (2012). "Standardisation and Legitimacy: Two Central Concepts in Research on Educational Borrowing and Lending," in G. Steiner-Khamsi and F. Waldow (eds.), *Policy Borrowing and Lending in Education*, 411–27, London: Taylor & Francis.

# 6

# PISA Rhetoric and the "Crisis" of American Education

Nancy Green Saraisky

## Introduction

The Programme for International Student Assessment (PISA) has become a widely used international measure of educational excellence, often dramatically associated with national education crises or scandalization (e.g., Steiner-Khamsi 2003; Takayama 2010; Takayama, Waldow, and Sung 2013). As the scholarship in this volume shows, however, reactions to education rankings are far from uniform, and local context mediates whether and how a country reacts to its performance in the ranking tables. This chapter explores one mechanism by which this mediation happens, that of media discourse. Media are an important channel through which international assessment results are linked to domestic education policy and politics. Media analysis not only reveals how meaning about PISA is created, but also how historical, geopolitical and cultural contexts influence the conditions under which PISA results resonate in national settings (Green Saraisky 2015).

More specifically, this chapter analyzes the use of reference societies in American media coverage of PISA from 2000 to 2012 to reveal how meaning about PISA in public discourse is created. As Waldow suggests in his introduction to this volume, the use of reference societies reveals more about the country doing the referencing than the country being referred to. Thus American media accounts of PISA can reveal the ways in which American education actors see PISA as useful in American education policy and politics. That is because references to top scoring countries on PISA are rarely merely empirical comparisons of scores. Instead, references to top scorers are engaged strategically to support or refute a variety of educational policy preferences. Nor is the choice of countries for comparison accidental. Certain country comparisons resonate more strongly than others. In the case of the United States, I find that Finland and China/Shanghai are the two most prominent reference societies in education discourse around PISA. The analysis confirms that comparisons with these other countries has little to do with any interest in adopting policies from other places, but much to do with education policy and politics in the United States.

Finland and China/Shanghai are in some ways obvious countries for comparison as they are consistently strong performers on PISA and are at or near the top of the PISA ranking tables. But as I discuss below, the data show that Finland and China/Shanghai are referenced in the discourse in very different ways, at different times, for different reasons. In fact, media coverage of PISA between 2000 and 2012 shows that though Finland is touted as an educational success in American discourse, there are no calls for policy borrowing based on a Finnish model. The analysis of references to China/Shanghai produces similar results; despite references to China/Shanghai as a model of educational success, there are no calls to look to China for actual policy change. Instead, the analysis suggests that the United States' geopolitical relationship with China drives the PISA discourse and is used to produce a round of crisis talk about American education. The chapter highlights the paradox of PISA scores. On the one hand, they provide a "blank screen" onto which all manner of interpretations about education can be projected. On the other hand, once these projections are made, PISA offers little actual policy guidance for policy-makers.

## Conceptual Framework

A growing body of literature has established that international large-scale assessments (ILSAs) are compelling forms of evidence in the policy process, and are often used as a kind of educational litmus test to determine how well a given education system is performing. Some studies have argued that country performance on ILSAs has led to a new cycle of education reform movements (Breakspear 2012; Meyer and Benavot 2013; Sellar and Lingard 2013). However, the extent to which any policy diffusion or reform has occurred as a result of ILSAs is unclear. PISA rankings have spawned an era of edu-tourism (Loveless 2012), as education experts from all over the world flock to Finland, a consistent top performer on PISA. Beyond that, however, there is scant evidence that PISA has led to educational policy change or that PISA participation has resulted in a convergence of educational pedagogy, methods, curricula or other reforms. In the United States, the media have used PISA to great discursive effect to make commonplace the notion that the United States lags behind its competition in educational performance. But PISA has not been the source of any clear policy change.

PISA is a particularly attractive ILSA in policy terms because of its comparative nature and the way in which it presents results. Kelley and Simmons (2015) argue that comparative assessments like PISA are part of a global phenomenon of systematic monitoring via numerical indicators. They theorize that global performance assessments like PISA operate through three distinct channels to affect policy: ranking systems can affect domestic politics; they can work through social pressure on elite networks; and they can activate transnational pressures that can affect markets or other material resources. For the purposes of this chapter, the domestic channel is most salient, as the analysis of media references is nested within the channel of domestic politics. Media play a key role in interpreting and disseminating ideas about public policy, and much has been written about the role that media play in agenda-setting, shaping public opinion and informing policy debate (e.g., McCombs and Shaw 1972; Gamson 1992; Snyder and Ballentine 1996; Henig 2008). Even in an age of declining newspaper readership, print journalism sources still provide a view into how policy elites perceive particular issues and which issues will be influential in the public sphere.

Rankings can influence domestic politics in at least two ways: by introducing new information about relative performance and by mobilizing actors to address the results insofar as the results are used as evidence of necessary policy change. If ranking results are in a particularly politically salient policy arena, and especially if the rankings are considered subpar, domestic policy actors may mobilize to create policy change to satisfy constituencies that demand action to address the ranking results (Kelley and Simmons 2015; Martens and Niemann 2013). Media become a venue in which these demands can be made, as various policy actors in the education system use media outlets as platforms to put forth ideas about what educational policy problems should be addressed as a result of PISA performance scores.

The key way in which PISA scores are used as policy evidence is through the comparison of one country to another. Typically, this involves comparing one's home country with top scoring countries elsewhere (though the comparison is sometimes also between the home country and lower performing countries). I argue that these comparisons increase and are more politically salient when a political rival is also a top scorer.

Theoretically, acts of reference to "elsewhere" in public discourse are important because they reflect how actors within the education sub-system feel they can best legitimize national policy programs. The rhetorical use of reference societies is interesting for at least two reasons. First, actors employ differing arguments (logics) depending on the time, place and institutional and political culture in which they are situated. Knowledge production is shaped by historical and cultural factors, and educational research responds to the problems and conditions of a specific society at a specific point in time. Schriewer and Martinez (2004) called this "socio-logic," describing the contextually bound reasoning behind the choice of references in educational knowledge production. On this view it is no accident that China is referenced in the US media more frequently than, say, Singapore, another Asian top performer. China's educational performance is far more politically salient than Singapore's, given the geopolitical and economic relationship between the US and China.

Second, references to top scorers on PISA demonstrate how actors legitimate their own policy preferences by admiring or rebuking policy approaches from elsewhere. Reference societies provide a "blank canvas" (Smithers 2004), a "projection screen," (Waldow 2012), or a "multiaccentual signifier" (Rappleye 2012) that are used as evidence to justify policy preferences. While comparative education has generally concerned itself with the borrowing and lending of educational policies and practices, less attention has been paid to the use of references in the construction of discourse (Silova 2006 being an exception). The policy studies literature has shown that comparative research provides an attractive form of evidence for policy actors with competing preferences looking to legitimize their positions (Kingdon 2011; Baumgartner and Jones 1993). In particular, research can be understood as a powerful source of political persuasion (Stone 2012; National Research Council 2012), especially in defining policy problems and solutions. The PISA discourse and its use of reference societies as a rhetorical device can reveal how policy actors problematize policy issues and what they see as potential policy solutions.

Previous studies that have looked at references to top scorers, especially Finland, have looked to understand how national political, economic and cultural rationales mediate the interpretation of PISA data. For instance, in the French case, Dobbins and Martens (2012) show how unions and political groups draw on PISA results in their rhetorical posturing while the Sarkozy government uses references to Finnish PISA performance to selectively promote policy change around teacher and school autonomy. Takayama (2008; 2010) provides a detailed analysis of the Japanese case. He uses press accounts to trace the construction of a crisis discourse in Japan, chronicling how progressives in particular used Finnish success as a rhetorical strategy of protest against conservative reforms. Takayama, Waldow and Sung (2014) show that the timing and intensity with which results were covered in the national medias of Australia, Germany and Korea varied considerably. The Finnish success trope is used to construct "crisis" narratives in domestic discourse that are "differently shaped by the preexisting of configuration of meanings in each country" (Takayama, Waldow, and Sung 2014, 33). The authors note two major commonalities in the cases: first, that the reference to "Finnish success" is used in the media discussions of the most contentious domestic education policy debates; and second, that all three countries show a linkage between the use of "crisis talk" and foreign models in education policy debates.

Martens and Niemann (2013) looked at reception of PISA in the United States and compared it to reception in Germany. Both the United States and Germany performed similarly in terms of raw scores and ranking, yet Germany went into "PISA shock," while the United States had a much more muted reaction. They theorize two conditions under which global performance assessments have an impact: when performance scores do not support the perception that elites have of their countries with regard to performance, and if the results are framed in such a way that they are made to seem vital to national interests. As I show later, however, these conditions may be necessary but are not sufficient to produce policy change.

## The US Case

The United States is an interesting analytical case for several reasons. First, policy elites have long used "crisis talk" in creating the narrative of American education. Comparison has a potent history in the United States of shaping and problematizing education. It was a major preoccupation of education experts in the early and mid-nineteenth century (Noah 1985) and continued throughout the twentieth century, with reports from travelers such as Horace Mann, John Dewey, and others. American education thinkers have long been interested in how education is done in other places, and what they might learn from those systems. Over time, comparison has become akin to problematization, as education rhetoric has engaged in comparison to highlight systemic strengths and weaknesses.

The tumultuous decade of the 1970s saw the United States coming out of the Vietnam War, into the oil crisis, and disillusioned with the level of success of the Great Society programs of the 1960s (Vinovskis 2009). Additionally, the US economy was in a recession; inflation and unemployment were high, productivity was down, and real income declined. American economic woes were only heightened as the press showered attention on the growing Japanese economy, which was avoiding double-digit inflation and growing their semiconductor and electronics industries to boot.

Against this backdrop of fear and uncertainty both domestically and internationally, US Secretary of Education Terrell Bell commissioned a blue-ribbon panel of business and education leaders to issue a report on the state of American education. The resulting publication, *A Nation at Risk: The Imperative for Educational Reform* (National Commission on Excellence in Education 1983), would prove seminal in framing the understandings of the US education system that remain today. The report painted an alarmist picture of America's education system, famously decrying "a rising tide of mediocrity that threatens our very future as a Nation and a people." It went on, "What was unimaginable a generation ago has begun to occur—others are matching and surpassing our educational attainments" (National Commission on Excellence in Education 1983, 4).

As scholars have shown, *NAR* led to an enormous shift in American education politics because it redefined the agenda status of education (Mehta 2006; Vinovskis 2009; Guthrie and Springer 2004; Manna 2006). Released during a recession, it offered an explanation of the relative success of such international competitors as Japan[1] and Germany. Underperformance in education was linked directly to the safety and security of the country vis-à-vis economic growth. In framing US education in an international comparative perspective, the economic goals of schooling were put front and center and were embraced by the business-oriented right. The focus on excellence for all students overtook debates about poverty and race that had dominated the previous decades (Mehta 2006).

Domestically, the report changed the agenda status of education, elevating it as a national priority. Due in large part to the decentralized, federal system of government that leaves educational decision-making powers in the hands of local and state officials, the US federal government has historically played a limited role in education policy. With the headlines from *NAR*, education policy became a cause for policy-makers at every level, and US presidents now prided themselves on being "education presidents." *NAR* also brought together previously disparate groups—legislators and business leaders—around a new common cause and a new language of education. This increased status of education prefaced greater federal involvement in what had been a highly decentralized system. In so doing, it set up a discourse that insisted on academic achievement as a bulwark against the pressures of an increasingly globalized and economically competitive world.

*NAR* was a media sensation. While some claimed that the crisis it invoked was artificial (Berliner and Biddle 1995), its narrative became the dominant trope in American education discourse. The report put its findings of American decline in a rhetorical context of international underperformance. American schools were failing their students and, as a result, America's economic competitiveness was suffering. Building on the fear and anxiety of the era, the report specifically referenced Japan, South Korea and Germany as our educated and ambitious economic competition. The report also foreshadows American demands for new ways to measure and compare educational performance, both domestically and internationally. This discourse has held fast since then and continues to contextualize the discourse in educational politics today.

Secondly, the US was critical to the early development of the OECD[2] and of PISA. The OECD, created as part of the post–Second World War reconstruction architecture, had no mandate for education specifically. But insofar as education was seen to be a component of economic growth and international competitiveness, education was on the OECD agenda. However it was only in the mid-1980s, thanks to a major push from the United States, that the education work of the OECD began to focus extensively on measurement. This was in spite of extensive opposition from other member countries and OECD staff.

The OECD strongly resisted the initial development of a PISA instrument because it ran counter to the OECD's understanding of country systems as entities that were separate and different. Nonetheless, the United States pushed for the development of PISA as an "objective" way to measure and compare education systems internationally.

The United States is also an interesting case because of its performance scores. United States performance on PISA has remained constant—with scores at or below the OECD average—since the test began more than a decade ago (Figure 6.1). This is in line with American performance on international assessments in general since the 1960s, on which American performance has been middling at best. Though critics have raised doubts about sampling bias (samples were not representative), test bias (curricular or cultural), and validity of the tests again and again as the United States has underperformed (Mehta 2006), the United States has remained a strong supporter of international assessment.

**Figure 6.1** US PISA performance over time

| Subject | Country | 2000 | 2003 | 2006 | 2009 |
|---------|---------|------|------|------|------|
| **Mathematics*** | OECD | 493 | 500 | 494 | 496 |
| | United States | 493 | 483** | 474** | 487** |
| **Reading** | OECD | 494 | 494 | 489 | 493 |
| | United States | 504 | 495 | — | 500 |
| **Science** | OECD | 494 | 499 | 498 | 501 |
| | United States | 499 | 491** | 489** | 502 |

\* *Significance tests were not available for 2000 mathematics scores*
\*\* *Score is statistically significantly lower than the OECD score, which represents the international average*

# Methods and Data

In order to understand the reception of PISA in the United States, I conducted a media content analysis of all articles that referenced PISA between 2000 and 2012, corresponding to the first decade of PISA testing. Media content analysis is a type of discourse analysis, as it refers to the analysis of communicative action. Media are generally acknowledged to play a key role in interpreting and disseminating ideas about public policy, as well as acting as a cipher for competing ideas in the public arena. As I have discussed elsewhere, systematic content analysis of the media can offer a nuanced view of the ways in which educational knowledge is created in national contexts (Green Saraisky 2016). It also sheds light on how media legitimate particular problem definitions that lead to specific proposed solutions. Media content analysis is one type of textual document analysis, but it is a useful method for understanding the ways in which historical, institutional, cultural, and political contexts are discussed in the public arena. It is most widely used to collect and analyze data to understand the meanings ascribed to an issue within a given context (Krippendorf 1989, 403).

As mentioned previously, the United States is chosen because of its historical background as a strong proponent of international assessment and PISA in particular, as well as its historically mediocre performance on international assessments. There has also been limited research on PISA reception in the United States, making it a reasonable selection for case study. In case study research the analytic approach centers on building an in-depth understanding of context and then exploring a bounded system over time through detailed analysis (Creswell 2008). This is a natural approach for a reception study, which undertakes a detailed analysis of local context.

The data come from four leading US newspapers (the *New York Times*, *The Wall Street Journal*, the *Washington Post*, and *USA Today*). Each of these sources is published daily and is considered a paper of record, often used is studies of American discourse (e.g., Fiss and Hirsch 2005).

Using Factiva, a subscription-based news service, I retrieved all texts from each source that contained the terms "PISA," "Programme for International Student Assessment," or "OECD and PISA." In order to ensure that Factiva was capturing all articles and blog posts, I also manually searched the online archives of each media source. This uncovered several more articles that included the search terms but had not been retrieved in the initial searches. Notably, I also employ a broad definition of what a reference is. Unlike other previous studies, I include both articles where PISA is the primary concern of the article and articles where PISA is referenced in passing. The inclusion of these simple mentions provides a subtler look at how ideas about PISA are created and change over time.

The date range was delimited from January 1, 2000, through December 31, 2012. This time frame covers the first decade (four cycles) of PISA. Sampling across the first decade of PISA allowed me to analyze reception over time and provide a more nuanced and systematic approach to understanding reception. The search resulted in seventy-three discrete newspaper articles (n=73). Of these, sixty articles referred to Finland and/or China. When articles appeared in two different formats (i.e., print and online), the article was counted once but the different formats were noted and coded as such.

Articles were coded according to a deductive coding scheme that was informed by similar previous analyses conducted on other literature (Green Saraisky 2015). The two-tiered analytic plan focused on framing and voice, first at the article level and then at the speaker level, across thirty-nine variable that explored explanations of PISA performance. Data were managed in Excel and descriptive statistics run using STATA 12.0.

# Findings

The analysis shows that American media rely on the use of reference societies to frame and direct the discourse about PISA. Comparison to other systems and use of ranking scores drives US media coverage. The data show that the ways in which the press frames PISA scores aligns with dominant interpretations of US education since the early 1980s. Education is constructed as a function of economic development, and there is cause for concern when the United States is not keeping up with its geopolitical rivals. Media anoint particular competitors—Finland and China—as successful, and the United States must take seriously calls for education reform or risk falling behind. However, there is no clear agreement on what path this reform should take.

The media capitalize on Shanghai's top scores in 2009 to create drama in the PISA discourse ("scandalization"), and references to the successes of top-scoring China and Finland ("projection") are most pronounced during and after this period. However, the references and analyses of top scorers do not result in calls for concrete policy change. Instead, they are discursive hooks that drive the discourse and scandalize the American education system.

## "China"

Before presenting descriptive data from the articles themselves it is important to note how the media references China throughout its coverage. Virtually all the articles that reference "Chinese success" note that in fact China's performance scores are based on the results of Shanghainese students only. However, as the articles go on, many of them subsequently conflate Shanghai with the entire People's Republic, discussing the scores of "Chinese" students. This conflation of Shanghai with the entire PRC is subtle yet misleading, as many feel that students sampled for PISA in Shanghai are not representative of the entire Chinese student population (Loveless 2014). Additionally, prior to 2009, other subnational units of China (e.g., Hong Kong, Macau) had participated in PISA but received no special media coverage; the media response is notably different when success comes from the mainland. In equating China with Shanghai, the coverage of PISA 2009 extends Shanghai's scores to the larger Chinese student population, numerically far larger and a more threatening comparison.

In the analysis that follows, I do echo the journalistic approach; when I refer to China I am including references to both China and Shanghai. Though this necessarily provides a less precise accounting of when each is used, it does follow the path of the media coverage that combines the more accurate use of "Shanghai" with the more general and politically weighty use of "China."

## Country References to PISA over Time

Figure 6.2 provides an overview of all country references in the media sample between 2000 and 2012. The figure does not report on the directionality of

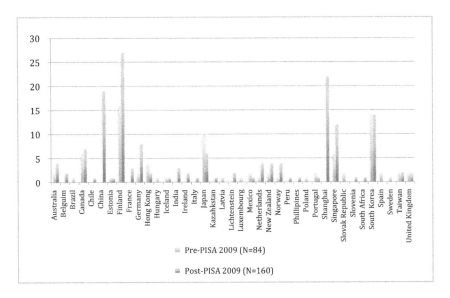

**Figure 6.2** All country references, pre- and post-PISA 2009

the references; that is, it does not show whether the references were positive or negative but rather provides an aggregate tally of each time the United States is compared to a foreign country in the media. The figure reveals several important points about media coverage of PISA. First, it shows that the use of country references in the media was quite different before and after PISA 2009. Before the 2009 results were released, there were eighty-four instances where articles compared United States results with those of another country, with the most references being made to Finland (16), South Korea (14), and Japan (10). After Shanghai participates and is ranked first on PISA 2009, the number of comparisons to other countries almost doubles in the media (to 160 references), showing how Shanghai's performance ignites both interest in PISA and a sense of competition between the United States and other countries.

## US Response to PISA over Time

During the first three cycles of PISA (2000, 2003, and 2006), the narrative can be characterized as a general narrative of decline, if fairly slow and even-keeled. The official government response acknowledged the mediocre results and called for continued improvement, but not much more. The first *New York Times* article about PISA (in which PISA was not even mentioned by name) was published in 2004, after the second round of testing was completed (Alvarez 2004).

The US Secretary of Education, as part of a conservative government, called the results "a blinking warning light" (Toppo 2004, P7D), a fairly measured response to US performance given that the United States scored below average in its mathematics literacy, at average in reading literacy, and below average in science literacy. Results from PISA 2003 and 2006, released under a conservative American government, evoked talk of the need for more radical change to ensure US competitiveness in the global economy but the public discourse remained rather bland.

During these years, the narrative used limited references to top scoring Finland as a reference society, as shown in Figure 6.3. The use of references before 2009 is minimal; there are few in-depth references to Finland and none specifically to China, since China had yet to participate. When Finland is referenced, it is often along with other top-ranked Asian countries (e.g., Japan, South Korea, Singapore) but without any discussion or possible explanation of those countries' successes. Instead, the country mentions are surprisingly short and simple, almost peripheral to the substantive reporting in the articles.

Before 2009, there are only two articles that discuss Finland in any depth. An associate editor for the *Washington Post* spent three weeks in Finland and

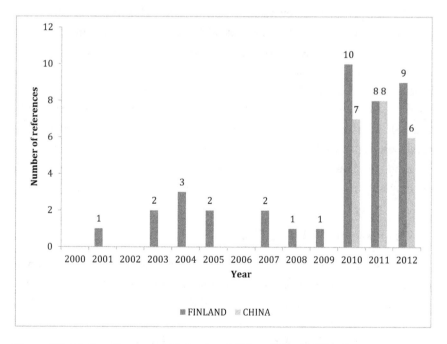

**Figure 6.3** Media references to Finland and China, 2000–12 (N=60)

published two features about its educational system. The articles praise Finland for its success, and the author credits combination of political will, culture, and teacher quality with Finnish success. Ultimately he concludes,

> I found Finnish society beguiling on many levels, but in the end concluded that it could not serve as a blueprint for the United States. National differences matter. (Kaiser 2005, B1)

Though Kaiser says that Finland should be an inspiration to education reformers, he stops short of pointing to specific policies that might be borrowed. Instead he argues that, like the Finns, if the United States wanted to make long-term systemic changes, it would be possible with the right combination of political will, political culture, and popular support.

The narrative is substantively changed after the 2009 results are released, and China is the top scorer in all three subject areas, while the United States remains in the middle of the pack. Fifty-three articles, or 72 percent of the sample, were published after the 2009 results were released, an average of more than seventeen articles per year, up from 2.3 articles per year prior to the 2009 release.

Articles that make reference to Finland project a vision of highly paid, autonomous and respected teachers, who are treated as professionals. In an op-ed written in support of elevating the teaching profession in the United States, the president of a teachers union says "Among the hallmarks of high performers such as ( . . . ) Finland are strong teachers unions ( . . . ) The lesson from PISA is clear: Respect teachers and treat them like professionals" (Van Roekel 2010, A8). Another article hopes that Americans will realize that our own reform models are failed but "we will understand the deep wisdom of Finland, with its love for children and its respect for educators" (Strauss 2011).

Figure 6.3 shows that after 2009, not only do references to China increase, but references to Finland do as well. China's top rank shifts the discourse to refocus on comparisons to reference societies, both the historic top-scorer, Finland, along with the new threat, China.

The *Wall Street Journal* publishes a blog post written by Chester Finn Jr., a leading conservative education thinker and then-president of the Fordham Institute, who likened China's success on PISA to the Soviet launch of Sputnik (Finn 2010, A21). Framing China's PISA performance as part of a larger geopolitical and economic rivalry, he writes,

> until this week we could at least pretend that China wasn't one of those countries that was a threat ( . . . ) We could allow ourselves to believe that China was only

interested in building dams, buying our bonds, making fake Prada bags ( . . . ) But we could comfort ourselves that their curriculum emphasized discipline and rote learning, not analysis or creativity.

Today that comfort has been stripped away. We must fact the fact the China is bent on surpassing us, and everyone else, in education. (Finn 2010, A21)

Finn's analysis becomes the meme of the reaction to PISA results, with then-President Barack Obama and then-Secretary of Education Arne Duncan taking up the same argument. Duncan, for instance states,

I know skeptics will want to argue with the results, but we consider them to be accurate and reliable, and we have to see them as a challenge . . . we can quibble, or we can face the brutal truth that we're being out-educated. (Dillon 2010, A22)

Duncan's "wake up call" was widely re-quoted throughout the blogosphere and in multiple news articles. China's scores quickly become evidence of America's decline, and experts suggest that the United States is in a dangerous position because of its PISA rank.

The media narrative is that China's top scores show that the world's best performing students are in China. This storyline states the American K–12 system must be "fixed" in order that the United States remain economically competitive in a global market. This is reflected in the coverage of Chinese performance in phrases like "The Chinese and others do it better. We must catch up" (Samuelson 2011, A17); the PISA scores illuminate the "sorry state of US education," which is a "broken system that contributes to our economic decline" (Huffman 2010, A13). China is "out-saving and out-hustling us" (Friedman 2010, 35). The head of PISA at the OECD suggests that Americans should go to their local superintendents and ask, "Why are we not doing as well as schools in China or Finland?" (Friedman 2012).

Figure 6.4 shows how each of the four media sources in the sample uses references to Finland and China. All media use both countries as reference societies in their PISA narratives, though *USA Today* uses this strategy the least. The *Washington Post* comprises the largest segment of the sample (54 percent) and unsurprisingly has the most references to foreign examples. Most of the *Washington Post* references to Finland and China come not from news articles but in blog posts, suggesting that references to elsewhere are being used as evidence not only in news stories but throughout the year by individual bloggers, raising the profile and discursive power of PISA.

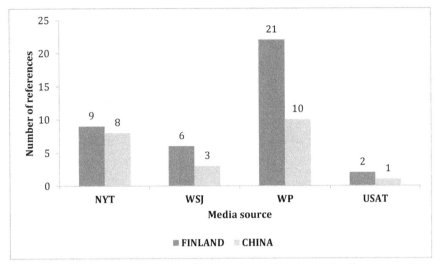

**Figure 6.4** References to Finland and China, by media source (N=60)

Figures 6.3 and 6.4 show how China's success on PISA shifted the public discourse. The release of 2009 results with China as the surprise leader in the ranking tables resulted not only in the publication of references to China, but in an increase in publication of references to Finland. On average, media published 1.2 articles a year with a reference to Finland through 2009, but once China came out on top, references to *both* China and Finland rise. Between 2010 and 2012, media published an average of fourteen articles per year referencing Finnish success and more than seven articles per year referencing China.

The number of articles in which top scorers are discussed in detail favors China over Finland. Of the articles that mention China, 35 percent of them discuss Chinese success on PISA in some detail, while only 26 percent of articles that mention Finland discuss Finnish success in depth. The United States being "beaten" by China gets more press attention and energizes the discourse by driving coverage about both reference societies. Chinese success seems to up the ante among education experts, and the narrative turns to portraying the rise of China at the expense of the United States. A *New York Times* column described it as follows:

> It can be win-win . . . for the world if China is doing better. But not for America . . . if [we are racing against] a country that is not just out-saving us and out-hustling us, but is also starting to out-educate us. (Friedman 2010, A35)

## Explanations of Top Scorers' Success

The references to Finnish and Chinese PISA performance emphasize different explanations of success between the two countries. Figure 6.5 compares what the media say about explanations for success in each country. Media discuss Finland and China both as systems to emulate and as systems from which the United States has nothing to learn. But the underperformance of the US relative to Finland and China is used repeatedly as evidence of a crisis in US education.

## Chinese Success

China, as an economic and geopolitical rival of the United States, is the catalyst that drives American PISA discourse. But there are no calls for lesson drawing from China. The media explain Chinese success by factors that are not associated with the US system and therefore offer little leverage as a model for emulation.

**Teaching to the test.** The reasons media employ when explaining Chinese success run the gamut. Media report that policy explanations account for much of China's success on PISA, with thirty of the articles referencing this explanation. The policy that is credited with Chinese success most often is that of "teaching to the test." On this view, the Chinese succeed because rote memorization is encouraged at the expense of creativity, and students spend excessive time in school preparing for the test.[3] This is an especially interesting argument since PISA is not tied to any school-based curricula and teaching to the test should be moot.

**Figure 6.5** Media explanations of Finnish and Chinese success

| CHINESE SUCCESS | FINNISH SUCCESS |
| --- | --- |
| **Education Policy (30%)**<br>• Teaching to the test<br>• Rote memorization<br>• Want to lead the world | **Teachers (28%)**<br>• Recruitment<br>• Rigorous training<br>• Ongoing professional development |
| **Culture (21%)**<br>• "Asian" model/commitment<br>• Confucian reverence for education | **Culture (26%)**<br>Communitarian (v. individual) |
| | **Equity (19%)**<br>• Inputs<br>• Outcomes<br>• Overall economic equity |

Though the United States has seen an increase in assessments domestically as part of the movement to hold schools and teachers more accountable for student success, here the notion of teaching to the test is dismissed, not only because it takes away instructional time from students but also because in the West there is an understanding that good education involves more than a chalk-and-talk, teach-to-the-test approach.

**Culture.** This argument dovetails with the next most frequently cited reason for Chinese success, Chinese culture. Twenty-one percent of references cite cultural explanations. Here, the media highlight a particularly "Asian" commitment to education linked with a Confucian history in which teachers and education are revered (Lynch 2008; Chua 2011; Kristof 2011). The reliance on cultural arguments is unexpected since these are arguments that place success at the mercy of a confluence of political, historical and social factors that are time and context specific. Culture is rarely transferrable. It is bounded by the political and social factors of a particular time and place. The public narrative employs cultural explanations frequently, but there is little to be offered from cultural explanations in terms of lesson drawing.

## Finnish Success

**Teachers.** Regarding Finland, media cite "teachers" as the most important explanation of Finnish success, 28 percent of the time. This argument captures a range of specific teacher-related features, including teacher recruitment, training, pay and/or ongoing teacher development. Finnish teachers are deemed successful because of highly systemic factors—Finnish teachers are recruited in a highly competitive process; they undergo rigorous teacher training with an emphasis on deep content expertise; teachers are given serious ongoing teacher development; their pay is good relative to other professions; and they are given a great deal of autonomy in the classroom. This is a potentially potent argument for reformers because it is possible to replicate these factors in other systems.[4]

In spite of this, there are no consistent calls for specifically borrowing from the Finnish system. Instead, a typical explanation includes reverence for Finnish teachers and the respect they receive in Finnish society: "The key . . . it's the people. The high quality of Finnish education depends on the high quality of Finnish teachers" (Kaiser 2005, B1). Teacher education programs are "highly competitive" and "rigorous," and principals and parents alike trust teachers (Ravitch 2011 blog post). All detailed articles about Finnish success reference teachers. Finnish experts are quoted as often as American commentators, but with the caveat that their success is specific to Finland.

**Culture.** Teacher explanations for Finnish success are closely followed by cultural explanations, referenced 26 percent of the time. References to culture refer to the Finnish orientation of putting community interests before that of the individual. Whereas in the United States education is often seen as a "private effort leading to a public good . . . in Finland, education is viewed as a public effort for a public purpose," (Sahlberg 2012) where the key beliefs are "collaboration, trust, responsibility and autonomy" (Ravitch 2010) not competition. The view in the American press is that the social democratic approach in the Scandinavian countries (which to many in the United States includes Finland) allows for a concern for the public good and a commitment to a social safety net that might be admirable, but would not be transferable to the US context.

**Equity.** The cultural explanations dovetail with the third explanation for success, which is equity. In 19 percent of the articles, equity is cited as the root of Finnish educational success. Equity in Finland is described both in terms of equity of inputs (equal allocation of resources to schools, a strong early childhood welfare system, and equality of opportunity for every child to succeed no matter what school he or she attends) and equity of outputs (the fact that the variation in between school performance is quite low, meaning that children get a similar education no matter what school they attend).

## Discussion

The use of Finland and China as reference societies in the American education narrative highlights the fact that PISA data are perfectly suited for use in both projecting idealized notions of educational success and for scandalizing the home country. Strikingly, none of this rhetoric seems to have presaged any concrete policy change. References to Finland, China or PISA in general are used as "one more reason" that the US education system is failing and needs reform, but the specifics of the argument—that certain policies regarding systems, teachers, and students should be adopted—never takes hold. In Finland, teachers and equity are seen as the most important variables; in China, it is government education policy. How should policy-makers determine the merits of each approach and decide which practices are best?

Take, for instance, explanations of culture as reasons behind China's and Finland's top performance. Why do elites use cultural explanations when they are naturally context specific and essentially non-transferrable? Culture is useful in that it gives actors a point of comparison, but is a slippery enough concept that it offers little in the way of policy prescription. It may be precisely for this reason that the media generally and elite policy actors specifically use the culture argument. It allows politicians and policy-makers to acknowledge the United States' mediocre performance without having to do much about it. The value of the reference is in the rhetoric rather than the substance, and allows actors to stake out their opposition to the state of American education without committing to any viable solution.

Finnish success is driven by a communitarian culture and by social democracy that provides a deep social safety net for its citizens. In China, the literature points to an "Asian" outlook that upholds a Confucian reverence for education as the culture of success. But these cultural explanations are a conundrum for policy-makers. Culture is contingent, and not easily replicable. PISA proponents see cultural differences as a threat to cross-national borrowing. While policies are seen as readily changeable—at least, according to the various reports about what can be learned from "strong" and "best" performing systems—cultural explanations are seen as pessimistic and even defeatist. On this view, "cultural and historical explanations for the success of education systems cannot be used to justify reforms in other nations, whereas pointing to specific policy settings as the cause of success can provide governments with leverage for internal reform agendas" (Sellar and Lingard 2013, 14).

These conflicting explanations of success are potentially problematic for US policy-makers since they offer divergent claims about successful practice. That the references to foreign examples can be all things to all people provides only weak policy guidance. On the other hand, this juxtaposition also potentially creates a space for debating US education reform. By employing PISA results generally, and Finland and China specifically, different actors can offer a range of claims about "what works" in education.

Additionally, in much of the discourse around reference societies success is predicated on a strong interventionist role for the state. In Finland, the historical contingencies of Soviet domination and a largely agrarian society led the state to commit to the development of a system of comprehensive schooling over decades of successive governments (Simola 2005; Porter-Magee 2012). More recently in China, government commitment to "national honor" and being a world leader in education is credited with pushing additional resources and pressure to Shanghainese students to achieve top scores (Finn 2010; Loveless 2014). PISA performance in these narratives is derivative of strong and specific government action. This discursive framing may offer little of interest to many reformers in the United States, where the state is often problematized in educational discourse. The state-as-roadblock-to-quality-education has been a prominent refrain of many American education reformers of the past three decades. Seen most obviously in the movement toward public schooling through mechanisms of choice, the dominant view toward the state in US education discourse has been one of distrust.

The data show that the ways in which the press frames PISA scores, as well as to whom the press gives voice in the debate, aligns with dominant interpretations of US education since the early 1980s.

Though US performance scores on PISA remained essentially the same during the entire first decade of assessment implementation, the response to the performance scores varied greatly. While Finland was seen as a blank slate onto which the United States could project its own education policy aspirations and fears, China's 2009 PISA scores were a far greater exogenous shock to the education policy narrative. The United States and China have a relationship that is deep, complex, and multifaceted. China has long been seen as one of the most important foreign policy relationships the US has. The two countries have a massive economic relationship—their trade and investment flows in 2012 reached a record half trillion dollars—and as the United States was crawling out of its 2009 recession, China continued to record near double digit annual economic growth rates. The United States narrative highlighted China's role as an economic adversary whose continued growth threatens US interests. This, coupled with geopolitical and philosophical differences, put China in a far more threatening position than Finland, about which most Americans likely had little knowledge, if any all. That Shanghai outscored all other international participants on PISA during its first time participating in the test resonated far more deeply with American policy-makers and elites than did Finland's ongoing high performance. This resonance is reflected in the narrative post-2009, in which American performance is scandalized but no serious policy solutions are offered.

## Conclusion

In this Chapter 1 have focused narrowly on the use of reference societies as a textual, rhetorical device to highlight how references to top scoring countries in PISA are used as evidence in national policy discourse in the United States.

The textual analysis of reference societies in the media is one form of content analysis that highlights when and why certain countries are used as yardsticks against which to compare US performance. Despite a choice of numerous top performers on PISA (e.g., Singapore, Hong Kong, Korea, Canada) the press consistently refers to Finland and China as the preferred reference societies in the media.

References to Finland and China suggest at least two things about American education politics and policy. The first is that preexisting historical, economic, geographic, and cultural relationships between the referrer and the referee matter. Clearly, the longstanding rivalries and power relations between the United States and China shaped the reaction in the US press to China's top scores on PISA. Prior to China's participation in PISA, US reaction was muted. But press coverage shifted in volume and in tone when a major geopolitical rival bested the United States in the ranking tables. China's top performance is used as evidence of a Sputnik-level crisis of the US education system and results in a shift in the discourse that focuses on scandalizing the level of performance of the United States. One area for future work in the analysis of international assessment data would be to focus on the directionality of the relationship between the press and PISA performance. That is, to further unpack the degree to which the media shape understandings of PISA and the degree to which preexisting national politics and culture shape press coverage.

The second point is that rhetorical scandal can ensue, but that is not enough to lead to policy change. Public discourse is an important conduit through which various interests can promote policy proposals with the hopes of getting them on the political agenda. But as Kingdon (2011) reminds us, policy change occurs within a window of opportunity when policy problems, solutions and politics align. Timing matters. As the data show, American performance scores on PISA remain flat though reception varies. It is not enough that projections are made and scandalization happens, but a myriad of other contextual factors must be present to mobilize actors to respond to any policy implications of PISA results. Absent this perfect storm of conditions, even the most compelling evidence will not lead to policy change. Thus scandalizing the US education system in the press is only one of many pieces of the policy process that would be necessary to result in actual policy change. The use of Finland and of China in the process of meaning making about PISA can be viewed as one step in defining educational problems and solutions on a political agenda.

As Pfetch and Esser (2004, 10) note, "The demand for comparative research in political communication is consequential because it requires abstracting from the implicit premises and the national idiosyncrasies in both politics and media communications in the search for generalizable communication patterns and their consequences." The analysis of the use of reference societies in the United States, as with many other cases presented in this volume, provides a step toward understanding how international assessment results are used as evidence in the policy process. References to elsewhere do not take place in a vacuum; they are a reflection of the interaction between content, context, and agency.

The question of which political ideas take hold is in part a battle among different constructions of evidence. Using top scorers as reference societies is one way in which PISA data becomes research evidence. Though there are many ways that analysts might talk about "top performers" (e.g., by the top five, or top ten scorers; by those countries with the smallest achievement gaps; etc.), the fact that Finland and China are the reference societies most frequently cited in the US media tells us something about the priorities and values of current education policy debates. Reference societies are not only about empirical scores; there are several comparable country scores from which one could choose. Reference societies are chosen because they provide specific value in legitimating preferred policy perspectives. Examining the ways in which PISA is talked about in education discourse elucidates not only how education actors construe PISA scores, but also more broadly how they problematize the educational landscape in contemporary politics.

# Notes

1  As Williamson recounts, in the 1970s US productivity was down to 1.9 percent annually from its long-term historical average of about 2.3 percent. At the same time, Japan experienced a 5 percent growth increase. Thus a narrative of Japanese strength and American decline was borne. This was in spite of the fact that Japanese growth was down from its growth rate in the 1960s, which had been about 10 percent annually (Williamson cited in Feuer 2011, 15).

2  See Henry, Lingard, Rizvi, and Taylor (2001) for a detailed treatment.

3  Some articles also mention the excessive out of school time spent in private tutoring, for example, Zhao (2012).

4  This is not to suggest that systemic reform is easy. It is of course highly contested and political. But all things being equal, calls to borrow policy are more concrete than calls for cultural or political changes.

# References

Alvarez, Lizette. (2004, April 19), "Educators flocking to Finland, land of literate children." Retrieved from www.nytimes.com.

Baumgartner, F., and Jones, B. (1993), *Agendas and Instability in American Politics*, Chicago: University of Chicago Press.

Berliner, D., and Biddle, B. (1995), *The Manufactured Crisis: Myths, Fraud and the Attack on America's Public Schools*, White Plains: Longman.

Breakspear, S. (2012), "The Policy Impact of PISA: An Exploration of the Normative Effects of International Benchmarking in School System Performance," *OECD Education Working Papers*, 71, Paris: OECD, http://dx.doi.org/10.1787/5k9fdfqffr28-en.

Chua, A. (2011), "How to Reshape US Education," *USA Today*, May 11, A9.

Creswell, J. (2008), *Educational Research: Planning, Conducting and Evaluating Quantitative and Qualitative Research*, 3rd ed., Upper Saddle River, NJ: Pearson.

Dillon, S. (2010), "US Must Raise Status of Its Teachers," *New York Times*, March 16, A22.

Dobbins, M., and Martens, K. (2012), "Towards an Education Approach à la Finlandaise? French Education Policy after PISA," *Journal of Education Policy*, 27(1), 23–43, http://dx.doi.org/10.1080/02680939.2011.622413.

Feuer, M. J. (2012), "No Country Left Behind: Rhetoric and Reality of International Large-Scale Assessment," The 13th William H. Angoff Memorial Lecture, Washington, DC: Educational Testing Service.

Finn, C. E., Jr. (2010), "A Sputnik Moment for US Education," *The Wall Street Journal*, December 8, A21.

Fiss, P. C., and Hirsch, P. M. (2005), "The Discourse of Globalization," *American Sociological Review*, 70(1), 29–52.

Friedman, T. (2010), "Skill Digging," *New York Times*, December 8, http://www.nytimes. com/2010/12/08/opinion/08friedman.html (accessed February 14, 2018).

Friedman, T. (2012), "New Rules," *New York Times*, September 9, SR13.

Gamson, W. A. (1992), *Talking Politics*, Cambridge: Cambridge University Press.

Green Saraisky, N. (2015), *The Politics of International Large-Scale Assessment: The Programme for International Student Assessment (PISA) and American Educational Discourse, 2000–2012* (Unpublished doctoral dissertation), ProQuest Dissertations and Theses Full Text.

Green Saraisky, N. (2016), "Analyzing Public Discourse: Using Media Content Analysis to Understand the Policy Process," *Current Issues in Comparative Education*, 18(1), 26–41.

Guthrie, J. W., and Springer, M. G. (2004), "'A Nation at Risk' Revisited: Did 'Wrong' Reasoning Result in 'Right' Results? At What Cost?" *Peabody Journal of Education* (A Nation at Risk: A 20-Year Reappraisal), 79(1),7–35.

Henig, J. R. (2008), *Spin Cycle: How Research Is Used in Policy Debates: The Case of Charter Schools*. New York: Russell Sage Foundation and the Century Foundation.

Henry, M., Lingard, R., Rizvi, F., and Taylor, S. (2001), *The OECD, Globalisation and Education Policy*, Oxford: Elsevier Science.

Huffman, K. (2010), "How to Get Top Grades in Education" (blog post), *The Washington Post*, January 2, http://www.washingtonpost.com/wp-dyn/content/article/2010/01/01/AR2010010101416.html (accessed February 14, 2018).

Kaiser, R. (2005), "In Finland's Footsteps: If We're So Rich and Smart, Why Aren't We More Like Them?" *The Washington Post*, August 7, B01.

Kelley, J. G., and Simmons, B. A. (2015), "Politics by Number: Indicators as Social Pressure in International Relations," *American Journal of Political Science*, 59(1), 55–70.

Kingdon, J. W. (2011), *Agendas, Alternatives, and Public Policies* (Updated 2nd ed.), New York: Longman.

Krippendorf, K. (1989), *Content Analysis: Departmental Papers at Annenberg School of Communications*, University of Pennsylvania.

Kristof, N. (2011), "China's Education System," *New York Times*, January 15, http://kristof.blogs.nytimes.com/2011/01/15/chinas-education-system/ (accessed February 14, 2018).

Loveless, T. (2012), "Misinterpreting International Test Scores," in *2012 Brown Center Report on American Education*, http://www.brookings.edu/research/reports/2012/02/16-brown-education (accessed February 14, 2018).

Loveless, T. (2014), "Lessons from the PISA Shanghai Controversy (Report)," *Part 1 of the 2014 Brown Center Report on American Education*, http://www.brookings.edu/research/reports/2014/03/18-pisa-shanghai-loveless (accessed February 14, 2018).

Lynch, D. (2008), "Learning from Korean Schools: US Could Use Some Tips on Preserving Competitiveness," *USA Today*, November 19, B1.

Manna, P. (2006), *School's In: Federalism and the National Education Agenda*, Georgetown: University Press.

Martens, K., and Neimann, D. (2010), "Governance by Comparison: How Ratings and Rankings Impact National Policy-Making in Education," *Tran-State Working Papers* (Sfb 597), 139, Bremen: University.

McCombs, M., and Shaw, D. L. (1972), "The Agenda Setting Function of Mass Media," *Public Opinion Quarterly*, 36(2), 176–87.

Mehta, J. D. (2006), *The Transformation of American Educational Policy, 1980–2001: Ideas and the Rise of Accountability Politics* (Unpublished doctoral dissertation), ProQuest Dissertations and Theses Full Text.

Meyer, H-D., and Benavot, A. (eds.) (2013), *PISA, Power and Policy: The Emergence of Global Educational Governance*, Oxford: Symposium Books.

National Commission on Excellence in Education (1983), *A Nation at Risk: The Imperative for Educational Reform: A Report to the Nation and the Secretary of Education, United States Department of Education*, Washington, DC: The Commission, https://www2.ed.gov/pubs/NatAtRisk/risk.html (accessed February 14, 2018).

National Research Council (2012), *Using Science as Evidence in Public Policy*, Committee on the Use of Social Science Knowledge in Public Policy.

Noah, H. J. (1985), "Comparative Education: Methods," in T. Husén and T. N. Postlethwaite (eds.), *The International Encyclopedia of Education*, 2nd ed., New York: Pergamon.

Pfetch, B., and Esser, F. (eds.) (2004), "Introduction," in *Comparing Political Communication: Theories, Cases, and Challenges*, New York: Cambridge University Press.

Porter-Magee, K. (2012), "Real Lessons from Finland: Hard Choices Rigorously Implemented," December 27, http://edexcellence.net/commentary/education-gadfly-daily/flypaper/2012/real-lessons-from-finland-hard-choices-rigorously-implemented.html (accessed February 14, 2018).

Rappleye, J. (2012), "Reimagining Attraction and 'Borrowing' in Education: Introducing and Political Production Model," in G. Steiner-Khamsi (ed.), *The Global Politics of Educational Borrowing and Lending*, New York: Teachers College Press.

Ravitch, D. (2011), "Why Finland's Schools are Doing Great (by Doing What We Don't)" (blog post), *The Washington Post*, October 13, http://www.washingtonpost.com/blogs/answer-sheet/post/ravitch-why-finlands-schools-are-great-by-doing-what-we-dont/2011/10/12/gIQAmTyLgL_blog.html (accessed February 14, 2018).

Sahlberg, P. (2012), "What the US Can't Learn from Finland about Education Reform" (blog post), *The Washington Post*, April 17, http://www.washingtonpost.com/blogs/answer-sheet/post/what-the-us-cant-learn-from-finland-about-ed-reform/2012/04/16/gIQAGIvVMT_blog.html (accessed February 14, 2018).

Samuelson, R. (2011), "An Achievement Gap that Won't Be Fixed in Schools," *The Washington Post*, January 10, A17.

Schriewer, J., and Martinez, C. (2004), "Constructions of Internationality in Education," in G. Steiner-Khamsi and F. Waldow (eds.), *World Yearbook of Education: Policy Borrowing and Lending in Education*, New York: Routledge.

Sellar, S., and Lingard, B. (2013), "Looking East: Shanghai, PISA 2009 and the Reconstitution of Reference Societies in the Global Education Policy Field," *Comparative Education*, 49(4), 464–85, doi: 10.1080/03050068.2013.770943.

Silova, I. (2006), *From Symbols of Occupation to Symbols of Multiculturalism: Re-Conceptualizing Minority Education in Post-Soviet Latvia* (Unpublished doctoral dissertation), ProQuest Dissertations and Theses Full Text.

Simola, H. (2005), "The Finnish Miracle of PISA: Historical and Sociological Remarks on Teaching and Teacher Education," *Comparative Education*, 41(4), 455–70, doi: 10.1080/03050060500317810.

Smithers, A. (2004), *England's Education: What Can Be Learned by Comparing Countries?* Liverpool: Centre for Education and Employment Research, University of Liverpool.

Snyder, J., and Ballentine, K. (1996), "Nationalism and the Marketplace of Ideas," *International Security*, *21*(2), 5–40 http://www.jstor.org/stable/2539069 (accessed February 14, 2018).

Steiner-Khamsi, G. (2003), "The Politics of League Tables," *Journal of Social Science Education*, *1*, doi: 10.4119/UNIBI/jsse-v2-i1-470.

Stone, D. (2012), *The Policy Paradox: The Art of Political Decision Making*, 3rd ed., New York: W. W. Norton.

Strauss, V. (2011), "Mobile Technology and School Reform: What's the Connection" (blog post), *The Washington Post*, February 16, http://voices.washingtonpost.com/answer-sheet/technology/mobile-technology-and-school-r.html (accessed February 14, 2018).

Takayama, K. (2008), "The Politics of International League Tables: PISA in Japan's Achievement Crisis Debate," *Comparative Education*, *44*(4), 387–407.

Takayama, K. (2010), "Politics of Externalization in Reflexive Times: Reinventing Japanese Education Reform Discourses through 'Finnish PISA Success,'" *Comparative Education Review*, *55*(1), 51–75.

Takayama, K., Waldow, F., and Sung, Y. L. (2013), "Finland Has It All? Examining the Media Accentuation of 'Finnish Education' in Australia, Germany and South Korea," *Research in Comparative and International Education*, *8*(3), 307–25, doi: 10.2304/rcie.2013.8.3.307.

Toppo, G. (2004), "US Teens Have Weak Practical Math Skill," *USA Today*, December 7, D7.

Van Roekel, D. (2010), "Elevate the Teaching Profession," *USA Today*, December 15, A8.

Vinovskis, M. (2009), *From A Nation at Risk to No Child Left Behind: National Education Goals and the Creation of Federal Education Policy*, New York: Teachers College Press.

Waldow, F. (2012), "Standardisation and Legitimacy: Two Central Concepts in Research on Educational Borrowing and Lending," in G. Steiner-Khamsi and F. Waldow (eds.), *World Yearbook of Education: Policy Borrowing and Lending in Education*, New York: Routledge.

Zhao, Y. (2012), "Yes, Numbers (on International Tests) Can Lie" (Blog post), *The Washington Post*, December 12, https://www.washingtonpost.com/news/answer-sheet/wp/2012/12/12/yes-numbers-on-international-tests-can-lie/?utm_term=.c53d13afb8f4.

Part Two

# Coping with Success: International Projections and National Counter Narratives

# 7

# The Use of PISA Results in Education Policy-Making in Finland

Piia Seppänen, Risto Rinne, Jaakko Kauko, and Sonja Kosunen

## Introduction

Finland has long been considered one of the top-performers in international large-scale assessments (ILSAs), including, most prominently, PISA. Scholars seeking to understand the reasons behind PISA outcomes have articulated the sociohistorical context of Finland's schooling system (Simola 2005, 2015; Chung 2009; Simola and Rinne 2011; Grek and Rinne 2011). Normative approaches have also been used, with some studies asking what the world can learn from the Finnish model (Sahlberg 2011a). Despite a few exceptions (Rautalin 2013), studies have focused on "cross-national policy attraction" (Steiner-Khamsi 2014) and investigated how non-Finnish policy actors have used an idealized story of "Finnish success" to criticize or justify reforms to their own system (e.g., Takayama 2010; Dobbins and Martens 2012). However, scholars and analysts have devoted much less attention to how Finnish policy actors have themselves used the PISA results for school reform in Finland. This study draws on the government's official press releases (see Appendix for full list) to understand policy usage of PISA in Finland.

This chapter traces the varied policy reactions to PISA 2000, 2003, 2006, 2009, 2012, and 2015. The first round results (PISA 2000) did not receive nearly as much attention within Finland as they did outside. It was only after PISA 2003 and PISA 2006 that Finnish politicians and policy actors discovered that their country's performance in international large-scale assessment could be a useful tool to argue for more resources for compulsory education. The preoccupation with PISA became further pronounced when the Finnish Ministry of Education and Culture (MoEC) launched an international campaign to showcase and promote various types of education export. However, after four rounds as the league leader, and three years of showcasing themselves for policy export, Finnish math scores for fifteen-year students in Finland slipped in 2012. In this chapter we will examine policy actors' reactions to grandeur and loss, and show that the (self-) projections into PISA success (2000, 2003, 2006, 2009) and slippage (2012, 2015), respectively, must be understood against the backdrop of national reform debates. It is the national policy actors who, after each round of results, determined anew whether the test could help support their reform agenda. As we show, the government-sponsored export of Finnish education[1] in 2009, and its subsequent marketization, mark a discursive shift from being to staying a league leader.

The agenda-setting literature is the starting point for this study. The notion of punctuated equilibrium suggests that change happens in bursts, supported by mounting positive feedback diffused through other systems, for instance, and as a growing number of policy actors become interested in the issue (Baumgartner and Jones 2009). The multiple streams approach similarly suggests that these actors hold on to their pet policies while searching for the right problem to implement them, as opposed to inventing new solutions in response to arising issues (see Kingdon 2003). What our analysis discusses is whether PISA can change the Finnish education policy agenda or whether PISA rather is used as a means to support the existing one.

In this chapter, we first describe Finland's national education policies in relation to its sociohistorical context and consider some of the latest trends toward social segregation in Finnish comprehensive schooling. Based on an analysis of policy documents, we propose two interpretations for how PISA-based scandalization and projection have been and are used as national education policy agenda-setting tools in contemporary Finland. These include one, an equality emphasis and the need to stay "a cutting-edge country" (Gov. 7, Doc. 37) and, two, building up education export policies with the country's PISA brand.

## Uniform Comprehensive School Model and Segregating Trends

The comprehensive school system for seven- to fifteen-year-olds in Finland relies on the Nordic model of one school for all. Like other countries in the region, Finland, a sparsely populated country with 5.5 million inhabitants, has a welfare-state organized to facilitate equality (e.g., Tjeldvoll 1998; Antikainen 2008). Since the post-war era, these ideals have been promoted through educational, labor, youth, and social policies, with inclusion, universalism, and equality as cornerstones (Rinne 2010).

Since the introduction of the comprehensive school (*peruskoulu*) in the 1970s, Finnish education policy has focused on diminishing differences in educational outcomes in relation to individuals' socioeconomic background, gender, place of residence as well as, more recently, ethnicity. The compulsory education system is publicly owned, funded, and governed. The Basic Education Act (628/1998) assigns responsibility for compulsory schooling to municipalities. Therefore, the role of private and even publicly funded private providers in pre-secondary schooling is very limited in comparison to, for instance, Sweden (Alexiadou and Lundahl 2016). Schools are not allowed to collect fees, and must provide warm meals as well as school supplies free of charge. In this sense Finland's comprehensive school system functions as a vast public service, which provides pupils with comprehensive social and welfare services.

Following the principal of equal educational opportunity for all, Finland has focused on developing compulsory education (grades 1–9) as "uniform instruction catering for the whole age group and securing equal prerequisites for all" (MoEC 2012, 26). Every school provides a similar broad national core curriculum, which is elaborated at the municipal and school levels. Officially, there are no ability-based groupings, and the aim is to include students with special educational needs. Children in densely populated areas have access to schools near their residences; otherwise, transport is offered to pupils free of charge. After completing compulsory education pupils are able to apply for further studies in general or vocational upper secondary schools. All secondary certificates provide eligibility to apply for further studies at the university level.

Despite these measures there is a growing body of research literature in Finland showing how seemingly uniform, neighborhood-based schooling and the public comprehensive school system are segmenting pupils in larger towns. Although social segregation between schools to some degree reflects the social segregation in cities, the more significant segmentation tendencies involve pupil selection and parental school choice policies in urban areas. Parental school choice policies in Finland have led to a corresponding rise in school selectivity, although both are still modest compared to some other countries (e.g., Seppänen, Carrasco et al. 2015). Empirical evidence from urban Finland shows that parental school choice as a pupil allocation practice divides along social class lines (e.g., Kosunen and Seppänen 2015; Seppänen, Kalalahti et al.

2015; Kosunen et al., 2016), resulting in significant achievement differences (Hautamäki et al. 2013; Berisha and Seppänen 2016).

## Research Task, Data, and Methods

This chapter addresses the question of how the PISA-based scandalization and projection have been used to formulate education policy in contemporary Finland. To answer it, we analyze two types of government policy documents (see Appendix):

1. Ministry of Education and Culture (MoEC) press releases, which refer to PISA results between 2000 and 2016. Out of the 1,774 press releases categorized as "Education and ECEC" from the MoEC we considered 43.[2]
2. Seven government programs, which focused on education after the 1999 Basic Education Act reform which were issued during four parliamentary election terms in 1999–2002, 2003–6, 2007–10, 2011–15, and 2015 to the present. The MoEC was run by the Social Democratic Party from 1999 to 2010, and by the Center-Right National Coalition Party since 2011.

Our analysis focused first on how PISA results set, confirmed, or changed education policy agendas in Finland, and second, on how PISA is referenced—if at all—in government education policies.

## Equality Nobility at Risk and the Need to Stay a "Cutting-Edge Country"

Despite global interest to Finland's outstanding PISA results, they have received comparatively little attention within Finland itself. This is evident in the fact that—as mentioned above—only 47 of the 1775 press releases (2 percent) issued by the MoEC between 2000 and 2016 mentioned PISA (see Appendix). Our analysis of these selected press releases reveals that, even in the early 2000s, PISA results were not focused on the highest performing educational systems. Rather, the PISA results were understood as a sign of education equality being in danger. The 2015 results in particular were interpreted to show how wide differences are in learning outcomes when considered in terms of gender, social class and geographic location (Gov. 7, Doc. 50). In this section, we analyze how the Finnish government dealt with the PISA results in press releases, and how it influenced their education policy agenda.

The first PISA round in 2000 happened during the period of the so-called Rainbow Government, a coalition of five parties ranging from left to right, which ruled the country from April 1999 to April 2003. The Rainbow Government's program emphasized equal rights in education, and introduced education policy as a tool for promoting people's belonging to society.

> Everyone has an equal right to education and training regardless of their place of residence, age, [first] language and economic situation in compliance with the principle of lifelong learning. Education policy is aimed to prevent marginalization and respond to the challenges of an elderly population. (Gov. 1, Doc. 1)[3]

The MoEC did not issue a press release regarding PISA 2000 when its results were internationally published in late 2001. However, when the national newspaper *Helsingin Sanomat* published two news items about the "World's Best Readers" in PISA 2000, Maija Rask, the Minister of Education and member of the Social Democratic Party, was asked to comment. According to the newspaper, regardless of Finland's PISA results she would increase the number of hours students were required to spend learning Finnish due to a need to improve writing skills across the boards, and raise the scores of young boys in reading (Helsingin Sanomat 2001a,b).

The June 2003 to April 2007 Center-Left government program which followed highlighted the importance of caring, inclusive, neighborhood schools, with a focus on different aspects of equality in education and the reinforcement of local decision-making in order to increase quality. This program did not mention PISA 2000 at all.

> The fundamental principle in the provision of basic education is a uniform comprehensive school. The principle of giving preference to the nearest school will be reinforced. . . . Quality recommendations for good comprehensive education and successful schools will be drawn up. Local evaluation will be enhanced. Remedial teaching will be increased in support of early intervention and preventive action, and special needs teaching and care for school pupils will be reinforced. The emphasis will be on cooperation between home and school. Access to basic arts education will be safeguarded. The integration of children with special needs into ordinary schools will be promoted in all levels of early education and education and training. (Gov. 2, Doc. 2)

The very first press release by MoEC of PISA evaluation was about PISA 2003 in December 2004 by Minister of Education Tuula Haatainen, a Social Democrat like her predecessor. Although she specifically addressed how "[y]oung Finns were among the OECD top in mathematics, science and reading literacy and problem-solving" (Gov. 2, Doc. 3), a separate press release by the MoEC set a policy agenda by interpreting results as "an incentive for improving low achievers' learning" (Gov. 2, Doc. 4). Also many policy issues such as exclusion in society, student welfare, and teachers' working conditions were addressed. The release emphasized that "excellent results" had been gained with "the same level of resources as in the other OECD-countries on average" and used Finland's PISA performance as a call for more funding to basic education:

> Finnish basic education must be able to meet future challenges and maintain the high standard we have achieved. A high level of knowledge is an asset in international contexts and we must make sure we keep it. Basic education resources need to be increased further because it will generate welfare for future generations. (Gov. 2, Doc. 4)

The following Center-Right government that subsequently held power from April 2007 to June 2010, which included the Green League and Swedish People's Party as minor partners, specified that "[r]esources available for basic education will be increased with a view to preventing and alleviating exclusion among children and young people" (Gov. 3, Doc. 5). Extra funding was allocated for achieving smaller study groups in schools, and the text included a discourse on quality improvement:

> The resources made available by smaller age groups will be used to improve the quality of education . . . to reduce group sizes, to strengthen remedial and special needs teaching, guidance counselling and student welfare, and to invest in extracurricular club activities. (Gov. 3, Doc. 5)

The government agenda in early 2007 did not emphasize literacy or mathematics, as would have been the case if their concern was PISA-focused. Instead, the program underlined skills and arts subjects, as well as foreign languages (Gov. 3, Doc. 5).

Once the PISA 2006 results were released showing Finnish students had achieved particularly well in science literacy, the government made the outcome of the focus of praise and celebration (Gov. 3, Doc. 6). The fact that the official remarks were published not only in the two official languages—Finnish and Swedish—but in English, French, and Dutch as well, shows this message was addressed to an international audience. This marked a shift in which it was now evident the government did indeed value Finland's outstanding performance and would allow it to influence their official discourse on education.

The subsequent interpretation of PISA 2006 by Sari Sarkomaa, Minister of Education from the National Coalition Party, was published in a Finnish language-only press release. Though she expressed satisfaction with the excellent results, she also stressed that policy must support "all sorts of talents" (Gov. 3, Doc. 7). She also pointed to the government's earlier decision (Gov. 3, Doc. 6) to allocate extra funding to the development of basic education.

> PISA researchers criticize our schools for lacking the highest top-performers. For this reason our goal is that comprehensive education better answers the needs of different children. It is important to support different types of talents to promote individual learning. Practical and arts subjects will be emphasized. . . . In addition to pure theory, teaching must offer aesthetic experiences and possibilities for developing practical skills, creativity and physical exercise. (Gov. 3, Doc. 7)

This comment reveals an interesting contradiction: PISA was used to show that the Finnish education system was failing its highest achievers, while also emphasizing the need for art subjects, aesthetic experiences, and practical skills not measured by PISA. The subsequent government, briefly led by the Center Party from June 2010 to June 2011, reversed this emphasis on comprehensive schooling (Gov. 4, Doc. 11).

When the results of PISA 2009 were released in December 2010 the MoEC press release was once again addressed to a global audience and published in multiple languages—including now Russian instead of Dutch (Gov. 4, Doc. 12). Minister of Education Henna Virkkunen of the National Coalition Party then published a separate press release in Finnish and English describing, "Excellent PISA results, with some worrying signals," meaning a deepening difference in achievement levels between particular schools (Gov. 4, Doc. 13).

The Minister also stated that the reason to improve schools is not "because we want our 15-year-olds to do well in the OECD comparisons," but rather to offer children, in addition to basic knowledge and skills, a "confidence, motivation and joy of learning that will carry them in further education and training and throughout their lives" (Gov. 4, Doc. 13).

The Right-left government which followed from June 2011 to June 2014, comprised primarily of an alliance between the National Coalition Party, the Social Democrats and four minor parties made strong reference to the ILSAs:

The Government aims to make Finland the most competent nation in the world by 2020. By 2020, Finland will be ranked among the leading group of OECD countries in key comparisons of competencies of young people and adults. (Gov. 5, Doc. 14)

Although this reference to ILSAs was finally incorporated into the government's program in 2011, there were numerous education policy agendas that were not connected to PISA by the government: continuing reduction of class size and strengthening special needs education (both already in the 2003 agenda; see Gov. 3, Doc. 5), multi-professional student care to prevent the social exclusion of children and young people, reducing bullying, consolidating extracurricular activities, fostering use of ICT in education, supporting the educational role of parents by schools, and enhancing parent–teacher cooperation. Due to the reformed national curriculum policy, the agendas also included strengthening the teaching of practical subjects, arts and sport, civic and citizenship education, environmental education, and collaboration between subjects, as well as diversifying language programs, focusing on communication skills and learning-to-learn skills (Gov. 5, Doc. 14).

When an analysis of the causes and trends in PISA 2009 (Gov. 5, Doc. 15) was published in April 2012, the new Minister of Education, the Social Democrat Jukka Gustafsson interpreted Finland's diminished performance stemmed from a faulty education policy:

The success of the Finnish school draws on our strong endeavour to support educational equality. New research shows that in many aspects, which we thought were national strengths, we see a worsening trend. The variation of the results between schools is also greater in the current than in the former PISA studies. (Gov. 5, Doc. 15)

Shortly afterward, in June 2012, the government announced (Gov. 5, Doc. 16) an educational equality program. To legitimate the stronger policy agenda toward equality in education, it used the PISA results indicating that children from families with low socioeconomic status are 1.5 years behind in reading skills compared to children from families that are better off and the difference between the weakest and the strongest schools is equivalent to 2.5 years.

In November 2013, just a couple of weeks before the release of PISA 2012 results, the MoEC published a press release (Gov. 5, Doc. 21) stating that a study conducted by Finnish academics on the learning-to-learn skills of Finnish fifteen-year-olds indicated they had deteriorated when compared to the results of studies published in 2001 and 2012. Once PISA 2012 results showing decline were announced, it was this time communicated in only three languages: Finnish, Swedish and English (Gov. 5, Doc. 25[4]). Despite highlighting the decreased results, the report framed them a relatively positive way.

> The national average score in mathematics has decreased significantly since the 2003 assessment. Reading and science literacy have also deteriorated markedly. Despite the clear downturn, Finnish students remain one of the best performers among the OECD countries. (Gov. 5, Doc. 25)

The following Minister of Education, also a Social democrat, Krista Kiuru saw the need for "a broad-based forum" committing diverse social groups to the development of basic education (Gov. 5, Doc. 25). Such a development project was launched soon after in February 2014 (Gov. 5, Doc. 26).

That year communications from the MoEC used discourse of failing to promote its work. An April 2014 press release announced that in the new area tested by PISA, problem-solving, the performance of Finnish students was among the best, but the Minister of Education simultaneously commented that "[t]he survey shows that one in seven students fails to gain sufficient knowledge and skills to cope in society" (Gov. 5, Doc. 27). When doing so she used the PISA results to legitimize recent government work to reform school education. Six months later the MoEC released additional messages concerning the "declining level of reading and counting competences" and the level of educational equality in a project report on the "Strengthening the national competence basis" (Gov. 5, Doc. 27).

The outcome of the government's development project was a report Tomorrow's Comprehensive School (Gov. 5, Doc. 29), published in March 2015, highlighting the education of entire age cohorts as Finland's most important advantage in the global arena. Achieving this focus was said to require, among other things, securing the neighborhood school principle, addressing socioeconomic equality, and developing continuing education for teachers (Gov. 5, Doc. 29). The following short-term government (June 2014 to June 2015) did not state anything about basic education in its program, "[a] new boost for Finland: growth and employment" (Gov. 6, Doc. 32).

The Center-Right government that has held power since May 2015 maintains a strong position on international education in its program (Gov. 7, Doc. 35). Its key aim to provide "[n]ew learning environments and digital materials [for] comprehensive schools" is meant to address the "problems" raised by previous PISA reports, while still addressing the perennial topic of student well-being:

This project will aim to improve learning outcomes and reduce differences between them. Steps will be taken to improve the learning environments so that students enjoy being at school and to raise the level of emotional and physical wellbeing of children and young people. (Gov. 7, Doc. 35)

Furthermore, the current government's reflections on ILSAs are more explicit than those of previous governments in that they promote the "goal to make Finland a cutting-edge country of modern and inspiring learning" (Gov. 7, Doc. 37). This goal clearly references ILSAs in the context of participating in international competition, as evident in the most recent press releases on PISA 2015 as well as TIMSS (Trends in International Mathematics and Science Study).

The results of the 2016 TIMSS, coordinated by the IEA (International Association for the Evaluation of Educational Achievement), indicated "a clear decrease in Finnish fourth graders' science and mathematics achievement between 2011 and 2015" (Gov. 7, Doc. 49). When the PISA results were released a week later in December 2016 (Gov. 7, Doc. 50) the MoEC highlighted its ongoing "key project New Comprehensive School" (Gov. 7, Doc. 43) focusing on curriculum and pedagogy reform and digitalization as reactions to PISA decline.

During its preparations for the centenary of Finnish independence in December 2017, the government established "a comprehensive school forum to participate in the work being carried out to improve and update the Finnish comprehensive school system" (Gov. 7, Doc. 48). This initiative repeatedly addressed the discourse surrounding the decline in education learning outcomes and equality.

The Finnish comprehensive school has opened doors to higher education and lifelong learning for all children irrespective of their family background. In recent years, the decline in the learning outcomes and fractures in the equality of education have caused concern. The efforts to improve and update the comprehensive school require the support of the entire nation. (Gov. 7, Doc. 48)

# Building Up Education Export Policies Using the Country's PISA Brand

The clearest impact of national policy actors' use of PISA assessment results in policy agenda-setting are also evident in areas besides national basic education. Since the late 2000s, governmental press releases have used interest from other countries to launch policies building a new type of export business to benefit from Finland's internationally established PISA reputation. Here projection to PISA was mentioned in 2009 as a source of anxiety in the sense that if Finland's performance declined the country's image would suffer correspondingly (Gov. 3, Doc. 9). In this section of the chapter, we track the developments that led several different governmental bodies to emphasize educational export.

Based on press releases by MoEC, the timeline to begin activities on education export was short, but expanded dramatically in recent years. In July 2009, Minister of Education Henna Virkkunen of the Coalition Party announced that she had established a working group to prepare "an export strategy" (Gov. 3, Doc. 8). Later that same year she argued for a whole "new area of export" (Gov. 3, Doc. 9), which was implemented by the government in April 2010 (Gov. 3, Doc. 10). The MoEC press releases portrayed Finland as prepared to contribute "significant know-how to highly competitive markets" (Gov. 3, Doc. 8), and argued that the three PISAs published in 2000 had established Finland's strong reputation in education. This, in turn, had supposedly attracted a flow of visitors from abroad "who have familiarized themselves with the Finnish educational miracle" (Gov. 3, Doc. 8), and from whom it was in turn possible to profit.

> Finland's internationally strong reputation in educational know-how should be utilized commercially. Educational export is a business with a lot of potential. The export of education and know-how requires strong co-operation between the public and private sector. (Gov. 3, Doc. 9)

The space in which education business could operate was created by government and PISA's effects on policy-making meant loosening regulations that hindered this emerging education export business. However, the state was also expected to support the export business via collaboration with the Ministry of Foreign Affairs. Despite these roles, the MoEC emphasized that private actors needed to take responsibility for both the business and its risks (Gov. 3, Doc. 9).

In the wake of these initiatives education export policies were strongly promoted in June 2013. At this point the MoEC announced that "education export has not grown as expected" and argued that there was an urgent need to analyze "what are the obstacles to the growth and what means could support it better" (Gov. 5, Doc. 17). Unlike previous policies, this new agenda created a joint effort among Finnish actors who were viewed as too small to act alone. Thus the government's initiatives in education export aimed to foster collaboration between different actors in the field.

Education export has been supported in the spirit of Team Finland by examples such as co-operation between the ministries of Work and Finance, Education and Culture, and Foreign Affairs, along with the help of the project Future Learning Finland, which has pooled stakeholders interested in education export and offered support ranging from productization to export delegations. (Gov. 5, Doc. 17)

Since then the MoEC has stayed busy sending delegations abroad to promote education export, an effort documented in numerous press releases. In October the Minister of Education travelled to Latin America to promote the possible use of Finnish expertise in higher education and research. The delegation also included representatives from the fields of vocational teacher training and learning technology (Gov. 5, Doc. 18). The MoEC's trip to East Asia in November 2013 was reported in the press as a means to foster collaboration and promote Finnish education expertise (Gov. 5, Doc. 22 and 23).

Document analysis shows how PISA has had fairly peculiar effects. In particular, Finland's education export has focused significantly on the university and vocational education sectors, although the PISA reputation is based on the scores of fifteen-year-olds and, thus, lower secondary education. The reported discussion topics, contracts or agreements produced by the Minister of Education's "education export tour" included higher education exchanges between Finland and Japan, and joint efforts with China, which were to provide "a more systematic platform for collaboration projects in education to encourage cooperation between businesses and higher education institutions" (Gov. 5, Doc. 22). A consortium of Finnish stakeholders and the regional administration of Shanghai was fostered to develop vocational education (Gov. 5, Doc. 23), an agreement with South Korea focused on university education as well as "school well-being" and bullying (Gov. 5, Doc. 24), and a March 2014 deal with Indonesia was intended to engage in "mutual collaboration in education" in forestry training and higher education (Gov. 5, Doc. 30).

A trip to the United States in May 2014 focused primarily on basic education in reference to PISA. Finland's Minister of Education stated she was glad that the U.S. Secretary of Education expressed his interest in establishing "a network of education superpowers" (Gov. 5, Doc. 31). The Finnish software company Rovio organized a Fun Learning Event in cooperation with the World Bank, which reportedly identified equality and motivation as keys to success (Gov. 5, Doc. 31). In June 2015, the MoEC declared an initiative for "expanding education collaboration" between China and Finland (Gov. 7, Doc. 36), and it seems education export will continue to remain on the Finland's policy agenda in the foreseeable future. "Education and research have become more international and obstacles to education exports have been removed," as a recent missive states (Gov. 7, Doc. 35) and here the focus is primarily on vocational and tertiary education (Gov. 7, Doc. 39).

The government's goal of benefitting from Finland's success on PISA—that is, to "turn Finland's strongest international brand into a thriving business" (Gov. 7, Doc. 45)—accelerated in August 2016, once three Ministries (Foreign Affairs, Education and Culture, and Economic Affairs and Employment) named a "Chief Specialist in Education Export" (Gov. 7, Doc. 43).[5] Each minister expressed the government's desire to use PISA to commercialize Finnish education to facilitate export in the language of economics (Gov. 7, Doc. 43). The inaugural Ambassador for Education Export, Marianne Huusko, stated that "the greatest challenge in education export lies in the commodification and marketing of big principles" (Gov. 7, Doc. 45) and in answering the question, "[a]t what point does international interaction and networking become [an] export[?]" As she stated, "we must not be so naive as to keep helping others out of the goodness of our hearts. After all, the goal is to achieve growth and success in business" (Gov. 7, Doc. 45).

## Conclusions and Discussion: What Does PISA Mean to Finnish Education Policy Agenda-Setting?

To answer the question asked in the beginning of this chapter—how PISA-based scandalization and projection have been used as national education policy agenda-setting tools in contemporary Finland—we conclude two things based on an analysis of press releases by MoEC and government programs in 2000–16. Overall in terms of policy content, international projections into "Finnish success" had an interesting impact on national agenda setting: the political discourse was fit into the framework of PISA, and to the success story and later to the slight decline the results showed.

First, measured quantitatively, references to PISA have been sparse. The tiny share—2 percent—of all MoEC press releases published between 2000 and 2016 that mention PISA argue allocating sufficient funds to basic education, and position PISA results as a source of concern as opposed to pride is connected to fears for education equality in Finland. Throughout the press releases mentioning PISA—not only after the "PISA decline"—there were signals of worries referring to the PISA results. In addition, government highlighted related policy issues, such as social exclusion, inequality and pupils' well-being. Based on evidence from these government policy documents, it is not possible to support Pasi Sahlberg's (2011b, 136) claim that international attention "made many decision makers and reformers careful not to disturb the high-performing education system." Regardless of PISA, Finland has initiated many reforms in comprehensive schooling. The defining factor in policy actions taken after the PISA results were published seems to be the government programs that steer and even limit the work of the MoEC (Kauko 2011; Kallunki, Koriseva, and Saarela 2015), rather than the PISA results themselves. Theoretically, this is supportive of the agenda-setting dynamics where policy actors stick to their pet ideas and try to offer them to arising problems (Kingdon 2003). Empirically, it demonstrates how PISA is not a major influence on the policy agenda in Finland, especially in contrast to the government program. This conclusion is supported also by a study suggesting that PISA, analyzed up until 2009, has been used domestically to bolster the interests of bureaucrats and teachers' unions, and that these groups faced little media criticism for their policy actions (Rautalin 2013).

Secondly, the programs and press releases we analyzed through 2016 indicate a gradual increase in the extent to which Finland's performance in PISA was referred to in the country's policy agenda. After the PISA results released in 2009, Finnish policy-makers began considering education not just domestically, but as a valuable commodity for export. Education as a form of industry, or a product to be promoted, bought or sold like any other product, is a significant contemporary global phenomenon (Verger, Lubienski, and Steiner-Khamsi 2016). As an interesting contradiction, while education export exists mainly in upper secondary and tertiary education, the marketing is based on the OECD-mediated reputation of the primary and lower-secondary school stage.

In the future, PISA projection might have more effects on compulsory schools in Finland, if the mission of education export will get attached to national education policy. Some recent national education policy goals have been framed rhetorically to exploit the PISA-led education reputation. An example is the plan announced by the Prime Minister's Office (2016, 30–1) "to make Finland into a world-class laboratory of new pedagogy and digital learning" by allocating significant funds to the digitalization of education. In this sense, the PISA reputation might be harnessed for turning Finland into a "laboratory" for global education business.

# Appendix
## List of Analyzed PISA-Related Ministry of Education and Culture (MoEC) Press Releases and Government Programs in Finland between 1999 and 2016

| | Time in office / Date of the document | Party of the prime minister (person's name) and ruling parties of government/Name of the document and topic of the government program [translations by authors] | Party of the Minister of Education (person's name) |
|---|---|---|---|
| Gov. 1 | April 15, 1999– April 7, 2003 | The Social Democratic Party (Paavo Lipponen). "Rainbow government" (Left, SDP, Right, Green, and Swedish parties). | The Social Democratic Party (Maija-Liisa Rask). |
| Doc. 1 | April 15, 1999 | Pääministeri Paavo Lipposen II hallituksen ohjelma. [Government program of Prime Minister Lipponen's second cabinet] Oikeudenmukainen ja kannustava—sosiaalisesti eheä Suomi. [Fair and encouraging—Socially harmonious Finland] | |
| | December 2001 | No documents mentioning PISA in the Ministry of Education's database between December 2001 (of seventeen press releases, all only in Finnish, in the field of "Education and ECEC") and December 2004. (http://www.minedu.fi/OPM/Tiedotteet/) | |
| Gov. 2 | June 24, 2003– April 9, 2007 | The Center party (Matti Vanhanen). Center-Left government (Center, SDP, and Swedish parties). | The Social Democratic Party (Tuula Haatainen and Antti Kalliomäki). |
| Doc. 2 | June 24, 2003 | The government program of Prime Minister Matti Vanhanen's government. Employment, entrepreneurship, and common solidarity: The keys to an economic rebound. | |
| Doc. 3 | December 7, 2004 | OECD PISA 2003: Young Finns among the world top in learning outcomes | |
| Doc. 4 | December 7, 2004 | Haatainen: PISA-tutkimustulokset kannustavat vahvistamaan heikoimmin menestyvien oppimisedellytyksiä [Minister Haatainen: PISA findings are an incentive for improving low achievers' learning] | |

| | Time in office / Date of the document | Party of the prime minister (person's name) and ruling parties of government/Name of the document and topic of the government program [translations by authors] | Party of the Minister of Education (person's name) |
|---|---|---|---|
| Gov. 3 | April 19, 2007– June 2, 2010 | The Center Party (Matti Vanhanen). Center-Right government (Center, National Coalition, Green and Swedish parties). | The Coalition Party (Sari Sarkomaa and Henna Virkkunen). |
| Doc. 5 | April 19, 2007 | Government program of Prime Minister Matti Vanhanen's second cabinet. A responsible, caring, and rewarding Finland. | |
| Doc. 6 | December 4, 2007 | OECD PISA 2006: Excellent results for Finnish students | |
| Doc. 7 | December 4, 2007 | Minister Sarkomaa: Hyviin PISA-tuloksiin pyritään myös tulevaisuudessa [We also strive for good PISA results in the future] | |
| Doc. 8 | July 14, 2009 | Minister Virkkunen: Koulutusosaamisesta vientituote [Making educational know-how an export product] | |
| Doc. 9 | November 27, 2009 | Minister Virkkunen: Koulutuksesta uusi vientiala [Making education the new branch of export] | |
| Doc. 10 | April 29, 2010 | Ministers Virkkunen and Pekkarinen: Koulutuksesta vahva tulevaisuuden vientiala [Making education the strongest future branch of export] | |
| Gov. 4 | June 22, 2010– June 2, 2011 | The Center Party (Mari Kiviniemi). Center-Right government (Center, National Coalition, Green and Swedish parties). | The Coalition Party (Henna Virkkunen). |
| Doc. 11 | June 22, 2010 | Government statement to parliament on the Government Program of Prime Minister Mari Kiviniemi's government, appointed on June 22, 2010. Finland toward a consistent path to growth, employment, and stability. | |
| Doc. 12 | December 7, 2010 | Finnish students high performers in PISA | |
| Doc. 13 | December 7, 2010 | Minister of Education and Science: Excellent PISA results, with some worrying signals | |
| Gov. 5 | June 22, 2011– June 4, 2014 | The Coalition Party (Jyrki Katainen). Left-right government (National Coalition, SDP, Green, Swedish, Christian Democrat, and Left parties), until March 25, 2014. | The Social Democratic Party (Jukka Gustafsson and Krista Kiuru). |

| | Time in office / Date of the document | Party of the prime minister (person's name) and ruling parties of government/Name of the document and topic of the government program [translations by authors] | Party of the Minister of Education (person's name) |
|---|---|---|---|
| Doc. 14 | June 22, 2011 | Program of Prime Minister Jyrki Katainen's government.<br>An open, fair, and confident Finland. | |
| Doc. 15 | April 11, 2012 | PISA 2009—raportti selittää PISA—tulosten syitä ja muutossuuntia [PISA 2009—Report explaining the causes and directions of change for PISA Results] | |
| Doc. 16 | July 28, 2012 | Gustafsson lupaa syksyllä esityksen koulutuksellisen tasa-arvon toimenpideohjelmaksi [Minister Gustafsson promises an action program for educational equality for the Autumn] | |
| Doc. 17 | June 13, 2013 | Minister Kiuru: Koulutusviennissä tarvitaan tiivistä yhteistyötä [Close cooperation is needed for educational export] | |
| Doc. 18 | October 25, 2013 | Opetusministeri Krista Kiuru koulutusvientimatkalle Brasiliaan ja Chileen, valtiosihteeri Pilvi Torsti Peruun [Ministry of Education to conduct education export journey to Brazil and Chile, State Secretary Pilvi Torsti to Peru] | |
| Doc. 19 | October 31, 2013 | Opetusministeri Kiuru Brasiliassa: Yhteistyö koulutuksessa Suomen ja Brasilian välillä laajenee merkittävästi [Ministry of Education Kiuru to Brazil: Cooperation in education between Finland and Brazil will expand significantly] | |
| Doc. 20 | November 4, 2013 | Minister Kiuru: Selvitys antaa pohjan sopia toimenpideohjelmasta koulutusvientiin [This account lays the groundwork for developing an agreement for an action program for educational export] | |
| Doc. 21 | November 14, 2013 | Assessment study: Learning skills of year nine students have deteriorated | |
| Doc. 22 | November 20, 2013 | Minister Kiuru in Tokio and Beijing: Significant increase in collaboration in the education sector | |
| Doc. 23 | November 21, 2013 | Minister Kiuru in Shanghai: Collaboration among top-ranking countries set in motion | |
| Doc. 24 | November 22, 2013 | Minister Kiuru in Soul: Kouluviihtyvyyteen panostaminen yhdistää Suomea ja Etelä-Koreaa [Investments in school well-being unite Finland and South Korea] | |
| Doc. 25 | December 3, 2013 | PISA 2012: Proficiency of Finnish youth declining | |

| Time in office / Date of the document | Party of the prime minister (person's name) and ruling parties of government/Name of the document and topic of the government program [translations by authors] | Party of the Minister of Education (person's name) |
| --- | --- | --- |
| Doc. 26 | February 28, 2014 | Kiuru: Broad-based project to develop future primary and secondary education | |
| Doc. 27 | April 1, 2014 | Finnish student performance in PISA 2012 problem-solving assessment among the best | |
| Doc. 28 | October 21, 2014 | Suomen osaamisperusta jää jälkeen kansainvälisestä kehityksestä [Finnish competence is falling behind in terms of international development] | |
| Doc. 29 | March 12, 2015 | Tulevaisuuden peruskoulu vastaa kehittyvän työelämän ja sosiaalisen elämän vaatimuksiin [The future's comprehensive school answers to the demands of developing work and social life] | |
| Doc. 30 | March 19, 2015 | Ministeri Kiuru syventämässä koulutusviennin mahdollisuuksia Indonesiassa [Minister Kiuru is deepening the possibilities of education export in Indonesia] | |
| Doc. 31 | May 6, 2014 | Opetusministeri Kiuru Washingtonissa: Yhdysvalloissa merkittävää kiinnostusta suomalaista koulutusosaamista kohtaan [Minister Kiuru in Washington: There is remarkable interest in Finnish educational expertise in the United States] | |
| Gov. 6 | June 24, 2014– May 9, 2015 | The National Coalition Party (Alexander Stubb). Right-left government (National Coalition, SDP, Swedish, Christian Democrat, and Green parties), until September 18, 2014) | The Social Democratic Party (Krista Kiuru). |
| Doc. 32 | June 24, 2014 | Program of Prime Minister Alexander Stubb's Government. A new boost for Finland: growth and employment. | |
| Doc. 33 | July 18, 2014 | Minister Kiuru: Suomi käynnistänyt kansainvälisen koulutusverkoston [Finland has established an international education network] | |
| Doc. 34 | May 19, 2016 | Opetushallituksesta ja CIMO:sta yksi virasto vuoden 2017 [Combining the Finnish education board and CIMO] | |
| Gov. 7 | May 29, 2015 | The Center Party (Juha Sipilä). Center-Right government (Center, National Coalition, and Finns parties). | The Coalition Party (Sanni Grahn-Laasonen). |

| | Time in office / Date of the document | Party of the prime minister (person's name) and ruling parties of government/Name of the document and topic of the government program [translations by authors] | Party of the Minister of Education (person's name) |
|---|---|---|---|
| Doc. 35 | May 29, 2015 | Strategic program of Prime Minister Juha Sipilä's government. Government Publications 12/2015. Finland, a land of solutions. | |
| Doc. 36 | June 12, 2015 | Kiinan ja Suomen koulutusyhteistyö laajenee [Educational cooperation between China and Finland is growing] | |
| Doc. 37 | 04 September 2015 | Osaamisen ja koulutuksen kärkihankkeilla uudistetaan suomalaista koulutusta [Finnish education is being reformed by the drivers of know-how and education] | |
| Doc. 38 | October 20, 2015 | Minister Grahn-Laasonen: Yritykset vauhdittamaan koulujen oppimisympäristöjen uudistamista [Enterprises to speed up schooling environment reforms] | |
| Doc. 39 | October 22, 2015 | Ministers Grahn-Laasonen and Toivakka: Esteet koulutusviennin tieltä puretaan [The hindrances of educational export have been overcome] | |
| Doc. 40 | November 24, 2015 | OECD: n koulutusvertailu Education at a Glance ilmestyi [The OECD "Education at a Glance" has been published] | |
| Doc. 41 | May 4, 2016 | Minister Sanni Grahn-Laasonen: Peruskoulun uudistamisessa keskitytään opettajien osaamisen kehittämiseen [Comprehensive school reforms focus on developing teachers' know-how] | |
| Doc. 42 | June 28, 2016 | Työryhmä esittää toisen asteen koulutuksen koulutusviennin esteiden purkamista [A working group is stating that the hindrances of educational export are reduced in the secondary education] | |
| Doc. 43 | August 19, 2016 | Press release 152/2016 by The Ministry for Foreign Affairs: Ambassador Marianne Huusko to boost education export | |
| Doc. 44 | September 9, 2016 | Ministeri Grahn-Laasonen: Uusi Peruskoulu -ohjelma julki—jokaiseen peruskouluun tutoropettaja tukemaan uudistumista [Minister Grahn-Laasonen: New comprehensive school program announced—every school will have a tutor—teacher to support the reform] | |
| Doc. 45 | October 5, 2016 | Webnews by Ministry of Education: Marianne Huusko—a trailblazer in education export | |

| Time in office / Date of the document | Party of the prime minister (person's name) and ruling parties of government/Name of the document and topic of the government program [translations by authors] | Party of the Minister of Education (person's name) |
|---|---|---|
| Doc. 46 | September 15, 2016 | Suomen koulutusta vertailtiin OECD: Education at a Glance—julkaisussa [Finland's education was compared in the OECD's "Education and a Glance"] |  |
| Doc. 47 | October 7, 2016 | Ministeri Grahn-Laasosen johtamalta koulutusvientimatkalta useita sopimuksia - suomalainen päiväkoti Dubaihin, jopa 1000 opettajaa Saudi-Arabiasta Suomeen koulutukseen [Several agreements from the education export trip led by Minister Grahn-Laasonen—Finnish day-care center to Dubai, including a thousand teachers from Saudi Arabia to Finland] |  |
| Doc. 48 | November 16, 2016 | Parliamentary working group to reform comprehensive school—Theses for the centenary of Finland's independence |  |
| Doc. 49 | November 29, 2016 | Neljäsluokkalaisten matematiikan ja luonnontieteiden osaaminen heikentynyt [Fourth class pupils' competence in mathematics and natural sciences has weakened] |  |
| Doc. 50 | December 6, 2016 | PISA 2015: Finnish youth still at the top, despite the drop |  |

Sources:

http://valtioneuvosto.fi/en/government/history/governments-and-ministers/report/-/r/v2

http://valtioneuvosto.fi/tietoa/historiaa/hallitusohjelmat

http://www.minedu.fi/OPM/Tiedotteet/ (except Docs 43 and 45, which come from http://www.minedu.fi/osaaminenjakoulutus/ajankohtaista/?lang=fi)

# Notes

1  *Education Finland* (http://www.eduexport.fi/the-role-of-flf) was created in 2015 to "bring together first-class private companies, vocational institutions, and higher education establishments in Finland, to help export their education expertise, which comes in rich and varied forms, from educational and learning products—technologies, programs, applications, digital learning suites and software, educational content and materials—to services covering teacher training, pedagogical and vocational programs, as well as multi-functional solutions in the physical and digital learning environments." The organization is government supported and managed by the Finnish National Agency for Education. Education

Finland is a part of the *Team Finland* network established to boost the success of Finnish companies abroad and promote Finland's country brand (team.finland.fi/en/). (See more in Schatz 2016)

2   One document (Doc. 43) was published jointly by the Ministry for Foreign Affairs and the Ministry of Education. One of the documents (Doc. 45) included in the data was online webnews by the Ministry of Education based on press release (Doc. 43).

3   The quotations from those documents with Finnish names (see Appendix) have been translated by the authors.

4   Unlike previous ministers, the current MoEC head Krista Kiuru did not issue a separate press release of PISA as previous ministers, but did refer to Finland's performance in a more general press release on education.

5   The position is also alternatively referred to as Ambassador for Education Export.

# References

Alexiadou, N., and Lundahl, L. (2016), "Reforming Swedish Education by Introduction of Quasi-Markets and Competition," in H. M. Gunter, E. Grimaldi, D. Hall, and R. Serpieri (eds.), *New Public Management and the Reform of Education: European Lessons for Policy and Practice*, 66–80, London: Routledge.

Antikainen, A. (2008), "Power, State and Education: Restructuring the Nordic Model," in J. Houtsonen and A. Antikainen (eds.), *Symbolic Power in Cultural Contexts: Uncovering Social Reality*, 93–106, Rotterdam: Sense.

Basic Education Act 628/1998. Finland, https://www.finlex.fi/en/laki/kaannokset/1998/en19980628.pdf (accessed March 28, 2018).

Baumgartner, F. R., and Jones, B. D. (2009), *Agendas and Instability in American Politics*, 2nd ed., Chicago: University Press.

Berisha, A-K., and Seppänen, P. (2016), "Pupil Selection Segments Urban Comprehensive Schooling in Finland: Composition of School Classes in Pupils' School Performance, Gender, and Ethnicity," *Scandinavian Journal of Educational Research*, doi:10.1080/00313831.2015.1120235.

Chung, J. (2009), "An Investigation of Reasons for Finland's Success in PISA." Doctoral dissertation, University of Oxford.

Dobbins, M., and Martens, K. (2012), "Towards an Education Approach à la Finlandaise? French Education Policy after PISA," *Journal of Education Policy*, 27(1), 23–43.

Grek, S., and Rinne, R. (2011), "Fabricating Europe: From Culture to Numbers," in J. Ozga, P. Dahler-Larsen, C. Segerholm, and H. Simola (eds.), *Fabricating Quality in Education—Data and Governance in Europe*, 19–31, London: Routledge.

Hautamäki, J., Kupiainen, S., Marjanen, J., Vainikainen, M.-P., and Hotulainen, R. (2013), *Oppimaan oppiminen peruskoulun päättövaiheessa: Tilanne vuonna 2012 ja muutos vuodesta 2001* [Learning to Learn at the End of Basic Education: The Situation in 2012 and the Change from 2001], University of Helsinki: Department of Teacher Education.

Helsingin sanomat (2001a), "Suomalaiset koululaiset loistivat 32 maan lukijatutkimuksessa: Suomi OECD-maiden kärkeä myös luonnontieteissä ja matematiikassa" [Finnish Pupils Shone in Reading Evaluation of 32 Countries: Finland Was also at the Peak of OECD Countries in Science and Maths], December 5, http://www.hs.fi/kotimaa/art-2000004016183.html (accessed April 1, 2018).

Helsingin sanomat (2001b), "Suomalaiset nuoret maailman parhaita lukijoita" [Finnish Adolescents the Best Readers in the World], December 5, http://www.hs.fi/kotimaa/art-2000004016147.html (accessed April 1, 2018).

Kallunki, J., Koriseva, S., and Saarela, H. (2015), "Suomalaista yliopistopolitiikkaa ohjaavat perustelut tuloksellisuuden aikakaudella" [Arguments Guiding Finnish Higher Education Policy in the Age of Efficiency], *Kasvatus ja Aika*, (3), 117–33.

Kauko, J. (2011), *Korkeakoulupolitiikan dynamiikat Suomessa* [Dynamics in Finnish Higher Education Politics], Helsinki: Faculty of Behavioural Sciences, University of Helsinki.

Kingdon, J. W. (2003), *Agendas, Alternatives, and Public Policies*, 2nd ed., New York: Longman.

Kosunen, S., Bernelius, V., Seppänen, P., and Porkka M. (2016), "School Choice to Lower-Secondary Schools and Mechanisms of Segregation in Urban Finland," *Urban Education*. https://doi.org/10.1177/0042085916666933.

Kosunen, S., and Seppänen, P. (2015), "The Transmission of Capital and a Feel for the Game: Upper-Class School Choice in Finland," *Acta Sociologica*, 58(4), 329–42.

MoEC = Ministry of Education and Culture (2012), *Education and Research 2011–2016: A Development Plan: Reports of the Ministry of Education and Culture, Finland 2012:3*.

Prime Minister's Office (2016), "Action Plan for the Implementation of the Key Project and Reforms Defined in the Strategic Government Programme," *Government Publications 1/2016*.

Rautalin, M. (2013), *Domestication of International Comparisons: The Role of the OECD Programme for International Student Assessment (PISA) in Finnish Education Policy*, Tampere: Tampere University Press.

Rinne, R. (2010), "The Nordic University Model from a Comparative and Historical Perspective," in J. Kauko, R. Rinne, and H. Kynkäänniemi (eds.), *Restructuring the Truth of Schooling—Essays on Discursive Practices in Sociology and the Politics of Education*, 85–112, Jyväskylä: Jyväskylä University Press.

Sahlberg, P. (2011a), *Finnish Lessons: What Can the World Learn from Educational Change in Finland?*, New York: Teacher College Press.

Sahlberg, P. (2011b), "PISA in Finland: An Education Miracle or an Obstacle to Change?" *CEPS Journal: Center for Educational Policy Studies Journal*, 1(3), 119–40.

Schatz, M. (2016), "Education as Finland's Hottest Export? A Multi-Faceted Case Study on Finnish National Education Export Policies," *Research Reports of the Department of Teacher Education 389*, University of Helsinki.

Seppänen, P., Kalalahti, M., Rinne, R., and Simola, H. (eds.) (2015), *Lohkoutuva peruskoulu—Perheiden kouluvalinnat, yhteiskuntaluokat ja koulutuspolitiikka* [Segmenting Comprehensive School—Parental School Choice, Social Classes and Education Policies], Jyväskylä: Finnish Educational Research Association.

Seppänen, P., Carrasco, A., Kalalahti, M., Rinne, R., and Simola, H. (eds.) (2015), *Contrasting Dynamics in Education Politics of Extremes: School Choice in Chile and Finland*, Rotterdam: Sense.

Simola, H. (2005), "The Finnish Miracle of PISA: Historical and Sociological Remarks on Teaching and Teacher Education," *Comparative Education*, 41(4), 455–70.

Simola, H. (2015), *The Finnish Education Mystery—Historical and Sociological Essays on Schooling in Finland*, London: Routledge.

Simola. H., and Rinne, R. (2011), "Education Politics and Contingency: Belief, Status and Trust Behind the Finnish PISA Miracle," in M. Pereyra (ed.), *PISA Under Examination: Changing Knowledge, Changing Tests, and Changing Schools*, 225–44, Rotterdam: Sense.

Steiner-Khamsi, G. (2014), "Cross-National Policy Borrowing: Understanding Reception and Translation," *Asia Pacific Journal of Education*, 34(2), 153–67, doi:10.1 080/02188791.2013.875649.

Takayama, K. (2010), "Politics of Externalization in Reflexive Times: Reinventing Japanese Education Reform Discourses through 'Finnish PISA Success,'" *Comparative Education Review*, 54(1), 51–75.

Tjeldvoll, A. (ed.) (1998), *Education and the Scandinavian Welfare State in the Year 2000—Equality, Policy, and Reform*, New York: Garland.

Verger, A., Lubienski, C., and Steiner-Khamsi, G. (2016), *World Yearbook of Education 2016: The Global Education Industry*, Oxon: Routledge.

# 8

# PISA and Self-Projection in Shanghai

Vicente Chua Reyes Jr. and Charlene Tan

## Introduction

Countries/economies that have performed well in international large-scale assessments (ILSAs) such as the Programme for International Student Assessment (PISA) are increasingly viewed and used as "projection screens" (Waldow 2012). The "projector" (i.e., the context from which the projection is made) and the "slide" (i.e., the conceptions that are being projected) constitute the "projection" undertaken by policy-makers to serve local agendas such as validating or criticizing certain educational policies and practices. That Shanghai is a choice projection screen is unsurprising, given its well-publicized success in PISA (Tan 2012; 2013). In both the 2009 and 2012 PISA, Shanghai emerged top in mathematics, reading, and science (OECD 2010; 2014a, b). Consequently, policy-makers such as those in the UK have selectively referenced policies in East Asia to advance their long preferred domestic policies (You and Morris 2015). But what about "self-projection," that is, how does Shanghai/China look at Shanghai's performance in PISA for 2009 and 2012? Focusing on the official Chinese responses to Shanghai's performance in PISA, this chapter examines "self-projection" in Shanghai (for a discussion of how other educational stakeholders in China respond to Shanghai's PISA success, see Tan 2017a). The chapter begins by introducing the conceptual framework for this study. This is followed by a discussion of the responses of local education officials in the light of Shanghai's PISA success.

## Self-projection, Introjection, and Projection

Countries are increasingly projecting their conceptions of "good" and "bad" education onto top-performers. The motivation, choice of locality, and target audience for the projection are determined by the site that carries out the projection (i.e., the projector). After all, it is the projector that creates and controls the slides and not the projection screen itself (i.e., the country/society that is chosen for the projection). The image that is projected does not necessarily and in most cases do not reflect the reality in the country/society being projected. Instead, the ensuing image serves to legitimate or de-legitimate one or more policies for the country making the projection (Waldow 2012). It follows that the projected image could be positive (in the case of emulating an education model or institution) or negative (in the case of reproving an educational model or institution). The image may also be designed to externalize to negative sentiments about one's own educational system by projecting features that induce tension or discontent onto other entities (Waldow, Takayama, and Sung 2014). An example is Finland where its education has been used as a projection screen for various ideals of "good education" and "good society" (Takayama, Waldow, and Sung 2013). Scholars have also observed the phenomenon of "looking East" where Shanghai as well as other East Asian societies such as South Korea and Singapore are regarded as "reference societies" (e.g. Sellar and Lingard 2013; Tan 2013; Auld and Morris 2014; Crossley 2014; You and Morris 2015; Tan and Reyes 2015, 2016).

Like projection, "self-projection" is concerned with a public display of one's normative standards and conceptions through a representative object. But what makes self-projection distinct from projection is that the representative object is not some other person, community, region or country but oneself. Put simply, the projector *is* the projection screen. By consciously constructing a self-image and presenting it to the target audience, the projector draws attention to oneself to convey one's intended message and achieve one's goal. Take for instance the popular practice of uploading our photos to social media platforms such as Facebook and Instagram. The choice of photos—what we wore, how we posed, who we were with, where we were, the captions that accompanied the photos, and so on—reveals the overall self-image we wish to project to the world. As in the case for projection, self-projection is less about what we really are and more about how we would like others to look at us. Put otherwise, self-projection serves the agenda of the projector by reflecting his or her imagined (rather than actual) reality of oneself. It is important to note that not all self-images are positive. A person may deliberately project a negative image of oneself before a specific target audience for a specific purpose. For instance, a person may paint a pitiful image of oneself for the sake of eliciting sympathy, garnering support and/or receiving donations. The choice of target audience is therefore crucial in self-projection: a change in the intended audience entails a corresponding change in the motivation for and self-image created by the projector.

It should also be added that not all cases of self-projections are carried out by individuals. Self-projection could also be undertaken by a group of people with shared commonalities such as a family, an ethnic community, a district or a nation. In such cases, the different self-projections (or what may be called "selves-projection") by various members of the group convey each member's interpretation of the group in which he or she belongs to. Take the example of self-projection by members of a family on the subject of one's family. An authoritarian father may project an image of himself to his relatives and friends as a strong head of the family surrounded by a submissive wife and docile children. His neglected and longsuffering son, in wishing to send a message to his father, may portray his ideal family as one with smiling parents hugging their children. Each self-image, in short, reflects the individual's projection of what he or she regards as a "good" family, parent and child onto their own family. Successful self-projection requires the projector to be cognizant of not just one's self-image but also how others view oneself. In order to achieve one's agenda, the projector may need to change the existing conceptions of oneself in the eyes of the intended audience so as to align these conceptions with one's ideal self.

In further elucidating on the concept of self-projection, we draw upon certain pertinent aspects from the very rich literature of psychoanalysis. The particular theoretical framework that inspires this inquiry comes from the seminal work of Melanie Klein (1975). Our focus is on her path breaking analysis of the phenomenon of how individuals position themselves as a response to "specific configuration of object relations" that invariably "persist throughout life" (Segal 1973, ix). Klein elaborates on the individual's positioning as a response to object relations (i.e., external stimuli):

> For if an object is taken into the self (introjected), the emphasis lies on acquiring some of the characteristics of this object and on being influenced by them. On the other hand, in putting part of oneself into the other person (projecting), the identification is based on attributing to the other person some of one's own qualities. (Klein 1975, 295)

For this chapter, we appropriate Klein's principles of introjection and projection originally applied to the acts of individuals onto groups and in this specific case, a jurisdiction. The leap from individual to group analysis, we argue, is appropriate and has historical as well as theoretical antecedents. Gordon Allport, another seminal figure in personality psychology, was one of the earliest thinkers to suggest that the phenomenon of direct projection can be applied to individual as well as group behavior in his highly-influential research that explores the theoretical nature of prejudice (Allport 1958). Moses argues convincingly that in looking at political processes, the notion of "projective identification can help us clarify our thinking about groups as well as about individuals" (Moses 1988, 150).

We define self-projection as a conceptual offspring of the Kleinian analytical concepts of introjection and projection. However, we refine it by claiming that self-projection becomes a powerful tool for groups, such as jurisdictions, to manage and fabricate an imagined identity: Self-projection allows one to exaggerate or diminish idealized images of external objects (i.e., the other) consistent with Kleinian introjection. Self-projection also allows embellishing or fading out fetishized depictions of one's own internal characteristics coherent with Kleinian projection. We further assert that consistent with Giddens' description of contemporary society in a period of late modernity, the jurisdiction of Shanghai and particularly its PISA-identity aptly captures the notion of a "reflexively ordered environment" (1991, 214): global influences impact local processes of identification and actualization which conversely impact world-wide trends. As we shall argue later, Shanghai's astute manipulation of the images (both positive and negative) that have arisen due to its remarkable PISA performance is an example of self-projection.

# The Study

## Method

This study is part of a larger study on the responses of and strategies adopted by the Chinese officials in the wake of Shanghai's remarkable achievement in PISA (Tan 2017a, b). The research findings reported in this chapter are guided by this research question: What is the self-image of Shanghai projected by Chinese education officials in the light of Shanghai's PISA performance? The term "Chinese education officials" is defined broadly in this study to refer to individuals who are involved in and have the power to influence, to varying extent, policy making in a given context. A prominent official was the team leader of the Shanghai PISA team in both 2009 and 2012 and a deputy director-general of Shanghai Municipal Education Commission. The newspaper articles were retrieved from an academic research database *China Core Newspapers*

*Full-text Database* (*Zhongguo zhongyao baozhi quanwen shujuku*) that collects articles published in 618 newspapers across China since 2000. Other sources such as documents and essays were obtained from two other academic research databases for publications in Mandarin: *China Knowledge Resource Integrated Database* (*Zhongguo zhiwang*) and *Wangfang Data* (*Wanfang shuju*). All the articles were selected through a keyword search on the three research databases of the words "PISA," "Shanghai PISA," and "education reform in Shanghai" (all in Mandarin). A total of fifty-two newspaper articles, official documents, and academic essays that were published in Mandarin between 2010 and 2016 were reviewed and analyzed. The data analysis process involved coding the data sources to identify initial patterns and categories as guided by the research questions set out in this study. The codes generated were subsequently refined, modified and developed, in an iterative manner, into themes that corresponded to the research question.

## Findings and Discussion

A content analysis of the data reveals a key finding: the self-image projected by the Chinese education officials is both positive and negative, that is, the strengths as well as the weaknesses of Shanghai's education system are highlighted.

## Self-image Projected by the Chinese Education Officials

A typical response from the officials when commenting on Shanghai's PISA performance comes in a "yes but" format. The leader of Shanghai PISA team maintains that "PISA gives us self-confidence but also prompts us to self-examine" (cited in Dong 2013). Observing that "the excellent result from PISA does not prove that all aspects of our basic education are good too," Zhang posits that "PISA enables us to know the obvious advantages of Shanghai students as well as the weakness in our basic education" (cited in Zou 2013; Gong 2013).

The "obvious advantages" mentioned by the team leader of PISA refers to Shanghai students outperforming other countries/economies in reading, mathematics and science in the 2009 and 2012 PISA. Underscoring the positive aspects of education in Shanghai, the Minister of Education highlights the traditional emphasis on knowledge transmission, training of foundational skills and the diligence of the teachers and students (*Zhongguo jiaoyu* 2016). Another prominent factor highlighted by the Chinese officials as giving Shanghai a competitive edge over other countries/economies is education reform in the municipality since the 1980s. The current reform is known as the "Second Phase Curriculum Reform" [*erji kegai*]. The "First Curriculum Reform" (1988–97) marked a series of major educational reforms aimed at helping schools to meet the needs of rapid economic developments in China. An integral component of the reform is pedagogical change. Specifically, the authority aims to replace the traditional didactic form of teaching where students are largely passive recipients of learning with a new form of learning. What is advocated is active, experiential and interconnected learning that fosters autonomy and cooperation (Shanghai Municipal Education Commission n.d.). Linking Shanghai's PISA achievement to the pedagogical reform, the team leader of Shanghai PISA commends Shanghai teachers for successfully shifting from the traditional method of rote-memorization to problem-solving learning methods (Wang 2013). Another distinctive feature of education reform in Shanghai is its focus on helping low-performing schools. A number of measures have been introduced such as assigning teachers with tertiary education to teach in the rural schools for a prescribed period so as to deal with the shortage of teachers in the remote areas, entrusting urban districts in Shanghai to manage the relatively weak schools in the outskirts and rural district, and selecting a high-performing school to replicate its academic and administrative success in a newly built school so that the latter will be able to become a top school in the shortest possible time (Tan 2012). Referring to the desired outcome of educational equity, the team leader of Shanghai PISA attributes Shanghai's success to decades of perseverance in implementing balanced development in basic education (Dong 2013).

The "weakness," on the other hand, is a reference to OECD report that Shanghai students have also emerged top in a related international survey, this time on the hours spent in doing homework. Shanghai students put in 13.8 hours per week to do their homework, a figure that was almost three times the report average of 4.9 hours (OCED 2014a, b). The Minister of Education in China states, "We have obtained outstanding results and nurtured some talents, but we indeed have our own deficiencies, such as excessive schoolwork burden for primary and secondary students, weak innovative spirit in our students, and inadequate practical ability" (cited in *Zhongguo jiaoyu* 2016). Other Chinese officials adopt the same measured and balanced approach; for example, an official from the teaching-research department of Shanghai Municipal Education Commission claims that PISA findings reveal that "Shanghai students' academic results are outstanding but their schoolwork burden is relatively heavy and their schoolwork pressure is relatively high" (Wang 2013, 17). The issue of excessive academic stress has been a longstanding concern in Shanghai and other parts of China. A culture of academic excellence, particularly in the *gaokao* (college entrance exam) has created and sustained an educational landscape where students devote long hours in studying, completing homework and attending extra classes outside school (Peng 2013). A Chinese official observes that students enrolled in prestigious schools tend to experience heavy schoolwork burden with insufficient music and art lessons and extracurricular activities (Hu 2012). It is reported that students in Shanghai/China have to wake up before 7 am and stay up to complete their homework until after 10 pm (He 2009; Wang 2012). A 2014 survey conducted with five thousand high school students across Shanghai confirms the realities of students experiencing heavy schoolwork burden coupled with insufficient sleep (Wang 2014).

The calm and moderated response from the authorities on Shanghai's PISA success in 2012 is not new. When Shanghai first participated in the 2009 PISA, the PISA team leader and fellow Shanghai PISA team members comment that Shanghai's groundbreaking average score of 556 for reading does not hide the weaknesses of the education system in the city (Zhang et al. 2011). Pointing out that it is not appropriate to compare the performance of a municipality like Shanghai with that of a country (as is the case for most of the participating countries in PISA), the PISA team leader cautions against being complacent and carried away by Shanghai's success (Gong 2010). It is instructive that the self-image is premised on PISA data that are described as objective, scientific, and authoritative by the local education officials. The PISA team leader declares that participation in PISA is a form of research that provides China with a more integrated approach to understanding basic education in Shanghai (Gong 2010; Zou and Han 2013). Likening PISA to a medical doctor, he avers that participation in PISA is like undergoing a diagnosis to discover the weaknesses of Shanghai education such as heavy academic burden (Dong 2013). It is also noteworthy that in projecting the self-image, the local education officials express their awareness of the public perceptions of the education system in Shanghai/ China. In particular, the officials acknowledge the prevailing grievance with the heavy schoolwork burden and attribute it to China's cultural beliefs in academic excellence, hard work and knowledge acquisition (*Jiefang Ribao* December 5, 2013).

## Kleinian Introjection and Projection

The research data reveals that self-projection in Shanghai is less about a society's actual performance in international assessments and more about domestic educational discourses. Prior to and following the PISA results, Shanghai educational reform context has been wrought with controversy and resistance from various educational stakeholders (Tan 2017b). Decades of education reform in Shanghai have generated concerns, tensions and hostility from anxiety-filled stakeholders. In such scenarios, the manufacturing of imagined identities and the proliferation of projection arise as deliberate policy choices and decisions. Specifically, the reference by the Chinese officials to PISA data is an example of Kleinian introjection. OECD's affirmation of Shanghai's performance in PISA allows the municipality to align itself with and champion OECD's appraisal of Shanghai as a High-Performing Education System (HPES). The Chinese officials draw attention to an idealized image of OECD as an internationally respected authority on student assessment. It is a significant point that the Chinese officials describe the PISA system as progressive, scientific and advanced (Tan 2007b). It is interesting that the team leader of Shanghai PISA announces that Shanghai has chosen to participate in PISA for the purpose of not participating in it in time to come (*canjia shi weile bu canjia*). What he means is that Shanghai will withdraw from participating in PISA once it has completed its learning from PISA and adequately developed its own appraisal system (Cao and Yan 2014). This strategy works on the basis that the assessment design, system and methods of PISA are worthy of emulation in the first place. This assumption is acknowledged by the team leader of Shanghai PISA who claims that Shanghai has developed its own scientific appraisal system by learning from and adapting the test evaluation ideology, theory and techniques of PISA (Cao and Yan 2014). Concurring with him is the deputy director and inspector of Shanghai Municipal Education Commission who asserts that Shanghai has benefitted from and borrowed PISA's evaluation ideology, method and techniques (Fan 2014).

Further indications of Kleinian introjection is seen in the Chinese officials' spotlight on the report by OECD on the long hours spent by Shanghai students on doing homework. By taking an object (i.e., OECD report), into the jurisdiction (i.e., Shanghai), the goal is to foreground and reinforce the existing problem of heavy schoolwork burden in the municipality so as to justify education reform. A case in point is the proclamation by the leader of Shanghai PISA team that Shanghai needs to research and implement effective measures to reduce the excessive schoolwork burden (Dong 2013). Existing alongside Kleinian introjection is Kleinian projection where one puts part of oneself into the other person by attributing to the other person some of one's own qualities. This is achieved by identifying OECD's notion of a HPES with Shanghai's educational paradigm of quality-oriented education. A quality-oriented education, in the

Chinese context, is an imagined reality that connotes an all-rounded education that is free of heavy schoolwork burden and exam stress. A quality-oriented education is contrasted with an exam-oriented education that centers narrowly on test scores, exam techniques and college entrance rate (Tan 2016). It is telling that the secretary-general of the Shanghai PISA team avers that Shanghai's 2009 result testifies to the effectiveness of the implementation of quality-oriented education and promotion of educational balance (Lu 2013). Self-projection by the Chinese officials therefore facilitates the playing up of fetishized depictions of one's own internal characteristics—in this case, the vision of quality-oriented education in Shanghai—that is coherent with Kleinian projection.

By employing both Kleinian concepts of introjection and projection, self-projection in Shanghai is designed to support ongoing education reform in Shanghai as part of reducing schoolwork burden and achieving quality-oriented education. An example of an education reform, the assessment changes to the *gaokao* (national college entrance exam) reform. An official document on the *gaokao* reform states that the foundational principle for the assessment reform is to "uphold quality-oriented education and focus on students' moral, intellectual, aesthetic and all-round development" (Shanghai Municipal Education Commission 2014, 1). Referring to an exam-oriented education and alluding to the heavy schoolwork burden of students, another document criticizes an over-emphasis in the traditional exam system on screening and selection of students based on their exam scores (Ministry of Education 2012). To support quality-oriented education, the *gaokao* system has been changed from "3+X" to "3+3" model. Previously, under the "3+X" model, students needed to sit for three compulsory subjects, namely Chinese language, mathematics and English language, plus an elective chosen by students: Politics, history or geography (for humanities students); or physics, chemistry or biology (science students). Under the current "3+3" model, students will still sit for the usual three compulsory subjects of Chinese, mathematics and English, but they now have to take three instead of one electives. And unlike the previous system where the choice of elective was restricted to a disciplinary specialization (sciences or humanities), students from 2017 will no longer specialize in either the sciences or the humanities. Instead, they can choose to be tested on any three subjects from the sciences such as chemistry and physics, as well as from the humanities such as geography and history (Yan 2014). The rationale for the introduction of a "3+3" model is to move away from a narrow disciplinary specialization to expose students to a more broad-based and well-rounded learning. In an attempt to reduce academic stress and by implication, the long hours spent on homework, the current *gaokao* system will no longer test the electives alongside the compulsory subjects during the *gaokao* exam that takes place in June. Instead, students will sit for the electives exams prior to high school graduation at the Ordinary Senior Secondary Level Academic Standard Graded Exam (*putong gaozhong xueye shuiping dengjixing kaoshi*). Also targeting at reducing the stress of high-stakes exam is the option for students to take the English language exam twice (once in January and once in June) and use the higher score for consideration in admission. The desired outcome of the *gaokao* reform is to enable Shanghai to retain its strengths of strong foundational knowledge and academic rigor while eliminating its main weakness of heavy schoolwork burden at the same time. Self-projection, in short, is the vehicle for the education authority to construct and manage its imagined reality of quality-oriented education.

## Conclusion

This chapter has examined how the local education officials in Shanghai/China project what they regard as "good" education—mastery in reading, mathematics and science—and "bad" education—heavy schoolwork burden—onto their own education system by relying on PISA findings. It was argued that the ensuing self-image in Shanghai is both positive and negative, with an emphasis not only on Shanghai's strengths in reading, mathematics and science, but also on its weaknesses, particularly the long hours spent by students on doing homework. Drawing upon relevant features of Kleinian psychoanalysis, particularly of introjection and projection, this chapter further argues how Chinese officials attempt to construct an imagined identity that centers on "quality-oriented education" (*suzhi jiaoyu*). Self-projection in Shanghai is designed to support ongoing assessment reform in Shanghai as part of reducing schoolwork burden and achieving holistic education. An example of an ongoing assessment reform are the refinements made to *gaokao*.

Overall, it can be observed that the self-projection—whether as Kleinian introjection or projection—by the local education authorities involves an intimate knowledge of the perceptions held by other policy actors, particularly the parents, in Shanghai. The perceptions of the Chinese consist of their expectations, assumptions and assessment of their own education system and achievement of Shanghai in PISA. A deep understanding of the existing self-image of fellow citizens is crucial for the Chinese education officials in projecting a self-image of Shanghai. This is because self-projection is unlike projection where the viewers of the projection screen are not well-acquainted with a referenced context. In the case of using Shanghai as a projection screen, the educational stakeholders in Shanghai have firm knowledge, presupposition and experience of their own educational system. Rather than projecting an image that ignores prevailing sentiments and grievances of fellow Chinese, the education officials judiciously present a self-image that takes cognizance of and incorporates the self-representations of the Chinese educational stakeholders. By projecting themselves into the horizon of the masses and understanding them within the context that shape their claims, the officials aspire to realize its imagined identity of quality-oriented education. The self-projection is made possible through the PISA discourse that is presented as a "new language" that is objective, scientific and neutral. This self-projection enables the policy-makers and other educational stakeholders in Shanghai to "talk undistortively" (Taylor 2002, 134) of each other, thereby expanding and combining the original horizons.

This study adds to the existing literature on the varying receptions across societies towards PISA findings and the diverse self-images that are projected. The example of Shanghai demonstrates that self-projection is less about a society's actual performance in international assessments and more about domestic educational discourses. The conceptual tool of self-projection has illuminated the educational discourses and policy-making in Shanghai in the wake of its PISA success. Self-projection is used by the local education authorities to simultaneously glorify Shanghai's education system as a product of effective education reform ("good education") and scandalize the same system for the long hours spent by students on completing homework ("bad" education) (Steiner-Khamsi 2006). Furthermore, the public spotlight on Shanghai students spending the most time doing homework is a form of "distortion" or "exaggeration"—the strategy used by policy-makers to magnify, whether intentional or otherwise, evidence from overseas with the purpose of foregrounding perceived deficiencies at home (Steiner-Khamsi 2009; Tan 2016). The experience in Shanghai brings to the fore the "context" argument: "because education is deeply culturally embedded, what works in one context may not work the same way in another context, so caution is to be exercised in such borrowing" (Gorur and Wu 2015, 654).

In an era that Giddens describes as late modernity typified by individuals and societies finding themselves enmeshed in a perpetual "reflexive project" (Giddens 1991, 258), transforming oneself to reflect global tendencies, it is inevitable that tensions occur:

Identification and projection form major means whereby potential spirals of anxiety and hostility are avoided. Identification is partial and contextual—the taking over of traits or patterns of behavior of the other which are relevant to the resolution or diminishing of anxiety-creating patterns. It is always a tensionful affair, because it is partial, because mechanisms of projection are involved, and because it is fundamentally a defensive reaction to potential anxiety. (Giddens 1991, 46)

The self-projection that Shanghai education officials have manifested, as indicated in the findings reported in this chapter, is a defensive reaction. This is their attempt at minimizing anxiety and eluding hostility from education stakeholders. It must be pointed out though that the defensive reaction is unique but not entirely unexpected. Through the strategic use of self-projection, a deliberate process of introducing a distinctive and ideal education alongside tacit acknowledgment of current education reform is accomplished. This is clearly manifested in the continuing discourse that can be found in descriptions of Shanghai education reform in the wake of PISA. The strategic approach does not openly challenge anyone in particular, making it a contextually suitable response. In this regard though, the behavior of the Shanghai education stakeholders should be no surprise. Goffman in his landmark tome about cultural rituals and interactions among people already documented more than fifty years ago, the cultural idiosyncrasy "to give face" that occurs in some places such as China (Goffman 1967, 9). This cultural peculiarity combined with self-projection creates an educational discourse that is seen predominantly as factual, logical, and impartial.

# References

Allport, G. (1958), *The Nature of Prejudice*, New York: Doubleday.

Auld, E., and Morris, P. (2014), "Comparative Education, the 'New Paradigm' and Caopolicy Borrowing: Constructing Knowledge for Education Reform," *Comparative Education*, 50(2), 129–55.

Cao, Ji, and Yan, W. (2014), "*PISA, huange shijiao kan jichu jiaoyu*" [PISA, Looking at Basic Education from a Different Angle], *Guangming Ribao*, February 7, 6.

Crossley, M. (2014), "Global League Tables, Big Data and the International Transfer of Educational Research Modalities," *Comparative Education*, 50(91), 15–26.

Dong, C. (2013), "Shanghai PISA xiangmu fuzeren: PISA rang women zixin ye rang women zixing" [Official in Charge of Shanghai PISA: PISA Gives Us Both

Self-Confidence and Self-Examination], *Dongfangwang*, December 4, http://sh.eastday.com/m/20131204/u1a7809993.html (November 11, 2017).

Fan, L. (2014), "Pingjia zhihuibang 'gaige': Fenshu cong weiyi biancheng shifen zhiyi" [Reform in the Appraisal Baton: Test Scores to Change from the Only One to One-Tenth], *Wenhui Bao*, March 21, 11.

Giddens, A. (1991), *Modernity and Self-Identity: Self and Society in the Late Modern Age*, Stanford: University Press.

Gong, Y. (2010), "Shanghai xuesheng PISA ceshi quanqiu diyi zhenjing oumei?" [Shanghai Students Top PISA Worldwide: A Shock to Europe and the U.S.?], *Zhongguo Qingnian Bao*, December 17, http://zqb.cyol.com/content/2010–12/17/content_3464771.htm (accessed November 11, 2017).

Goffman, E. (1967), *Interaction Ritual: Essays on Face-to-Face Behaviour*, New York: Pantheon.

Gong, Y. (2013), "Shanghai xuesheng canjia PISA zai duoguan" [Shanghai Students Participated in PISA and Won Again], *Zhongguo Qingnian Bao*, December 4, http://blog.sciencenet.cn/blog-521242–747663.html (accessed November 11, 2017).

Gorur, R., and Wu, M. (2015), "Leaning Too Far? PISA, Policy and Australia's 'Top Five' Ambitions," *Discourse: Studies in the Cultural Politics of Education*, 36(5), 647–64.

He, R. (2009), "Zhongxiao xuesheng jianfu diaocha—Xuesheng jianfu chengxiao ruhe?" [Survey on Burden for Secondary and Primary Students—How Effective Is Reducing the Burden for Students?], *Yangzhou Ribao*, February 6, B1.

Hu, X. (2012), "Ba xuexiao daidao hefang" [Where Are the Schools Heading Towards], *Shanghai Education*, 4A, 66–67.

*Jiefang Ribao* (2013), "PISA Shanghai xiangmu fuzeren: Xuexi shijian yu chengji chengzheng bili" [Official in Charge of PISA Item: Learning Time Is Proportionate to Performance], December 5, http://blog.sina.com.cn/s/blog_519169510101j3iz.html (accessed November 12, 2017).

Klein, M. (1975), "Our Adult World and Its Roots in Infancy," *Human Relations*, 12(4), 291–303.

Lu, J. (2013), "Lu Jing: Diyi de guanjian shi jianyu junheng" [Lu Jing: The Key Is Educational Balance], *Zhongguo Jiaoyu XinwenWang*, December 12, http://sh.qq.com/a/20131212/012605.htm (accessed November 12, 2017).

Ministry of Education (2012), "Jiaoyu bu guanyu jiji tuijin zhongxiaoxue pingjia yu kaoshi zhidu gaige de tongzhi" [Notice of the Ministry of Education to Actively Promote the Reform of Appraisal and Examination System for Primary and Secondary Schools], www.gov.cn/gongbao/content/2003/content_62173.htm (accessed November 12, 2017).

Moses, R. (1988), "Projection, Identification, and Projective Identification: Their Relation to Political Process," in J. Sandler (ed.), *Projection, Identification, Projective Identification*, 133–50, London: Karnac.

OECD (2010), *PISA 2009 Results: Executive Summary.* https://www.oecd.org/pisa/pisaproducts/46619703.pdf (accessed November 12, 2017).

OECD (2014a), *PISA 2012 Results in Focus What 15-Year-Olds Know and What They Can Do with What They Know.* https://www.oecd.org/pisa/keyfindings/pisa-2012-results-overview.pdf (accessed November 12, 2017).

OECD (2014b), *PISA in Focus 46,* http://www.oecd-ilibrary.org/docserver/download/5jxrhqhtx2xt.pdf?expires=1464329970&id=id&accname=guest&checksum=3DAEBE4F6130674C6442FD730A43D51F (accessed November 12, 2017).

Peng, W. (2013), "Kaoshi buying shi jiaoyu de weiyi zhihuibang" [Exam Should Not Be the Only Baton in Education], *Jiefang Ribao,* December 6, 2.

Segal, H. (1973), *Introduction to the Work of Melanie Klein,* London: Karnac Books.

Sellar, S., and Lingard, B. (2013), "Looking East: Shanghai, PISA 2009 and the Reconstitution of Reference Societies in the Global Education Policy Field," *Comparative Education,* 49(4), 464–85.

Shanghai Municipal Education Commission (n.d.), "Shanghaishi putong zhongxiaoxue kecheng fangan (shixing gao) shuoming (shehui ban)" [Explanation for the Trial Curriculum Plan for Ordinary Secondary and Primary Schools in Shanghai (Social Version)], www.shmec.gov.cn/attach/article/72.doc (accessed November 12, 2017).

Shanghai Municipal Education Commission (2014), "Shanghai shi shenhua gaodeng xuexiao kaoshi zhaosheng zonghe gaige shishi fangan" [Implementation Plan to Deepen the Comprehensive Reform for College Entrance Exam in Shanghai City], http://gaokao.eol.cn/zui_xin_dong_tai_2939/20140919/t20140919_1177783.shtml (accessed November 12, 2017).

Steiner-Khamsi, G. (2006), "The Economics of Policy Borrowing and Lending: A Study of Late Adopters," *Oxford Review of Education,* 32(5), 665–78.

Steiner-Khamsi, G. (2009), "Comparison: *Quo Vadis?*" in R. Cowen and A. M. Kazamias (eds.), *International Handbook of Comparative Education,* 1141–58, Dordrecht: Springer.

Takayama, T., Waldow, F., and Sung, Y.-K. (2013), "Finland Has It All? Examining the Media Accentuation of 'Finnish Education' in Australia, Germany and South Korea," *Research in Comparative and International Education,* 8(3), 307–25.

Tan, C. (2012), "The Culture of Education Policy Making: Curriculum Reform in Shanghai," *Critical Studies in Education,* 53(2), 153–67.

Tan, C. (2013), *Learning from Shanghai: Lessons on Achieving Educational Success,* Dordrecht: Springer.

Tan, C. (2016), *Educational Policy Borrowing in China: Looking West or Looking East?,* Oxon: Routledge.

Tan, C. (2017a), "Chinese Responses to Shanghai's Performance in PISA," *Comparative Education,* 53(2), 209–23.

Tan, C. (2017b), "PISA and Education Reform in Shanghai," *Critical Studies in Education,* 1–16, doi: 10.1080/17508487.2017.1285336.

Tan, C., and Reyes, V. (2015), "Neo-liberal Education Policy in China: Issues and Challenges in Curriculum Reform," in S. Guo and Y. Guo (eds.), *Spotlight on China: Changes in Education under China's Market Economy*, 3–18, Rotterdam: Sense.

Tan, C., and Reyes, V. (2016), "Curriculum Reform and Education Policy Borrowing in China: Towards a Hybrid Model of Teaching," in C. P. Chou and J. Spangler (eds.), *Chinese Education Models in a Global Age: Transforming Practice into Theory*, 37–50, Singapore: Springer.

Taylor, C. (2002), "Gadamer on the Human Sciences," in R. J. Dostal (ed.), *The Cambridge Companion to Gadamer*, 126–42, Cambridge: University Press.

Waldow, F. (2012), "Standardisation and Legitimacy," in G. Steiner-Khamsi and F. Waldow (eds.), *World Yearbook of Education: Policy Borrowing and Lending in Education*, 411–27, New York: Routledge.

Waldow, F., Takayama, T., and Sung, Y.-K. (2014), "Rethinking the Pattern of External Policy Referencing: Media Discourses over the 'Asian Tigers'' PISA Success in Australia, Germany and South Korea," *Comparative Education*, *50*(3), 302–21.

Wang, J. (2012), "Kandong PISA, kandong Zhongguo jiaoyu" [Understand PISA, Understanding Education in China], *Wenhui Bao*, April 21, A.

Wang, M. (2013), "Shanghaishi zhongxiao xuesheng xueye zhiliang lüse zhibiao zonghe pingjia gaige yanjie" [Research on the Green Indicator Integrated Appraisal Reform for the Academic Quality of Secondary and Primary Students in Shanghai], http://www.cnsaes.org/homepage/Upfile/2013126/2013120665257661.pdf (accessed November 12, 2017).

Wang, W. (2014), "Shanghai gaozhongsheng redian wenti diaocha baogao: Shuimian buchu renwei jiejue" [Survey Report on a Hot Topic for Senior Secondary Students in Shanghai: The Problem of Insufficient Sleep Is Still Unresolved], *Xinmin Wanbao*, August 18, http://edu.people.com.cn/n/2014/0818/c1053-25482363.html (accessed November 12, 2017).

Yan (2014), "Shanghai, Zhejiang to pilot gaokao reforms," *China Daily*, September 20, http://usa.chinadaily.com.cn/china/2014-09/20/content_18632195.htm (accessed November 12, 2017).

You, Y., and Morris, P. (2015), "Imagining School Autonomy in High-performing Education Systems: East Asia as a Source of Policy Referencing in England," *Compare: A Journal of Comparative and International Education*, 1–24, doi:10.1080/03057925.2015.1080115.

Zhang, M., Lu, J., Zhan, S., Zhu, X., and Wang, T. (2011), "Zhuanye shiye zhong de PISA" [A Professional Perspective to PISA], *Jiaoyu Yanjiu*, *6*(6), 3–10.

*Zhongguo jiaoyu zongti shuiping jinru shijie zhong hanglie, jiaoyu buzhang yuan guiren da jizhe* (2016), [The Overall Standard of Education in China Has Joined the Ranks of the World, the Minister of Education Yuan Guiren Responds to Reporters], http://learning.sohu.com/20160311/n440167620.shtml (accessed November 11, 2017).

Zou, J. (2013), "Shanghai jiang gongbu xin pingjia tisi: lùse zhibiao ceshi" [Shanghai to Announce a New Evaluation System: Green Indicator Assessment], *Dongfang Zaobao*, December 4, A7, http://blog.sciencenet.cn/blog-521242–747663.html (accessed November 12, 2017).

Zou, J., and Han, X. (2013), "Shanghai chengji xizhong youyou: Zuoye shijian quanqiu diyi shuxue yingyong nengli eruo" [Worry in the Midst of Joy for Shanghai Results: Homework Hours Are Top in the World, Slightly Weak Application of Mathematics], *Dongfang Zaobao*, December 4, A6, http://blog.sciencenet.cn/blog-521242–747663.html (accessed November 12, 2017).

# 9

# Curse or Blessing? Chinese Academic Responses to China's PISA Performance

Barbara Schulte

## Introduction

Over the past fifteen years, China has been struggling with educational reform in order to transform from an exam-oriented system into a system that values holistic and creative approaches to education and learning. Persisting mechanisms of competition and selection were to be reconciled with considerations that would reach beyond test performance and take into account innovative thinking, students' well-being and genuinely equal access to educational resources. China's comparatively weak performance (in proportion to its population size), for example, in terms of patents or international academic citations seemed to underline the urgency of educational reforms.[1]

The Chinese—or rather, Shanghainese—high performance in PISA 2009 and 2012 implied a potential break with China's continuous striving for educational improvement and its orientation toward Western educational models: through the OECD ranking, the Chinese educational system was testified to produce internationally outstanding students, assessed by indicators that had been developed at an institution who symbolized the quintessence of Western-dominated, global power. Did this mean that China would stop looking elsewhere for educational improvement and reform, and could instead of *importing* educational models and ideas, engage in global educational *export* (see e.g. Sellar and Lingard 2013, on the reconstitution of educational reference societies)?

This chapter will look at the academic responses to China's PISA performance as articulated in Chinese academic journals and educational newspapers.[2] These responses belong largely to four different types: (1) Learning from PISA and its implications for assessing educational quality; (2) establishing China as an educational role model; (3) contrasting the Chinese system's exam-efficiency with individual or social welfare; and (4) questioning the positive correlation of educational assessments with educational quality. An ensuing section will then discuss the potential motives and agendas behind the Chinese embrace or, alternatively, rejection of PISA. The conclusion will relate these perceptions and projections to the wider transnational, hegemonic educational policy regimes that permeate the implementation of, and conclusions drawn from, PISA.

## China's Participation in PISA

China has participated in PISA four times, but never as an entire country. In 2009 and 2012, China was represented by Shanghai, which achieved top results, separating Shanghainese students from the rest of the OECD countries by up to several school years (e.g., OECD 2014). While data in regions other than Shanghai were collected, they were never made publicly accessible; researchers who were given exclusive access note, among other things, the prevalent rural-urban divide in educational performance (Lu 2017) and more generally problems of educational inequality (Wang, Jing, and Tong 2017). In PISA 2015, the Chinese sample was extended to also include students from Beijing as well as from the provinces of Jiangsu and Guangdong. Probably due to the greater diversity of the sample, China dropped to the tenth place in the PISA ranking (OECD 2016b). Only the aggregated data can be retrieved (OECD 2016c); it is therefore impossible to make any data-supported assumptions about performance disparities within or between the four regions included. For PISA 2018, Guangdong province is reported to have been replaced with Zhejiang province. This may lead to a higher total ranking, since Zhejiang province is known for its excellent schools and high prioritization of education among families.

Already during the early days of PISA-Shanghai, those in charge would stress that the participation in PISA was only a temporary solution, and that the ultimate goal was to develop a Chinese version of PISA. As Zhang Minxuan, the person in charge of PISA-Shanghai, already remarked in 2013, China "participated in order to not participate [in the future; BS]" (quoted in Wang 2013). Prior to PISA 2015, news went out that China would drop out of PISA altogether. In March 2014, *Xinmin Evening News* (*Xinmin Wanbao*) reported on the decision that China would not take part in PISA 2015. It specified that the aim should not be to find the most efficient cram school, but to diminish the burden on teachers and students (e.g., arising from excessive homework) (Wang 2014). However, due to the many contextual data that PISA was able to deliver—such as regarding the socioeconomic background of students, gender differences, and stress factors, and their correlation with student performance— China renounced the decision to withdraw, and instead enlarged the student sample. Similarly, China's participation in PISA 2018 had long been uncertain; consequently, the preparation work, which usually requires one and a half years, had to be completed within four months.

In addition to China's international PISA participation, a nation-wide assessment system was put in place in 2015. This system is to a large extent based on a pilot assessment system developed since 2012 in Shanghai—the so-called green indicators (*lüse zhibiao*) (see Xu et al. 2016)—which in turn draw on the Shanghainese experiences from PISA. According to these indicators, test results play only a minor role (of approximately ten percent); further factors to consider are attitudes toward learning, moral behavior, mental and physical health, individual development, identification with the school, teaching methods, school management skills, and the correlation between socioeconomic background and student performance. Besides, in the newly developed, national Chinese PISA, "softer" subjects such as physical education, art, and moral education are also part of the assessment. As the chairman of the Ministry of Education's School Inspection Commission, He Xiuzhao, concedes, China had previously lacked the ability and the tools to assess the quality of compulsory education and to adequately diagnose existing problems and their causes; PISA was to be employed to learn about effective assessment methods, in order to build up an indigenous system of performance and quality assessment (MOE 2015b). Even though the Chinese PISA has been conducted twice so far, involving each time ca. 6,500 schools, 200,000 students, and between 70,000 and 100,000 teachers (MOE 2015a; 2016), data have so far not been made accessible.[3]

## Chinese Academic Responses to Shanghai's PISA Success

The successes of the Shanghainese PISA performance in 2009 and 2012 were met with both skepticism and enthusiasm among Chinese educationists. On one side, the high PISA performance was seen as having seriously undermined the argument for reform: why change a system that has proven to be of high quality, even according to international standards? Similar to the reaction of some Finnish reformers in light of the Finnish PISA success story (see e.g. Sahlberg 2011; Lundgren 2013), also Chinese educationists worried that the excellent PISA results would bring an end to educational reform—of a system that was considered highly problematic in many aspects (see e.g. Fang 2015). Many educational scholars chose to not reciprocate the overly admiring Western reactions regarding the Shanghainese performance and rather displayed wariness and self-criticism (Yang 2011).

On the other side, the Shanghainese success story was used to argue for the effectiveness of the educational reforms implemented so far. Shanghai had long been considered a pioneer of educational reform. Particularly the above-mentioned PISA representative Zhang Minxuan—who had also been responsible for implementing educational reforms in Shanghai prior to PISA—interprets the excellent performance of Shanghainese students as reflecting the extensive investment in educational reform (see e.g. Zhang and Kong 2013; 2012; Zhang, Xu, and Sun 2014). Conversely, others attribute China's drop to the tenth place in the most recent PISA ranking to the negative effect of educational reform: rather than seeing the extended sample (and thereby greater socioeconomic diversity of participants) as a reason for the deteriorated results, it is assumed that effective traditional teaching and learning methods have been abandoned too quickly in favor of Western imports, leading to poorer student performance (Lü 2017).

The academic responses to and utilizations of China's PISA performance can be categorized into four types: a first faction of academics holds that China can learn from PISA, as PISA is seen to epitomize the idea of a modern, future-oriented education; besides, this faction regards PISA as providing valuable knowledge about how to adequately assess educational quality. A second faction uses the Shanghai example to argue that the time has come for China to teach something to the world (rather than the other way around), for example in terms of study discipline and respect for the teacher. A third faction concedes that the Chinese educational system may lead to better test results but doubts whether this can justify the sacrifices that Chinese families are forced to make in order to attain these results. A fourth type of response is to regard the PISA results as a non-finding: this group is not surprised over the fact that Chinese students are best at passing tests, but is reluctant to draw any conclusions from this in terms of educational quality. Some push this attitude of reluctance further and maintain that PISA does not measure aspects that should be regarded relevant for Chinese students and schools, such as space for creativity, leisure time, and inclusive education. It should be noted that this categorization only takes into account the instances when PISA is utilized as an argument in the educational-political debate; it excludes the large group of researchers who, like their Western counterparts, use PISA for data-mining purposes, without taking a clear normative stance on PISA.[4] Hence, only articles of a clear debate character were included for this categorization.

## Looking West: Learning from PISA

Learning from PISA is understood differently, depending on the respective educational-cum-political agenda. First, and closest to the official mission, PISA is supposed to improve China's ability to professionally assess its educational system, as has been mentioned above with regard to both the Ministry of Education and those who were in charge of implementing PISA in Shanghai. As researchers point out, prior to China's participation in PISA, only exams and grades were used as indirect indicators for assessing the system's quality (Wang and Jing 2013). The multidimensional approach as employed for PISA has turned out to be an eye-opening experience for Chinese educationists (Yang 2011). In a slight twist of the mission of improving the *system's* assessment, some see PISA also as a useful instrument for re-thinking the way that *examinations* are designed and organized in China. Over recent years, experiences from PISA have helped to improve the design of the nation's university entrance examination (*gaokao*), by putting more emphasis on critical thinking (Wang and Jing 2013).

Secondly, PISA is expected to modernize and raise the quality of Chinese education and school management. Since PISA is judged to reveal a nation's quality of education and foresee this nation's "competitiveness" in the "global society of the future," it is also expected to show "which way Chinese education should go" (Pan 2012, 47). As PISA is considered to assess what is needed for the future, it is expected to support China in modernizing its education system; this modernization entails above all the need to acquire skills in interactive problem-solving, flexible knowledge application, and abstract thinking beyond school subject boundaries—all areas where Chinese students, despite their otherwise stunning results, continue to reveal weaknesses (Ren et al. 2016). In terms of school management, the PISA results show, according to many educational researchers, the need for more school autonomy, as this would have a positive effect on student performance (Wang and Jing 2013).

The ideological base of this modernization process is interpreted differently. Some relate the process to domestic policies like the Ten-Year Plan for educational development in China and its stress on quality and equality of education, thus seeing the PISA participation as the natural extension of national policy implementation (Wang and Jing 2013). The assessment tools provided by PISA, according to these researchers, will help to level out inequalities in terms of family background and urban-rural divide (Lu 2017). Others regard PISA as a sort of break with the socialist tradition, according to which education had primarily been expected to adjust to a society's economic, political, and cultural needs. This socialist outlook is judged to have resulted in a continuous reproduction of the past, turning graduates into "standardized educational products" (Pan 2012, 51). In contrast to this social engineering mind-set, PISA is seen as nurturing an orientation toward the future and a positive attitude toward taking risks and moving toward the unknown. Instead of simply acquiring knowledge, students, so it is argued, are now pushed toward learning how to learn.

Thirdly, PISA is seen to improve policy-making in a context that has long been characterized by arbitrary, despotic governing. Becoming integrated in a transnational assessment regime is judged to enhance the pressure on policy-making to become based on scientifically substantiated arguments. As Wang and Jing express it, "[c]urrently, regarding many hard-to-solve problems in education, there is no lack of experts with the knowledge, skills and wisdom, but unfortunately there is a gap between research in education and administrative work in education" (2013, 175). PISA, so it is hoped, would transplant the international logic of scientific assessment and policy recommendations to the Chinese context, and thereby professionalize Chinese policy-making.

## Looking East: China as an Educational Role Model

"Chinese students'" intelligence, skills and knowledge, as well as their hardworking spirit are stronger than among foreign students, and in particular stronger than among American students, who are admired by "everyone," rejoices Ji with "a feeling of gratification" (2011, 18). But rather than simply showing that Chinese students perform better than their American peers, PISA seems to prove to these researchers that it is still important to accumulate knowledge and skills, as these lie at the base of all innovation and creativity. This faction dismisses the more child-centered approaches as have been influencing educational reform, arguing that "a so-called creative education, which encourages the child to play as much as he likes, is a lie that deceives oneself and others" (Ji 2011, 18).

The better performance of China and more generally Asian countries is attributed to "many influential factors from Chinese traditional culture"; these traditional patterns, researchers caution, should not be changed through reforms, but "Western educational thought" should be "appropriated through indigenization" (Lü 2017, 14). Likewise, Zhou notes that for many educational experts, the good PISA results mean that China should stop reforming its education along Western lines, as the results "prove that . . . our basic education has many bright spots, and there is no need for all kinds of chaotic reform, lest we reform away our own strengths and advantages" (2011, 37). In general, educationists in this faction emphasize the necessity of China choosing its own path (Zhao 2010): PISA has shown that China is on the right way and is capable of building its own, both modern and indigenous, system of education.

Some take this argument further and claim that the West can learn from China, both with regard to the quality and equality of education. Huang (2016) describes his experiences from a Chinese-English teacher exchange in mathematics instruction that, following Shanghai's PISA success, was initiated in 2014, noting the British teachers' insufficient subject knowledge, excessive curriculum decentralization, and too little time spent on homework. Interestingly, many of the aspects that he regards negatively have previously been noted positively by Chinese reform-minded educationists. For example, he judges the English teacher and school autonomy as much more inefficient than the Chinese centralized model; he criticizes the strong focus on the student's own creativity in solving problems, instead of having more teacher-led discussion; and he is highly skeptical toward dividing students into different groups according to their abilities while teaching: "'Differentiated teaching' is an important reason for why today so many [English; BS] students have fallen behind in mathematics; differentiation, individuality have already become 'excuses' for abandoning students!" (Huang 2016, 27). By introducing "Asian mathematics education," which contains elements such as frequent exercise and repetition for all, England, according to Huang, has embarked on the right journey.

Even with regard to educational equality, PISA is thought of being able to teach the West a Chinese lesson. Lu and Zhu (2011) note that there were no large performance differences among students and schools in Shanghai,[5] and how this has prompted a variety of researchers becoming interested in the Shanghainese model of managing low-performing schools, including OECD researchers. Some propose openly to turn Shanghai into an "educational trade zone" (Song, Yu, and Mi 2014, 35); through branding the Shanghainese model and actively copying the marketing policies of the United States, Australia, and Singapore, this zone should become a strong competitive player in the global educational market.

## Students as Testing-Machines, or Individual Welfare?

"If it is weekend, and you are not sitting in a tutoring class, you are on your way to a tutoring class," Zhou (2011, 37) quotes a popular saying. As he and many others criticize, there is little learning outside the spaces constrained by school and parents, and learning only serves to achieve high exam results; students generally find no joy in studying, as all learning occurs under pressure (Li 2012). Many educationists in this faction do not disagree that China's educational model is efficient and successful, but wonder whether it is worth the price that students and their parents are paying. Besides, the huge investment does not seem to be economical: when correlating time investment and performance, Chinese students turn out to be inefficient in comparison with their peers in other countries (Wang and Jing 2013)—an aspect that was also frequently remarked upon in the Chinese social media, which noted the high performance of Finnish students while enjoying a low amount of homework and tutoring. Chinese education is seen as following a paradoxical logic: basic education focuses on talents and exerts high pressure on students, while university students enjoy carefree lives; the reverse would be appropriate (Zhou 2011).

Scholars in this group do not question the high performance or the validity of PISA, but they show themselves shocked by the contextual factors, such as homework overload, lack of enthusiasm and low extent of self-directed learning; as well as an excessive focus on exceptional talents and exaggerated expectations toward what the school can deliver—which after all is only one part of the social whole (Yang 2011). The ultimate goal of this kind of education, these critics argue, is the optimization of students who are already privileged in the first place, as they are found to profit much more from tutoring classes than their less fortunate peers, in contrast to US-American students (Zhou and Zou 2016). Thus, most scholars in this faction do not see PISA itself as a problem but rather the uncritical embrace of the high Chinese results, and the overly optimistic interpretation of these results regarding the present state and future direction of Chinese education; this naive enthusiasm, these scholars worry, may dampen reform efforts to make learning more of a joy and less of a burden for Chinese students. PISA as an assessment tool, rather than as a ranking tool, is mostly welcomed by these scholars since they can use the PISA data to demonstrate their argument.

## Do Assessment Tests Reflect Educational Quality?

In March 2017, *China Education Daily* reported on a roundtable on PISA with three prominent Chinese educationists, who expressed their concerns that the Chinese high performance in PISA would be conflated with a general high quality of Chinese education. PISA, it is argued, can by no means be used to understand the educational quality of an entire country; persistent problems such as the excessive focus on exams and results, rather than on learning and processes, cannot be adequately reflected in assessments like PISA (Yu, Lai, and Shi 2017). High test scores are judged to disguise the fact that Chinese students are largely extrinsically motivated, have little self-efficacy, little epistemic and procedural knowledge, a rather weakly developed attitude of scientific inquiry, and a lack of global and environmental awareness—all aspects that are of paramount importance for today's global knowledge society (Zhang, Wan, and Xue 2017).

The PISA successes show above all one thing, according to Wu (2015): the conducive influence of the Chinese, or Asian/Confucian, traditional educational culture for achieving high test results; while Western, reform-oriented countries all performed poorly, he maintains, Confucian cultures achieved top results. Wu concludes from this that it was not educational reform in Shanghai that played a role for the good PISA results, but rather Shanghai's continued embeddedness in the Confucian culture. In the end, however, the PISA results reveal nothing more than that Asian students are good at solving test items; important qualities like creativity, critical thinking, and application of knowledge are largely missing from these formalized assessments. Consequently, Wang, Jing, and Tong (2017) argue that China should move toward more diversified assessment methods; educational quality means also spending less time on cramming and more time on innovative thinking and character building.

Putting too much faith in PISA as a valuable and trustworthy instrument of assessing educational quality may lead to severe disappointment in the future, when China's excellent students may not be able to deliver what is expected of them, as the judgment of their potential was based on the wrong premises, incorrectly assuming that PISA had the power to foresee how these students would develop in the future: "in a few years, the public will wonder: with all these Chinese fifteen-year olds who had become 'the world's best' early on, why is it that in the end they have not turned into outstanding talents?" (Zhou 2011, 38).

# International Student Assessments and Their Discontents: Agendas behind the Debate

As can be seen from this debate, China's PISA success is judged to be both a curse and a blessing. The following sections will probe into the agendas behind these different stances.

## Mixed Blessings: Grounding Educational Reform, or Making China Great Again?

Those who welcomed PISA did so with very different motives: while some point to the worrisome contextual factors, which indicate the stress and pressure that the Chinese school system is putting on students, others instrumentalize the general high Chinese ranking for proving the system's excellence and superiority to Western models. The latter motive can be differentiated into two underlying rationales, which may however partially overlap. On one side, Shanghai's success is used for internal, domestic distinction. People like the above-mentioned Zhang Minxuan, who both represent PISA-Shanghai and stand for educational reform, use various channels to praise the innovativeness and efficiency of the Shanghainese education system (for an English version, see for example Zhang, Xu, and Sun 2014), highlighting how Shanghai has been able to "introduce great reforms in order to raise the quality of the teaching force" "in a short span of about 30 years" (Zhang, Xu, and Sun 2014, 160). While this strategy can be read as using PISA in order to legitimate educational reform domestically (see e.g. Tan 2017), the special role that Shanghai has been playing—both in domestic politics and in educational policy-making—has to be taken into account too: Since the early 1980s, Shanghai has been the vanguard of educational modernization and experiment, and this role has not always been unquestioned by the central leadership and other, regional governments (Deng and Zhao 2014). PISA can therefore serve to reassert Shanghai's role of an educational pioneer.

On the other side, PISA has been increasingly used to brand the Shanghainese system as a model for global export. Particularly PISA 2012 gave rise to what could be called an educational branding literature, advocating and selling educational policy innovations by pointing to high-performing educational systems, including Shanghai (see e.g. Lee, Lee, and Low 2014). Such a marketing strategy was reciprocated on the Chinese official side. For example in 2014, the temporary Vice Minister of Education, Liu Limin, expressed his pride to finally not just *receive* expert-teachers in order to develop Chinese education, but to be able to *dispatch* expert-teachers to improve foreign education systems—in this case, math teachers to the UK (see Dong 2016). Or as expressed even more blatantly by the Deputy Head of Shanghai's Educational Bureau, Ding Xiaoding: "As concerns pushing Chinese education to reach the world and increasing the influence of Shanghai and of our country in the global educational structure, this is of strategic importance" (see Dong 2016).

## PISA's Threefold Curse

Just like the embrace of PISA, caution or even suspicion toward this international assessment program originate also in differing concerns and agendas connected to these concerns. Three types of concerns can be considered most relevant in the Chinese context: (1) PISA as undermining reform and making the undesirable visible; (2) PISA as disturbing the balance in national-regional educational policy-making; and (3) PISA as compromising China's national independence in assessment, judgment, and policy-making.

Regarding the first, and as has become apparent from the discussion presented so far, many educationists fear that too positive results in PISA would undermine the drive for educational reform, as China's high ranking would confirm the status quo, or even reverse some of the previous reform efforts that have been striving for more child-centered and less exam-oriented learning. Additionally, we can observe a shift in performance in regions where public school reform has been extensive—namely, a performance shift in favor of private schools, which unlike their public counterparts can afford to implement educational reform to a much lesser extent (HZJS 2015). Parents in wealthy, pro-reform regions increasingly opt for private schools and can thereby continue to expose their children to conventional ways of teaching and learning. This is a trend that has so far not received much attention in the Chinese educational literature, although the public-private performance gap can even be read from the PISA data (Schulte 2017b). Perhaps the obvious conclusion to draw is too inconvenient: conventional schooling and cramming seem to be more conducive for achieving outstanding test results than their modernized counterparts. The government's recent ban of for-profit private schools from compulsory education may indicate that it is not willing to tolerate a two-track development, that is, a school system characterized by a conventional pedagogy, and a reform track (see NPC 2016). Disengaging from PISA may therefore be motivated by the fear that such assessment programs will reveal the conduciveness of the pre-reform system for achieving good learning results, which in turn could lead to an exodus of families from public to private schools.

As concerns national-regional educational policy-making, Shanghai's special role in the reform process has been pointed out in the previous section. The relationship between Shanghai as the center of reform and the rest of the country has been no easy-to-keep balance, and the continuous emphasis on Shanghai as an exemplary model of educational reform risks to irritate educationists and policy-makers outside Shanghai. The notable drop in rank in PISA 2015, after other regions had joined Shanghai in the sample, may have been the final straw to break the Shanghainese dominance in the educational reform discourse. As Zhu Yongxin remarks at the above-mentioned roundtable on PISA, "for China to build self-confidence in education, it is not Shanghai or Beijing where things are done and self-confidence is gained, but only if we work on the education of the entire country will we really succeed in building self-confidence" (Yu, Lai, and Shi 2017). To even out the educational-political landscape and dispose of factionalism is also a distinct characteristic of the present administration under leader Xi Jinping in general (see Lam 2015). The data and information that become available through PISA threaten to disturb the national-regional balance in educational reform and development.

Finally, questioning PISA may also reflect the quest for national independence from global assessment and ranking systems, whose tools and strategies China has only limited means to control (i.e., as one of many participant countries). On one side, China may be generally both tired and wary of taking part in what by many participants is regarded a competition in who has the best educational system. Chinese educationists have frequently pointed out that contrary to for example, the US-American perception of PISA as a world-wide educational race, PISA's value lies in providing data for recognizing strengths and weaknesses in international comparison, rather than coming first in any ranking:

> The unhealthy trend of putting excessive emphasis on the ranking of PISA or other assessments is the old custom of "grade-ism"; as a nation with a particularly long history and culture of examinations, Chinese educational circles ought to be the first to realize this. (Wang and Jing 2013, 177)

On the other side, education is still considered a national core project whose leaders do not tolerate any unfiltered influence, or even interference, from abroad. It is no coincidence that a translated journal article by Thomas Popkewitz (2015), which discusses PISA as a colonizing instrument that imposes Western norms on other countries, has attracted comparatively wide attention in China.[6] From this perspective, the fact that a potentially malevolent power like the United States sheds excessive praise on the Shanghainese system seems particularly suspicious. As Yang (2011, 9) remarks, the instinctive Chinese reaction is that "everything the enemy praises, we should oppose," assuming that the Western powers intend to hinder China from choosing the right path in educational development.

# Conclusion

The publication of the PISA 2015 results was followed by a conspicuous official silence. While the Chinese-language BBC reported on the deteriorated Chinese performance already on the same day, and Chinese social media were buzzing with the news and possible underlying reasons, the Chinese government only published a short, descriptive press release the day after, without any comments or suggestions (Liang 2016). The National Institute for Education Assessment, who was in charge of PISA 2015 in China, has until today not issued any press release on the results (the last news release being from the beginning of 2016). Also the Ministry of Education's Bureau of Education Inspections, who oversees educational quality and who according to the OECD (2016a) plays a key role in educational management, did not react. Instead, the Ministry of Education's news outlet was dominated by an initiative for strengthening ideological education, which had just been launched by president Xi Jinping (see Wu and Hu 2016). In light of the various agendas and strategies as discussed above, this official reaction is somewhat ambivalent: it could mean that the decreased PISA rank was unexpected, and interfered with plans to brand and market Chinese education globally. Alternatively, the silence could reflect the Chinese government's reluctance to let global assessment regimes dictate national news and agendas.

Interestingly, many of the academic responses as presented in this chapter have gone through various stages of reflection and projection: reflecting and projecting upon foreign educational systems; upon these scholars' own, Chinese educational system; and, in a sort of double hermeneutic move, upon foreign reflections and projections upon the Chinese school system. These reflections and projections are not simply interpretative-cognitive processes, but are embedded in transnational, hegemonic educational regimes that attempt to define and sanction ways of assessing educational quality, often at odds with local understandings of educational quality and political constraints. Chinese educational scholars are well aware of the Western reactions to the Chinese PISA performance (Yang 2011). Some have specifically studied and categorized these reactions, just as this chapter is doing with regard to the Chinese responses.[7] Others treat, again in parallel with this and many other contributions to this volume, claims regarding PISA, and school systems assessed by PISA, not as analytical facts but as discursive positions in processes of policy negotiations and justifications. Wu talks specifically of "analyses based on blackbox-like thinking" (2014, 69) when referring to the West's numerous speculations about China's PISA success. He maintains that rather than departing from contextual knowledge, Western scholars like the PISA coordinator Andreas Schleicher "produce explanations from perspectives [that are fed by; BS] their own imaginations" (Wu 2014, 69).

Imagining the other as a means to project something on one's own educational wish list upon a foreign context, to then argue for educational borrowing from this context, has been an often-observed and analyzed phenomenon within comparative education (see e.g. Zymek 1975, as one of the earliest examples of this strand of research). Regarding more recent argumentative projections for the purpose of policy borrowing, You and Morris (2016) have shown how policy-makers in the UK have projected their ideas of school autonomy on East Asian countries, to then argue for more school autonomy in their own system. As mentioned earlier in this contribution, also Chinese researchers and debaters reference, both in a positive and in a negative way, to school autonomy, which they assume to be the dominant form of school governance in England (on negative referencing, see e.g. Waldow, Takayama, and Sung 2014). Just like their British colleagues, they construe school autonomy as a phenomenon to their liking (or disliking), in order to frame their own standpoint, get their argumentative point across, and woo for (or argue against) a tool of educational governance that has allegedly proven to work (or fail) in other contexts. Similarly, to scandalize PISA as suspicious, and as a potential weapon of Western imperialism, supports the Chinese quest for national independence from transnational assessment regimes, or alternatively, the Chinese intention to continue with educational reform despite deteriorating PISA results. Thus, both positive and negative referencing is not a mere statement of facts, or a presentation of analytical findings, but constitutes (1) a *conceptual tool* for ordering, categorizing, and interpreting empirical reality; (2) a *strategic tool* for arguing for or against a particular approach or reform; and (3) a *political tool* for legitimizing (or delegitimizing) the ideology underlying these approaches or reforms.

To establish references to other educational systems, or even to construe entire reference societies that for longer periods of time affect and dominate national educational discourses (see e.g. Steiner-Khamsi 2012, on reference societies), can therefore be considered an academic and ideological struggle about which direction to take in educational development and reform (or counter-reform). Drawing originally on Luhmann, comparative educationists have framed these processes as externalization (Schriewer 1990; Takayama 2010). In the literature, most attention so far has been paid to how local, regional, national, and transnational actors externalize to the outside world: to alleged phenomena and developments internationally, located in contexts other than their own. It has been noted how ideas, such as reforms and new pedagogies, need to resonate in the host context if they are to successfully integrate with their new environment (e.g., Steiner-Khamsi 2004). Schriewer and Martinez (2004), however, point to processes that alternate with externalizations to the outside, and which they consider at least as important as international externalization: referencing to a constructed "inside," in the sense of construing traditions (national) pasts, and heritages that are "rediscovered" and established as exemplary models (or alternatively, as deterrent examples). Schriewer and Martinez conclude that there is no continuous, ever expanding internationalization and establishment of reference societies; rather, over the course of history, the two different forms of externalization—to the international world, and to one's own history—occur in what could be best described as a cyclical process. Judging from China's growing unease about PISA, and its recent attempts at reviving and rejuvenating socialist and partially Maoist traditions in educational development, it seems that the country is on the point of switching its externalization mode to a strengthened reflection, and thereby modeling, on its own history, which emphasizes above all self-assertion, self-control, independence, and the primacy of ideology.

# Notes

1  China has been able to considerably improve its performance with regard to both patents and international, high-impact journal publications, although the surge in research citations may be at least partially attributed to practices of internal, localized citations (George and McKern 2014; Tang, Shapira, and Youtie 2015).

2 English translations of Chinese article titles, if provided with the article, were included in the bibliography, even if the translation was faulty; in case no translated title was provided, my own translation was added. All direct quotes from the articles are my own translations.

3 To date, the National Assessment Center for Education Quality has only published one which summarizes the results for the years 2015 to 2017.

4 However, most of these researchers would implicitly feel at home in the first category, in that they accept the basic methodological and normative premises of PISA as an adequate instrument for assessing educational quality.

5 This was not confirmed in PISA 2015, which on the contrary attested Chinese schools a comparatively strong segregation of low and high performing schools (see Schulte 2017a).

6 To utilize postmodern arguments for purposes of national self-assertion has been a Chinese strategy since the 1990s (see Schulte 2004). In academia, this strategy was reflected in attempts at establishing an indigenous social science, claiming that "what is called social science today is Western social science" (Yang 1994, 51).

7 For example labeling these reactions as admiration of the Chinese school system; self-reflection upon one's own shortcomings vis-à-vis the Chinese success; pointing to the lack of innovative thinking among Chinese students (despite or because of their excellent performance); and emphasizing the excessive focus on academic performance within the Chinese school system, at the expense of other activities such as arts and sport (Lu and Zhu 2011).

# References

Deng, M., and Zhao, Z. (2014), "The Education System in Shanghai: Negotiating the Nature of Education," *The Asia-Pacific Education Researcher, 23*(4): 805–12.

Dong, S. (2016), "Yingguo weihe san ci pai jiaoshi fu Shanghai qujing" [Why England Sent Teachers to Shanghai Three Times to Collect Experiences], *Jiaoyubao*, November 11, http://news.jyb.cn/world/gjgc/201611/t20161111_682231.html. ,

Fang, F. (2015), "Meiguo de jiaoyu zhen de bi Zhongguo cha ma" [Is American Education Really Worse than Chinese Education], *Dangdai Jiaoyujia, 9*: 67–8.

George, Y., and McKern, B. (2014), "Innovation in Emerging Markets—The Case of China," *International Journal of Emerging Markets, 9*(1): 2–10.

Huang, X. (2016), "Yingguo shuxue jiaoyu de xianshi yu xiangwang— jianyu Zhongguo shuxue jiaoyu bijiao" [Reality and Dream of Mathematics Education in England: Comparison to China], *Bijiao Jiaoyu Yanjiu, 319*(8): 24–56.

HZJS = Hangzhou Zhongxiaoxue Jiaoyu Shixun (2015), "2015 Hangzhou minban chuzhong he gongban chuzhong zhongkao chengji duibi" [Comparing the 2015 Results from Middle School Entrance Examinations among Private and Public

Lower Middle Schools in Hangzhou]. *Bendibao*, June 24, http://hz.bendibao.com/edu/2015624/56868.shtm (accessed December 7, 2017).

Ji, L. (2011), "Shanghai xuesheng PISA duoguan dailai de xinwei" [The Gratification of Shanghainese Students Becoming the World Champions in PISA], *Nei Menggu Jiaoyu*, 5, 18.

Lam, W. W.-L. (2015), *Chinese Politics in the Era of Xi Jinping. Renaissance, Reform, or Retrogression?*, New York: Routledge.

Lee, S. K., Lee, W. O., and Low E. L. (2014), *Educational Policy Innovations. Levelling Up and Sustaining Educational Achievement, Education Innovation Series*, London: Springer.

Li, B. (2012), "PISA di yi bing bu yiwei Shanghai you quan shijie zui hao de jiaoyu tixi—bu yuan zhudong xuexi shi Zhongguo jiaoyu de da wenti" [Ranking First in PISA Does Not Mean That Shanghai Has the Best Educational System in the World: The Unwillingness of Learning Actively Is the Big Problem of China's Education], *Jichu Jiaoyu Luntan*, 5, 37.

Liang, X. (2016), "Jinghe zuzhi fabu zuixin guoji xuesheng pinggu xiangmu ceshi baogao: Zhongguo Dalu paiming xiahua" [OECD Report on the Newest PISA: Mainland China Sliding Down in Rank]. *Xinhua*, December 7, http://www.gov.cn/xinwen/2016-12/07/content_5144617.htm.

Lu, J. (2017), "Quanmian, keguan de renshi Zhongguo jiaoyu de chengjiu yu buzu" [Comprehensively and Objectively Recognizing the Accomplishments and Shortcomings of Chinese Education], *Renmin Jiaoyu*, 2, 25–32.

Lu, J., and Zhu, X. (2011), "Ruhe kandai Shanghai 2009 nian PISA ceping jieguo—Zhongguo Shanghai zhongxuesheng shouci canjia guoji ceping jieguo fanxiang shuping" [How to Regard the Assessment Results from PISA Shanghai 2009: Discussing the Reaction to the Results from the First-Time Participation of Chinese-Shanghainese Middle School Students in the International Assessment], *Shanghai Jiaoyu Keyan*, 1, 17–19.

Lü, L. (2017), "Quanqiu shiye xia de Zhongguo xuesheng shuxue suyang bijiao yu qishi: lai zi PISA de zhengju fenxi" [Comparison and Insight of Mathematical Literacy of Chinese Students under Global Vision: From Evidence Analysis of PISA Data], *Jiaoyu Shengwuxue Zazhi*, 5(1): 10–14.

Lundgren, U. P. (2013), "PISA as a Political Instrument: One History behind the Formulating of the PISA Programme," *Profesorado*, 17(2): 15–29.

MOE = Ministry of Education of the People's Republic of China (2015a), *2015 nian guojia yiwu jiaoyu zhiliang jiance ceshi shunli wancheng* [2015 Monitoring Test of Quality of State Compulsory Education Successfully Completed], http://www.moe.edu.cn/jyb_xwfb/gzdt_gzdt/moe_1485/201506/t20150629_191522.html.

MOE = Ministry of Education of the People's Republic of China (2015b), *Jiaoyu zhiliang jiance: kaoshi pingjia zhidu gaige de tupokou* [Educational Quality Monitoring: Breakthrough Regarding the Reform of the Examination and Evaluation System], http://www.moe.gov.cn/jyb_xwfb/xw_fbh/moe_2069/xwfbh_2015n/xwfb_150415/150415_mtbd/201504/t20150416_187221.html.

MOE = Ministry of Education of the People's Republic of China (2016), *2016 nian guojia yiwu jiaoyu zhiliang jiance ceshi shunli wancheng* [2016 Monitoring Test of Quality of State Compulsory Education Successfully Completed], http://www.moe.edu.cn/jyb_xwfb/gzdt_gzdt/s5987/201605/t20160527_246761.html.

NPC = The National People's Congress of the People's Republic of China (2016), *Yiwu jiaoyu bude ban yinglixing minban xuexiao* [Compulsory Education not Allowed to Run For-Profit Private Schools], http://www.npc.gov.cn/npc/xinwen/lfgz/2016-11/01/content_2000338.htm.

OECD (2014), *PISA 2012 Results: What Students Know and Can Do—Student Performance in Mathematics, Reading and Science*, Paris: OECD.

OECD (2016a), *Education in China: A Snapshot*, Paris: OECD.

OECD (2016b), *PISA 2015 Results (Volume I): Excellence and Equity through Education*, Paris: OECD.

OECD (2016c), *PISA High Performers: China (Country Note)*, Paris: OECD.

Pan, Y. (2012), "PISA jiazhiguan he pingjiaguan dui Zhongguo jiaoyu chuangxin de qishi" [The Implications of the PISA Concept of Values and Evaluation on the Education Innovation of China], *Jiaoyu Fazhan Yanjiu*, 2: 47–52.

Popkewitz, T. (2015), "Guoji xuesheng pinggu xiangmu (PISA) dui xuexiao kecheng yingxiang—chengji paiming, biaozhunhua ji xuexiao kecheng lianjinshu" [The Influence of PISA on School Curriculum—Ranking, Standardization and the Alchemy of the School Curriculum], *Jiaoyu Xuebao*, 11(2): 73–86.

Ren, Y., Chen, C., Wu, M., and Yu, C. (2016), "Jujiao 'wenti jiejue', buqi wo guo gongmin kexue suzhi 'duanban'" [Focusing on "Problem Solving": A Research on Remedy Limitation of Scientific Literacy of Chinese Citizens], *Kexue yu Shehui*, 6(2): 9–17.

Sahlberg, P. (2011), "PISA in Finland: An Education Miracle or an Obstacle to Change?" *CEPS Journal: Center for Educational Policy Studies Journal*, 1(3): 119–40.

Schriewer, J. (1990), "The Method of Comparison and the Need for Externalization: Methodological Criteria and Sociological Concepts," in J. Schriewer and B. Holmes (eds.), *Theories and Methods in Comparative Education*, 3–52, Frankfurt a.M.: Lang.

Schriewer, J., and Martinez, C. (2004), "Constructions of Internationality in Education," in G. Steiner-Khamsi (ed.), *The Global Politics of Educational Borrowing and Lending*, 29–53, New York: Teachers College Press.

Schulte, B. (2004), "East is East and West is West? Chinese Academia Goes Global," in J. Schriewer, C. Charle and P. Wagner (eds.), *Transnational Intellectual Networks. Forms of Academic Knowledge and the Search for Cultural Identities*, 307–29, Frankfurt a. M.: Campus.

Schulte, B. (2017a), "China," in S. Trumpa, D. Wittek and A. Sliwka (eds.), *Die Bildungssysteme der erfolgreichsten PISA-Länder: China, Finnland, Japan, Kanada und Korea* [The Educational Systems of the Most Successful PISA Countries: China, Finland, Japan, Canada, and South Korea], 21–49, Münster: Waxmann.

Schulte, B. (2017b), "Private Schools in the People's Republic of China: Development, Modalities and Contradictions," in T. Koinzer, R. Nikolai and F. Waldow (eds.),

*Private Schools and School Choice in Compulsory Education. Global Change and National Challenge*, 115–31, Berlin: Springer.

Sellar, S., and Lingard, B (2013), "Looking East: Shanghai, PISA 2009 and the Reconstitution of Reference Societies in the Global Education Policy Field," *Comparative Education*, *49*(4): 464–85.

Song, C., Yu, G., and Mi, H. (2014), "Zhongguo (Shanghai) zimao shiyanqu jiaoyu fuwu maoyi guoji hezuo jizhi gouxiang" [Political Innovation of Education Internationalization in Shanghai], *Kexue Fazhan, 72*: 32–5.

Steiner-Khamsi, G. (2004), "Blazing a Trail for Policy Theory and Practice," in G. Steiner-Khamsi (ed.), *The Global Politics of Educational Borrowing and Lending*, 201–20, New York: Teachers College Press.

Steiner-Khamsi, G. (2012), "Understanding Policy Borrowing and Lending: Building Comparative Policy Studies," in G. Steiner-Khamsi and F. Waldow (eds.) *Policy Borrowing and Lending in Education*, 3–17, London: Routledge.

Takayama, K. (2010), "Politics of Externalization in Reflexive Times: Reinventing Japanese Education Reform Discourses through 'Finnish PISA Success,'" *Comparative Education Review, 54*(1): 51–75.

Tan, C. (2017), "PISA and Education Reform in Shanghai," *Critical Studies in Education, 53*(2): 1–16.

Tang, L., Shapira, P., and Youtie, J. (2015), "Is There a Clubbing Effect Underlying Chinese Research Citation Increases?" *Journal of the Association for Information Science and Technology, 66*(9): 1923–32.

Waldow, F., Takayama, K., and Sung, J-K. (2014), "Rethinking the Pattern of External Policy Referencing: Media Discourses over the 'Asian Tigers'' PISA Success in Australia, Germany and South Korea," *Comparative Education, 50*(3): 302–21.

Wang, J. (2013), "PISA hou Shanghai jiang tui ziji pingjia tixi—'Lüse Zhibiao'" [After PISA Shanghai Will Push Their Own Evaluation System—the "Green Indicators"], *Dongfangwang*, December 4, http://sh.eastday.com/m/20131204/u1a7809994.html (accessed December 7, 2017).

Wang, L., and Jing, A. (2013), "Women cong PISA xuedao le shenme—jiyu PISA Zhongguo shice de yanjiu" [What Have We Learned from PISA? Research on the PISA China Trial], *Beijing Daxue Jiaoyu Pinglun*, 1, 172–80.

Wang, L., Jing, A., and Tong, W. (2017), "PISA Zhongguo duli yanjiu shijian dui goujian Zhongguo tese jiaoyu zhiliang pingjia tixi de qishi—jiyu PISA 2009 Zhongguo duli yanjiu" [Transition from PISA China Trial to Education Evaluation System with Chinese Characteristics—Based on PISA 2009 China Trial], *Jiaoyu Yanjiu*, 444, 114–23.

Wang, Y. (2014), "Shanghai huojiang tuichu xiaci PISA ceshi" [Shanghai Maybe Dropping out of Next PISA], *Xinmin Wanbao*, March 7, http://www.ecnu.edu.cn/_s64/b2/5e/c1835a45662/page.psp (accessed December 7, 2017).

Wu, G. (2014), "Shanghai de PISA ceshi quanqiu di yi de aomi hezai—jiyu Zhongguo jiaoyu wenhua chuantong de shijiao" [Where is the Secret of Shanghai Being No. 1 in PISA—From the Perspective of the Tradition of Chinese Educational Culture], *Tansuo yu Zhengming*, 1, 68–9.

Wu, G. (2015), "Zhongguo jiaoyu wenhua chuantong dui PISA ceshi jieguo de yingxiang" [The Influence of the Tradition of Chinese Educational Culture on the PISA Results], *Jiaoyu Yanjiu yu Pinglun*, 1, 91–2.

Wu, J., and Hu, H. (2016), "Xi Jinping: ba sixiang zhengzhi gongzuo guanchuan jiaoyu jiaoxue quan guocheng" [Xi Jinping: The Entire Process of Connecting Ideological-Political Work with Education and Pedagogy], *Xinhua News*, December 8, http://www.moe.gov.cn/jyb_xwfb/s6052/moe_838/201612/t20161208_291306.html (accessed December 7, 2017).

Xu, D., Ji, M., Wang, M., and Liu, Z (2016), "Ruhe jiang lüse biaozhi zhenzheng yongyu tisheng jiaoyu zhiliang" [How to Genuinely Use the Green Indicators to Raise the Quality of Education], *Renmin Jiaoyu Zazhi*, June 2, http://www.jyb.cn/Theory/jyfz/201606/t20160602_661591.html (accessed December 7, 2017).

Yang, G. (1994), "'Jiangcun jingji' zai renshi" [A Re-Evaluation of the Book "The Economy of the Village Jiang"], *Du Shu*, 10, 50–7.

Yang, H. (2011), "Zhongguo chuzhongsheng 'shijie di yi' de sikao—PISA ji qi ceshi jieguo de qishi" [Reflections on Chinese Primary and Secondary School Students Being 'The World's First'—PISA and What the Assessment Results Reveal], *Renmin Jiaoyu*, 3–4, 8–10.

You, Y., and Morris, P. (2016), "Imagining School Autonomy in High-Performing Education Systems: East Asia as a Source of Policy Referencing in England," *Compare: A Journal of Comparative and International Education*, 46(6): 882–905.

Yu, H., Lai, P., and Shi, J. (2017), "Zhongguo de jiaoyu zixin zai naili" [Where is China's Educational Self-Confidence], *Zhongguo Jiaoyubao*, March 3, http://www.moe.gov.cn/jyb_xwfb/s5147/201703/t20170303_298082.html (accessed December 7, 2017).

Zhang, H., Wan, D., and Xue, Y. (2017), "PISA 2015 Zhongguo xuesheng kexue chengji xiahua tedian ji yuanyin tantao" [Investigation to Decline of Science Score of Chinese Students in PISA 2015], *Jiaoyu Shengwuxue Zazhi*, 5(1): 1–9.

Zhang, M., and Kong, L. (2012), "An Exploration of Reasons for Shanghai's Success in the OECD Program for International Student Assessment (PISA) 2009," *Frontiers of Education in China*, 7(1): 124–62.

Zhang, M., and Kong, L. (2013), "Why Shang Hai's Students Rank No. 1 in PISA (2009). An Exploration of Reasons for Shanghai's Success in the OECD Program for International Student Assessment (PISA) 2009," *China Daily*, July 16, http://blog.chinadaily.com.cn/blog-1142759-11219.html (accessed December 7, 2017).

Zhang, M., Xu, J., and Sun, C. (2014), "Effective Teachers for Successful Schools and High Performing Students: The Case of Shanghai," in S. K. Lee, W. O. Lee and E. L. Low (eds.), *Educational Policy Innovations. Levelling Up and Sustaining Educational Achievement*, 143–61. Heidelberg: Springer.

Zhao, Y. (2010), "PISA neng fou chengwei Zhongguo jiaoyu gaige de qiji" [Can PISA Become the Turning Point in Chinese Educational Reform?], *Shanghai Education*, 12(B): 44.

Zhou, D. (2011), "Shanghai PISA ceshi gaosu Zhongguo shenme" [What Does PISA Shanghai Tell China?], *Jiaoyu Xunkan*, 6, 37–8.

Zhou, J., and Zou, X. (2016), "Zhongmei xuesheng jiaoyu buxi jihui de yingxiang yinsu bijiao—jiyu 2012 nian Zhongguo Shanghai he Meiguo PISA shuju de shizheng tansuo" [Comparing the Private Tutoring Options between Students in China and the United States—Evidences from 2012 PISA Survey and Investigation], *Jiaoyu yu Jingji*, 2, 44–52.

Zymek, B. (1975), *Das Ausland als Argument in der pädagogischen Reformdiskussion: Schulpolitische Selbstrechtfertigung, Auslandspropaganda, internationale Verständigung und Ansätze zu einer vergleichenden Erziehungswissenschaft in der internationalen Berichterstattung deutscher pädagogischer Zeitschriften, 1871–1952* [Foreign Countries as an Argument in the Discussion of Educational Reform: Self-Justification in School Policy, Foreign Propaganda, International Understanding and Approaches to a Comparative Education Science in International Reporting of German Pedagogic Journals, 1871–1952] (Schriftenreihe zur Geschichte und politischen Bildung 19), Ratingen: Henn.

# 10

# Excellence and Envy: The Management of PISA Success in Singapore

Søren Christensen

Over the past two decades, Singapore has consistently been one of the top scorers in international educational league tables such as TIMSS and, more recently, PISA. In December 2016, Singapore's rise to international fame in education reached a high point when the results of PISA 2015 were released, showing Singapore's students to be the top performers ("PISA with all the toppings," as a local newspaper had it [Davie 2016a]) in all three categories of reading, math, and science.

Surprisingly, perhaps, these impressive results did not meet with unmixed enthusiasm among Singaporeans. A few weeks after the release of PISA 2015, an article in the *Straits Times*, Singapore's largest newspaper, noted that many Singaporeans remained "unconvinced" about Singapore's status as "world-beaters" (Davie 2016b), ascribing Singapore's performance mainly to "rote learning" and the pervasiveness of "tuition" (the local term for private supplementary teaching or 'shadow education'). The entire article was dedicated to repudiating this (mis-)interpretation of Singapore's PISA performance, citing for this purpose the Ministry of Education (MOE) as well as the head of PISA, Andreas Schleicher. Specifically, Schleicher was quoted as saying that PISA 2015 had shown Singaporean students to excel, not only in their mastery of scientific and mathematical content (which can be acquired through cramming and rote-learning), but especially in their capacity for mathematical and scientific thinking (which cannot).

These two conflicting interpretations of Singapore's PISA performance are not limited to the specific case of PISA 2015—or even PISA more generally. They pervade current debates about education in Singapore. In this chapter, I explore how they play out in two different, but closely interconnected, settings: in the context of global educational comparison and policy benchmarking, on the one hand, and in the context of domestic education reform in Singapore, on the other.

In the first part of the chapter, I distill, from a number of influential reports on the policy implications of PISA and other international league tables, a specific model of educational excellence, which (borrowing an expression from Mourshed, Chijiote and Barber 2010) I call the model of "most improved systems." Taking a cue from Waldow, Takayama and Sung (2014), I argue that the importance of this kind of meta-discourse on league table performance resides in the fact that, by explaining high performance as an expression of superior policies and learning orientations, it transubstantiates mere league leaders into icons of educational excellence. I also argue that this is especially consequential for Singapore (and other East Asian systems) since this gives rise to new projections of East Asian excellence, which contrast starkly with entrenched culturalist stereotypes of East Asian "exam hell" and "tiger mothers."

In the second part of the chapter, I show how this new projection of Singaporean excellence interacts with education reform in Singapore. I argue that, while international league tables have so far played a very subdued role in education reform in Singapore, in recent years PISA has acquired an important role as an external endorsement of reform efforts. The reason for this is not simply Singapore's PISA results themselves. Rather, it is the image of globalized, twenty-first-century excellence, in terms of which PISA explains superior performance and which correlates closely with the policy objectives of education reform in Singapore.

Policy-makers thus have very good reasons to buy into this projection of Singaporean excellence since it seems to confer an external stamp of approval on education reform. However, as I show in the last part of the chapter, this projection remains hotly contested at the domestic level. In public opinion in Singapore, the traditional projection of East Asian educational performance as springing from repetitive drilling and test obsession still seems to resonate much more than the PISA projection of Singaporean "excellence." In this sense, it is not only the rest of the world, which must be convinced that Singapore is succeeding for the right reasons (superior policies and learning orientations) and not for the wrong ones (long hours and mechanical drilling). It is above all Singaporeans themselves.

## Most Improved Systems: League Leaders and Icons of Excellence

The release of PISA 2015 has brought Singapore's reputation as a global leader in education to a new level. Singapore's rise to fame did not happen overnight, however. Over the past two decades admiration for Singapore education has grown steadily in policy circles around the world and in the last decade Singapore has increasingly come to feature among the handful of education systems—including also systems like Finland and Ontario—from which policy-makers around the world seek inspiration in order to improve their own systems.

Why has this happened? The most obvious explanation is, of course, Singapore's performance in international comparisons of educational achievement. Ever since Singapore entered the world of educational league tables in the mid-1990s, it has consistently been among the top performers in the world.

However important, this reference to league table performance is not itself sufficient to explain the global reputation that Singapore education enjoys today. In a recent article on media discourses on East Asian PISA success, Waldow et al. (2014) have made the important point that one does not automatically become a reference society by being a top scorer in PISA or other international league tables. As Waldow et al. point out, this applies most conspicuously to East Asian education systems whose league table performance is frequently interpreted in terms of a negative cultural stereotype, which tends to dismiss East Asian educational achievement as an expression of a highly undesirable educational culture marred by constant testing, rote learning and excessively pushy parents ("tiger mothers").

This stereotype remains tremendously important to interpretations of East Asian PISA success. As Waldow et al. (2014, 315) point out, it does so also as an "auto-stereotype," an image in terms of which East Asian societies criticize and call for changes in their own approaches to parenting and education. As I shall show in the last section, this applies also very much to Singapore. Nevertheless, the admiration that Singapore—along with other East Asian systems—has come to enjoy among educationists and policy-makers, can be taken as an indication that this culturalist stereotype is increasingly being challenged by new interpretations of East Asian educational performance.

Here the proliferation of international league tables in education has played a crucial role—not simply by drawing attention to the high achievement of East Asian systems, but by laying the foundation of a new model of educational excellence, which breaks in a very explicit way with the premises of the culturalist explanation. Borrowing a term from a McKinsey report, I call this the model of "most improved systems" (Mourshed, Chijiote, and Barber 2010). As I have just suggested, this term does not refer to league table results as such,[1] but to a certain "meta-discourse" that seeks to synthesize the bewildering array of data generated by international league tables into a coherent model of systemic excellence, from which policy-makers around the world can draw lessons for improving their own systems.

This model of most improved systems does not have a single inventor, of course. I piece it together here from a number of reports by various think tanks and consultancy firms, which seek to distill policy lessons from international league tables for various national and global audiences.[2] These reports characterize such model systems in slightly different ways. Still, I believe they converge enough to be viewed as different versions of a single model of educational excellence.

The most important feature of this model is its exclusive focus on leadership and policy. Educational excellence is viewed as a matter of "effective leadership, both at the level of the system and at the level of individual schools" (Barber and Mourshed 2007, 40) and of the ability to implement policies with "fidelity," "rigor and discipline" (Mourshed, Chijioke, and Barber 2010, 20). Furthermore, they are characterized as efficient systems, which are not among the top spenders in education (in some versions, this is made an explicit prerequisite of being considered a "leading system" (Tucker 2011). They are aggressive benchmarkers (Tucker 2011, 205) who systematically use international comparisons to improve themselves. Most importantly, however, they focus on the quality of teaching as a precondition for the improvement of learning outcomes for students and they are therefore characterized by excellent policies for the selection, education and professional development of teachers (Tucker 2011).

According to this discourse, there is very little that cannot be accomplished by policy. If only its fundamental policy precepts are observed, stagnating education systems can be turned around "in a short period of time" (Barber and Mourshed 2007, 40). Conversely, any reference to culture or context comes to be viewed as spurious. As Andreas Schleicher puts it in his foreword to one of the McKinsey reports,

> The world is indifferent to tradition and past reputations, unforgiving of frailty and ignorant of custom and practice. Success will go to those individuals and countries which are swift to adapt, slow to complain and open to change. (Schleicher 2007)

In this perspective educational performance is clearly not determined by culture. As Barber and Mourshed state categorically, the attribution of educational performance "to variables seemingly outside the control of the policymaker" is groundless since "the same broad policies are effective in different school systems irrespective of the cultural context in which they are applied" (Barber and Mourshed 2007, 16). While this does not mean that context disappears altogether, it means that policy is fundamentally independent of context. Context registers only as an object, a set of exterior circumstances, which must be managed "tactically" by policy: "Contextualizing is all about the tactics the system leaders use in tailoring the set of interventions needed on their performance journey to their specific context" (Mourshed, Chijioke, and Barber 2010, 21).

This discourse on most improved systems can therefore be seen as construing a new kind of reference society. As such it differs, however, from traditional reference societies in several respects. It emerges from ILSA data and therefore claims to be not simply a work of social imagination, but an "evidence-based" reference society. Second, it is an abstract and disembodied reference society, which is derived from a variety of empirical systems.

Even if it does not coincide with any really existing society, this model serves as a mold for creating new real-world reference societies. It subjects the education systems from which it derives its data, to a process of purification where they are relieved of their contextual messiness and elevated into empirical approximations of this model. It is in this process that mere league leaders are transubstantiated into "icons of excellence"—that is, reference societies.

The logic, in terms of which this conversion proceeds, can be characterized as a form of inverted causality. Systems are included into the discourse on most improved systems on the basis of being league leaders. The work of this discourse, however, consists in developing a model of educational excellence, which explains why they are league leaders. Thus, causality is reversed in the sense that they are no longer among the most improved systems because they are league leaders. Instead, they have now become league leaders because they are among the most improved systems. Thanks to this logic, high scores are transubstantiated into educational excellence.

While the model of most improved systems does also include a number of non-Asian systems (Finland, Ontario, etc.), it is especially consequential for East Asian systems like Singapore since these are the systems whose educational performance is most frequently interpreted in negative terms—not as an expression of educational excellence, but as an expression of a pathological educational culture.

It is therefore no wonder that the discourse on most improved systems takes special pains to repudiate the culturalist interpretation of East Asian educational performance. Thus, McKinsey cites the reference to "Confucian values" as a prime example of the misguided attribution of educational performance to variables outside the control of the policymaker (Barber and Mourshed 2007,

16). Even more categorically, an Australian report on East Asian school systems states that East Asian educational success is not "culturally determined, a product of Confucianism, rote learning or Tiger Mothers" (Jensen et al. 2012, 2). Characteristically, this conclusion is justified by referring to the OECD's own interpretation of PISA:

> Success cannot be explained by rote learning, either. PISA assesses meta-cognitive content knowledge and problem solving abilities. These skills are not conducive to rote learning. In fact, rote learning in preparation for PISA assessments would lead to lower scores. (Jensen et al. 2012, 12)

In recent years, Singapore has become one of the most prominent examples of this kind of de-culturalized' discourse on East Asian education. As a result of the purification or "de-territorialization" (Steiner-Khamsi 2002) performed by this discourse, there is no longer anything specifically Asian about Singapore's education system. Around the world, Singapore is commended for its prudent and efficient spending on education (Barber and Mourshed 2007), for its global orientation and for being among "the most determined and disciplined benchmarkers in the world" (Tucker 2011, 172). Most of all, perhaps, Singapore education is praised for its excellent policies in selecting, educating and developing teachers. In all this, no mention is made of all the favorite themes of the "Asian stereotype" (except, perhaps, for the purpose of dismissing them): no tiger mothers, no exam hell, no cram industry. Here, even the incredibly hard work performed by students in Singapore results from excellence in policies: it is attributed not to nagging parents or excessive competition, but to "clear and ambitious goals" and "rigorous, focused and coherent standards" (Stewart 2011, 133).

In the next section, I explore how these two interpretations of East Asian education play out in the context of education reform in Singapore. After having provided an account of education reform in Singapore, I focus, more specifically, on the way in which PISA, as the most important embodiment of the model of most improved systems, has been mobilized in media and policy discourse to endorse education reform—as a testimony that Singapore education has, indeed, become reformed and future-ready.

## PISA Success and Education Reform

Since the mid-1990s Singapore has participated on a regular basis in international studies of student achievement. In the same period Singapore has also gone through a process of sustained education reform. In this combination Singapore resembles many other countries. However, whereas in most countries international league tables have been deeply implicated in education reform, creating (or, more rarely, alleviating) reform pressure, this is not the case with Singapore. Here education reform has generally been very loosely coupled with international league tables. For the most part education reform and benchmarking through international league tables have proceeded along separate tracks. It is only in recent years that policy-makers have begun, in a more systematic fashion, to make such data relevant in the context of education reform.

## Education Reform: From Efficiency to Excellence

To understand why this is so, a brief account of the reform agenda may be relevant. The current wave of education reform in Singapore is usually traced back to the late 1990s. In 1997 the then Prime Minister Goh Chok Tong gave a speech on education, which has since acquired the status of an inaugural speech of education reform in Singapore. In this speech Goh called for a fundamental change in the Singaporean mindset in relation to education. More specifically, he chastised Singaporean students for lacking a "passion for learning," studying instead "for the sake of getting good grades in their examinations." In contrast, he praised the United States for its

> ability to produce highly creative, entrepreneurial individuals. Their best schools produce well-rounded, innovative students by putting them through a diverse and challenging curriculum. Their academic institutions and research laboratories are at the forefront of ideas and scientific breakthroughs, and infused with entrepreneurial spirit (Goh 1997).

This way of contrasting Singapore with the United States was a significant reversal of established policy rhetoric at the time. In the 1980s and early 1990s education policy in Singapore had been focused on creating an efficient and competitive education system stressing academic rigor and high performance. Policy-makers (led by Goh himself) consistently legitimized this approach to education in terms of Confucian or (more broadly) Asian traditions that supposedly set Singapore apart from Western countries. According to this view, the "soft" liberal approach to education in the West had led to a significant decline in educational standards. In Singapore, on the other hand, a Confucian approach to education, stressing diligence, competition and high performance ensured the upholding of high educational standards (Goh 1992; Christensen 2015).

Now, however, the very "Asian" traits which had been used to set Singapore apart from the West—the focus on examinations and academic competition—came to be seen as potential obstacles to Singapore's future progress. Probably, the single most important reason for this change of perspective was the gradual diffusion in that period of the OECD-sponsored "imaginary" of "the knowledge-based economy" (Jessop 2008) among policy-makers around the world. While this imaginary views education as crucial to economic competitiveness, it does not put a premium on the Confucian values of discipline, diligence, and academic competition. Instead, it promotes qualities like independent, critical and creative thinking, entrepreneurialism and innovation as crucial to individual employability as well as national competitiveness in the twenty-first century.

It is precisely with reference to such notions of "twenty-first-century education" that Singapore's education system has been reformed over the last twenty years. Curricula have been trimmed to make teaching less content-heavy and to free up space for more experimentation and exploration. New didactic approaches have been introduced in order to move away from repetitive rote learning and toward student-centered pedagogies, encouraging each student to take charge of her own learning. Non-academic domains like sports and the performing arts have been prioritized in order to make students more independent, more resilient and more creative. This has been accompanied by a concerted effort to change mindsets. In stark contrast to the celebration of "Confucian values" in the early 1990s, government officials (led by Singapore's "founding father" Lee Kuan Yew) openly criticize "the East Asian reverence for scholarship" (Hamlin 2002). Educators, parents, and students are therefore encouraged to move away from a single-minded focus on examinations and academic results. Instead, the focus should be on instilling a passion for learning among all students and to transcend the prevailing "fear of failure" (*kiasuism*, to use the local term) in Singapore so as to create a culture of initiative, independence, and entrepreneurialism.

Through education reform Singapore has thus set out to effect on itself the conversion, described in the previous section, from a mere high-performing Asian system to an excellent twenty-first-century system. In this process references to (mostly disembodied and future-oriented) "international standards" (Steiner-Khamsi 2012) have played a crucial role. International league table results, however, have not. At no point in the process of education reform have references to international league tables served as significant drivers of, or references for, reform.

While at first sight this may seem paradoxical, it makes good sense on the background of Singapore's performance in international educational league tables in this period. Singapore entered, in earnest, the world of international league tables with TIMSS 1995, which showed Singapore's students to be the top performers globally in mathematics at both the 4th and the 8th grades. Since then Singapore has been performing at similar levels in one international league table after another.

Ironically, from the perspective of policy-makers such league table results would have been much more immediately useful in the previous "Confucian" phase of education policy in Singapore. Corroborated by the equally impressive performance of other East Asian countries like Korea and Japan, they might have served as compelling evidence of the superiority of the Confucian approach to education. In the context of education reform, it is, however, much harder to put such league table results to use. They blatantly fail to perform any kind of scandalization effect, which might be used to support or generate pressure for education reform. In fact, they are even potentially inconvenient to policy-makers to the extent that they lend themselves easily to a counter-argument against reform, claiming that "if it ain't broken, why fix it."

Even more importantly, perhaps, in the context of education reform in Singapore, the reference to league table results would seem to be fundamentally beside the point. It is not the ability to perform which is at stake in education reform in Singapore. It is the ability to go beyond mere performance. Here the reference to mere performance—in the form of league table results—would seem not only to miss the point but to jeopardize the whole enterprise of education reform by endorsing the very approach to education, which education reform itself is seeking to transcend.

## PISA as an Endorsement of Education Reform

It is on this background that the reception of PISA in Singapore becomes of interest. With PISA (in which Singapore started to participate in 2009) the previously separate paths of international league tables and education reform seem finally to have come together—although uneasily so, as I shall show. This is precisely because PISA explicitly claims to go beyond mere performance. In PISA educational performance is an expression of something more—the "future-readiness" (MOE 2016) of students, their ability to solve problems and apply knowledge in real-world situations.

In the official reception of PISA in Singapore—in media coverage, and especially in statements by education officials and experts—this understanding of PISA plays a pivotal role. In most countries news media tend to present PISA simply as a test, which measures students' proficiency in math, science, and reading. In Singapore newspapers, reporting on PISA results routinely explains that PISA is a test "that measures how well students use mathematics, science and reading to solve real-world problems" (Davie 2013a). Additionally, to educate readers on the "correct" interpretation of PISA, reporting on PISA is frequently accompanied by interviews with education experts (including Andreas Schleicher himself) who explain how PISA is a new kind of test, which does not assess curricular knowledge ("book-learning"), but the ability of students to apply knowledge and solve problems under unfamiliar conditions (Davie 2013a, 2013b, 2016a; Teng 2013).

Education officials are even more explicit in promoting this interpretation of PISA. In a press release, issued in response to the release of PISA 2015, the MOE summed up Singapore's performance by stating that "Singapore's 15-year-olds have demonstrated competencies that enable them to navigate the challenges of the 21st century" (MOE 2016). The Ministry went on to note that Singapore's students "not only possess strong fundamentals in literacy and numeracy, but are also equipped with higher-order thinking skills," citing Andreas Schleicher, to the effect that Singapore's students are "leading the world ( . . . ) in the way they creatively use and apply their knowledge" (MOE 2016). Likewise, on Facebook the Education Minister himself summed up Singapore's PISA results as showing that "our students are equipped with some of the needed skills for the future." He reinforced his message by calling on his fellow citizens to keep up the collective effort to move Singapore toward twenty-first-century education:

> Let's continue to encourage our students to be curious learners, able to apply knowledge in unfamiliar contexts. May they also find joy in their learning and seed an intrinsic motivation to continually improve and prepare for the future. (Ng 2016)

The importance of this interpretation of PISA resides in the fact that it turns PISA into an endorsement, not only of Singapore education in general, but of education reform more specifically. PISA comes to serve as evidence that education reform has succeeded in turning Singapore from a mere high performer into an excellent, "future-ready" education system. In a domestic context where the transformative effects of education reform remain very much in doubt (as I shall show in the last section), this external stamp of approval is of crucial importance. Thus, in its press release on PISA 2015, the MOE categorically stated that the

> results of the 2015 and past PISA cycles reflect the deliberate curricular shifts we have made over the years towards a greater emphasis on higher-order, critical thinking skills, and our pedagogical shifts in moving learning beyond content to mastery and application of skills to solve authentic problems in various contexts. (MOE 2016)

This point was duly echoed in national media coverage of PISA 2015. Thus, one newspaper on its front page announced the results of PISA under the heading "from rote learning to critical thinking" (Foo 2016a)—thereby presenting PISA 2015 as a kind of arrival of education reform. Similarly, a different article in the same newspaper carried the headline "Test shows Singapore students move from regurgitating to critical thinking" (Foo 2016b). Other newspaper articles explained how both rote learning and "tuition" (use of shadow education) were associated with lower PISA performance, not higher (Davie 2016a; Cheng 2016)—thus repudiating the notion that Singapore's PISA success could in any way be explained by the traditional, non-reformed aspects of the system.

Thus, the official reception of PISA in Singapore consistently interprets PISA as a statement on the accomplishments of education reform. Conversely, other interpretations of PISA are similarly dis-emphasized. This applies above all to the understanding of PISA as a global ranking of education systems. In media coverage of PISA in Singapore, metaphors likening PISA to a sports competition regularly pop up. Thus, the *Straits Times* announced the results of PISA 2015 under the heading "Singapore students bag education 'World Cup'" (Davie 2016c) and other news stories stated that Singapore had taken a "gold" or "pole" position in PISA (Davie 2016b).

However, in statements by education officials and experts this aspect of PISA is carefully dis-emphasized. Most conspicuously, bragging rights are meticulously—almost ostentatiously—left unexploited. Thus, at no point in the MOE's press release on the "key findings of PISA 2015" did it make any mention whatsoever of the fact that Singapore was the top scorer in PISA. Similarly, in their responses to PISA 2012 both the MOE and the then Education Minister Heng Swee Keat explicitly dismissed the ranking aspect of PISA. In a reply to the Parliament, the MOE made clear that the "purpose of our participation is not to get a good global ranking" (MOE 2014,), while Minister Heng stated that Singapore was not out "to chase a rank" and added that the important thing about PISA was not how Singapore's students compared to students from other countries, but how they compared to themselves—that they had improved compared to the previous PISA study: "Regardless of how they rank relative to students from elsewhere, our students' own scores are better this time than when we first took part in PISA in 2009" (Heng 2013).

This dismissal of the competitive or ranking aspect of PISA should probably not be read as an expression of (false or genuine) modesty. Rather, it is an indication that even in the case of PISA, the appeal to league table results in the context of education reform in Singapore remains highly problematic and demands careful management.

As should be clear from Singapore's sustained participation in international league tables during the reform period, the new orientation towards "authentic" and "holistic" learning does not imply an indifference to performance and ranking at the international level. Rather, education reform in Singapore can be viewed as an enterprise to keep performance constant (if not improving) while changing the causes of performance. The education system should continue to rank highly and deliver results, but this should no longer be because the education system is driven by the desire for results and high rankings. Instead, high rankings should result spontaneously, so to speak, from the joy of learning and student-centered teaching strategies permeating a twenty-first-century education system. It is only then that Singapore has truly become a leader in education and not merely a league leader.

Thus, if international league tables have an important monitoring role in the context of education reform, it is equally imperative that they do not acquire a motivational role—that education is not (re-)captivated by the desire to perform and to top the rankings. This is why, even in the case of PISA, the appeal to league tables in the context of education reform remains a highly tricky matter. On the one hand, PISA success can be used to argue that education reform is succeeding—that Singapore is, indeed, overcoming its obsession with rankings and high performance. On the other hand, the very reference to league table success risks playing to, and encouraging, this orientation toward rankings and high performance. The highly managed and guarded policy reception of PISA in Singapore can be viewed as an attempt to perform the almost impossible feat of keeping apart these two aspects of PISA success.

## PISA Envy: Projections of Educational Enjoyment

As I noted in the introduction to this chapter, Singapore's success in PISA has not been received with unmixed enthusiasm among the Singaporean public.[3]

If the government's (and the OECD's) interpretation of PISA is rehearsed over and over again in the media and in statements by the MOE, this is also because many Singaporeans stubbornly continue to believe that Singapore's performance in PISA and other league tables is caused by repetitive drilling and inordinately long hours in schools and tuition centers. Thus, only two months after the MOE had announced the PISA 2015 results under the headline "Equipped, Primed and Future-Ready: Singapore's Students Have What It Takes To Thrive In the 21st Century Workplace" (MOE 2016), the *Straits Times* published an article with the headline "Let's kill the drill approach in schools." Noting that Singapore's students work longer hours "than a McKinsey consultant," and that they are subjected to "regular 'kill and drill' routines from young," the author claimed that "the high scores in the international Pisa benchmark—dubbed the World Cup of Education—that make Singapore proud every year can be rightly attributed to the drilling culture" (Jayaraman 2017). Such skepticism is shared even by many educationists, including education researchers, who express their disbelief in claims like the one made in the MOE statement (quoting Andreas Schleicher) that Singapore education is "leading the world" in the creative use and application of knowledge (MOE 2016). Instead, they refer to surveys of foreign employers who characterize Singaporean employees as reliable, hardworking and competent, but as lacking in independence, creativity and can-do spirit. Or they refer to the fact that, in spite of Singapore's allegedly excellent education system, no Singaporean scientist has ever been awarded a Nobel Prize.

While the government actively buys into the projection of Singapore as a global leader in education, using it as a testimony to the accomplishments of education reform, this projection seems to resonate very little with the public at large. This stubborn refusal to adopt—or sometimes even acknowledge—the official interpretation of PISA does of course not reflect a philosophical disagreement about what PISA measures. It reflects a different perception of the realities of educational life in Singapore.

In much of the literature on "most improved" systems, discussed in the first section, the use of the Asian or Confucian stereotype as a framework for understanding East Asian achievement in education is explicitly dismissed as prejudiced and complacent (Jensen et al. 2012). However, in local discussions about education in Singapore, including much of media debate, the Asian stereotype remains firmly in place as an "auto-stereotype" (Waldow et al. 2014) that serves, in a much more powerful way than the projection of Singaporean "excellence," to make sense of the realities of educational life in Singapore. In this sense, the writer quoted above speaks for much of public opinion in Singapore when he depicts Singapore education as organized around a "grueling regimen" of "kill and drill," massive workloads and extra classes.

In this context, education reform often counts for very little. As a Singaporean parent put it some years back, during a public dialogue session on education convened by the MOE:

> Our education system is so stressful because of the high stakes. Even though the government says that there are alternate paths, the truth is you will lag behind if you fail early on in life. If you don't do well in the Primary School Leaving Examination [after grade 6] you will fall behind others. (MOE 2013)

This perception of educational realities in Singapore makes most Singaporeans immune to a projection of Singaporean PISA success, which praises Singapore education in terms like "curiosity", "joy of learning" and ' "intrinsic motivation" (Ng 2016). Even in the case of PISA, high performance remains associated with the "old," un-reformed aspects of the education system: long hours, drilling, grit and determination. Here high performance is just that—"mere" performance— not an expression of educational excellence.

While this makes the PISA projection of Singapore as a global leader in education fall flat with Singaporeans, it simultaneously provides a fertile soil for a whole range of different educational projections—that is, images of an "elsewhere" where educational life is better. Since education in Singapore is overwhelmingly associated with stress and hard work, it is not surprising that such projections are above all concerned with places where education is imagined to be more enjoyable. They are, to borrow a phrase from Lacanian psychoanalysis, fantasies about how the (cultural) Other enjoys in education.

For Singaporeans at large the most significant projections of this kind are probably America and Australia. These are places where many Singaporeans dream of migrating and where education is imagined to be much happier, freer, and more humane. However, for many professional educators in Singapore (as in other East Asian systems [Takayama et al. 2013]), there is one projection that looms larger—that is, Finland. While the idea of a coincidence between joyful and curious learning and high PISA performance is dismissed in Singapore's own case, many educators enthusiastically embrace it in the case of Finland. In the Singapore case, joy and high performance in education are experienced as mutually exclusive. Educational performance presupposes the sacrifice of enjoyment—in education as in life more generally. In Finland, however, this is not the case. The "Finnish miracle" is here imagined precisely as the miraculous overcoming of this impossible split between enjoyment and performance—hence the glowing fascination that permeates this portrait of Finland in a prominent Singaporean education magazine:

> Finnish education is known for its long breaks, short hours, and the total absence of supplementary classes, enrichment lessons, examinations, ranking and stress. The result of such a unique education system is consistently high placings in all three categories—Math, Science and Reading—in the Programme for International Student Assessment (PISA). (Poon 2013, 23)

In this sense, it is perfectly possible for a PISA top scorer like Singapore to be struck by PISA envy. This envy, however, does not concern performance itself, but that which is more than "mere" performance. Whereas Singaporean PISA success tends to be dismissed as mere performance (as resulting mechanically from long hours and repetitive drilling), Finnish PISA success is represented as more than just performance—as miraculously coinciding with enjoyment in education (short hours, no competition, no stress). A local high-school teacher expressed this peculiar kind of PISA envy more succinctly than anyone else when, during an interview with me, he burst out:

So for me as an educator and as a parent, I ask myself, okay, if Finland can do it, and their kids won't have to work so hard, then why the hell are we working so hard?

## Conclusion: "Changing Parents' Mindset"

From the preceding account, it would therefore seem that there are two incompatible tales of Singapore education—and of education reform more specifically. On the one hand policy-makers in Singapore refer to Singapore's brilliant performance in PISA as evidence that education reform, with its focus on authentic and higher-order learning, is very much on track. On the other hand, in public debate on education in Singapore, the education system is often portrayed as essentially unreformed—as infested with all the stereotypical ills of Asian education.

It often appears as if these two accounts of education in Singapore live separate lives and never really meet. This, however, is only partially true. In recent years the government has been increasingly open in recognizing that, in spite of all the efforts of education reform, education in Singapore is still pervaded by stress and ruthless competition for academic success. Thus, a few years back the MOE convened a number of public dialogue sessions in order to discuss these issues of "stress" and "excessive focus on academic examinations" with concerned Singaporean parents and educators (MOE 2013).

In this sense, the understanding of Singapore education as un-reformed—as driven by long hours and stress, and not by curiosity and critical thinking—does actually register at the policy level. Still, it registers here mainly in forms which leave intact the projection of Singapore as a most improved twenty-first-century system. Even if stress and excessive focus on academic examinations are acknowledged as problems, they are rarely acknowledged as problems that have any inherent relation to education policy itself.

Instead, such problems tend to be acknowledged mainly in "externalized" forms (Schriewer 1988). Here one might speak more specifically of an "externalization to parents" since, in recent years, Singaporean parents have increasingly been singled out by education officials as the main reason why stress and excessive focus on academic examinations remain seemingly intractable problems of educational life in Singapore. From the perspective of education officials (and many educators, as well), it is above all because parents cannot let go of the well-worn tiger mother precepts of pressuring and drilling their children for academic success that education reform seems, in certain respects, to make very little headway.

"Changing parents' mindset" has therefore become something of a mantra among policy-makers and educationists in Singapore in recent years. This view of parents as undermining reform goals was expressed very clearly by PM Lee Hsien Loong himself when, in his 2012 National Day Rally Speech, he delivered this admonishment to Singaporean parents:

> Please let your children have their childhood! . . . Education experts, child development specialists, they warn against over teaching pre-school children. You do harm, you turn the kid off, you make his life miserable. Instead of growing up balanced and happy, he grows up narrow and neurotic. . . . . I read of parents, who send their kindergarten age children to tuition, please do not do that. (Lee 2012)

Here the two stories of education in Singapore meet—and yet do not meet. The persistence of stereotypically Asian features like stress, over-teaching and obsession with results are here acknowledged by policy-makers and yet simultaneously disavowed—that is, externalized to parents. While education reform aims to make children grow up "happy and balanced," the traditional attitudes of parents make them grow up "narrow and neurotic" instead. Thus, it is not the system which is stereotypically Asian. It is the parents.

# Notes

1 PISA forms a partial exception here because this model is built into PISA in a much more explicit way than is the case with other league tables. As I show in the next section, this is why PISA acquires a special status in the context of education reform in Singapore.
2 I draw here especially on four reports/books: Barber and Mourshed 2007: Mourshed, Chijioke, and Barber 2010; Tucker 2011, and Jensen et al. 2012.
3 In addition to written documents, this section draws on fieldwork in Singapore in 2013 (four months) and 2017 (three months). As part of my fieldwork I conducted ethnographic interviews (around thirty in all) with parents and educators, focusing especially on their experiences with and views on education reform in Singapore.

# References

Barber, M., and Mourshed, M. (2007), *How the World's Best-Performing School Systems Come Out on Top*, http://mckinseyonsociety.com/how-the-worlds-best-performing-schools-come-out-on-top/ (accessed January 22, 2018).

Cheng, K. S. K. (2016), "Kids with Tuition Fare Worse," *Straits Times*, December 8, http://www.straitstimes.com/opinion/kids-with-tuition-fare-worse (accessed January 22, 2018).

Christensen, S. (2015), "Healthy Competition and Unsound Comparison: Reforming Educational Competition in Singapore," *Globalisation, Societies and Education*, 13(4), 553–73.

Davie, S. (2013a), "Singapore Students Shine in PISA Test," *Straits Times*, December 4, http://ifonlysingaporeans.blogspot.dk/2013/12/singapore-students-shine-in-pisa-test.html (accessed January 22, 2018).

Davie, S. (2013b), "Scaling Education Heights in PISA," *Straits Times*, December 5, http://ifonlysingaporeans.blogspot.dk/2013/12/singapore-students-shine-in-pisa-test.html (accessed January 22, 2018).

Davie, S. (2016a), "Useful Pisa Takeaways for Singapore Education," *Straits Times*, December 8, http://www.straitstimes.com/opinion/useful-pisa-takeaways-for-singapore-education (accessed January 22, 2018).

Davie, S. (2016b), "PISA and the Creativity Puzzle," *The Sunday Times*, December, 25. http://www.straitstimes.com/singapore/education/pisa-and-the-creativity-puzzle (accessed January 22, 2018).

Davie, S. (2016c), "Singapore Students Bag Education 'World Cup'," *Straits Times*, December 7, http://www.straitstimes.com/singapore/singapore-students-bag-education-world-cup (accessed January 22, 2018).

Foo, J. Y. (2016a), "Global Test? Piece of Cake," *The New Paper*, December 7, 1.

Foo, J. Y. (2016b), "Test Shows Singapore Students Move from Regurgitating to Critical Thinking," *The New Paper*, December 7, http://www.tnp.sg/news/singapore/test-shows-singapore-students-move-regurgitating-critical-thinking (accessed January 22, 2018).

Goh, C. T. (1992), *PM's National Day Rally Speech*, National Archives of Singapore, http://www.nas.gov.sg/archivesonline/speeches/record-details/73e734df-115d-11e3-83d5-0050568939ad (accessed February 18, 2018).

Goh, C. T. (1997), "Shaping our Future: Thinking Schools, Learning Nation," http://ncee.org/2017/01/singapore-thinking-schools-learning-nation/ (accessed February 18, 2018).

Hamlin, K. (2002), "Remaking Singapore," http://www.littlespeck.com/informed/2002/CInformed-020607remake.htm (accessed January 22, 2018).

Heng, S. K. (2013), "Singapore's Students Ready for the 21st century," Facebook post December 4, 2013, http://ifonlysingaporeans.blogspot.dk/2013/12/singapore-students-shine-in-pisa-test.html (accessed January 22, 2018).

Jayaraman, B. (2017), "Let's Kill the Drill Approach in Schools," *Straits Times*, February, 17 (accessed January 22, 2018).

Jensen, B., Hunter, A., Sonnemann J., and Burns, T. (2012), *Catching Up: Learning from the Best School Systems in East Asia. Full Report*, Grattan Institute, http://grattan.edu.au/wp-content/uploads/2014/04/130_report_learning_from_the_best_detail.pdf (accessed January 22, 2018).

Jessop, B. (2008), "A Cultural Political Economy of Competitiveness and Its Implications for Higher Education," in B. Jessop et al. (eds.), *Education and the Knowledge-Based Economy in Europe*, Rotterdam: Sense.

Lee, H. L. (2012), *Prime Minister Lee Hsien Loong's National Day Rally Speech 2012*, http://www.pmo.gov.sg/newsroom/prime-minister-lee-hsien-loongs-national-day-rally-2012-speech-english (accessed February 18, 2018).

MOE = Ministry of Education Singapore (2013), *Education Dialogue Session: 13th April 2013*, Anderson Junior College.

MOE = Ministry of Education Singapore (2014), 'PISA Ranking and the Role of Schools', April 14, https://www.moe.gov.sg/news/parliamentary-replies/pisa-ranking-and-the-role-of-schools (accessed January 31, 2018).

MOE = Ministry of Education Singapore (2016), "Equipped, Primed & Future-Ready: Singapore Students Have What It Takes to Thrive in the 21st Century Workplace," https://www.moe.gov.sg/news/press-releases/equipped--primed-and-future-ready--singapore-students-have-what-it-takes-to-thrive-in-the-21st-century-workplace (accessed February 12, 2018).

Mourshed, M., Chijioke, C., and Barber, M. (2010), *How the World's Most Improved School Systems Keep Getting Better* (Report November, 2010) McKinsey and Company, http://www.mckinsey.com/industries/social-sector/our-insights/how-the-worlds-most-improved-school-systems-keep-getting-better (accessed January 31, 2018).

Ng, C. M. (2016), Facebook post on TIMSS 2015 and PISA 2015, December 6, https://www.facebook.com/NgCheeMengforSG/posts/1260894520597945:0.

Poon, S. W. (2013), "The Finnish Experience: Lessons for Singapore," *EduNation 1*(1), 18–27.

Schleicher, A. (2007), "Foreword," in M. Barber and M. Mourshed (eds.), *How the World's Best-Performing School Systems Come Out on Top*, New York: McKinsey.

Schriewer, J. (1988), "The Method of Comparison and the Need for Externalization: Methodological Criteria and Sociological Concepts," in J. Schriewer and B. Holmes (eds.), *Theories and Methods in Comparative Education*, Frankfurt a. M.: Peter Lang.

Steiner-Khamsi, G. (2002),"Reterritorializing Educational Import: Explorations into the Politics of Educational Borrowing," in A. Nóvoa and M. Lawn (eds.), *Fabricating Europe: The Formation of an Education Space*, Hingham: Kluwer Academic.

Steiner-Khamsi, G. (2012), "Understanding Policy Borrowing and Lending: Building Comparative Policy Studies," in G. Steiner-Khamsi and F. Waldow (eds.), *World Yearbook of Education 2012: Policy Borrowing and Lending in Education*. London: Routledge.

Stewart, V. (2011), "Singapore: A Journey to the Top, Step by Step," in S. M. Tucker. (ed.), *Surpassing Shanghai: An Agenda for American Education Built on the World's Leading Systems*, Cambridge: Harvard Education Press.

Takayama, K., Waldow, F., and Sung, Y.-K. (2013), "Finland Has It All? Examining the Media Accentuation of 'Finnish Education' in Australia, Germany and South Korea," *Research in Comparative and International Education*, 8(3), 307–25.

Teng, A. (2013), "Students Know Their Stuff and How to Apply It," *Straits Time*, December 4, http://ifonlysingaporeans.blogspot.dk/2013/12/singapore-students-shine-in-pisa-test.html (accessed January 31, 2018).

Tucker, M. S. (2011), "How the Top Performers Got There: Analysis . . . and Synthesis," in S. M. Tucker (ed.), *Surpassing Shanghai: An Agenda for American Education Built on the World's Leading Systems*, Cambridge: Harvard Education Press.

Waldow, F., Takayama, K., and Sung, Y.-K. (2014), "Rethinking the Pattern of External Policy Referencing: Media Discourses over the 'Asian Tigers': PISA Success in Australia, Germany and South Korea," *Comparative Education*, 50(3), 302–21.

# 11

# Perceptions of the East Asian Model of Education and Modeling Its Future on Finnish Success: South Korean Case

Yoonmi Lee and Youl-Kwan Sung

## Introduction

Finland and South Korea have attracted worldwide attention for their consistently high performance in education. However, Korean educators across the political spectrum only rarely regard their students' high rankings in the Program for International Students Achievement (PISA) as cause for celebration (Ahn 2008). Instead, as the South Korean media repeatedly reports, educators tend to downplay students' high rankings in PISA results and instead call for reforming their educational system to fit the Finnish model. Despite the fact that the South Korean education system is globally recognized as effective, this success is never acknowledged in domestic discourse (Jung 2012). As Deborah Stone states, educational policy problems have a narrative structure—"stories" that are told to explain achievement or failure (Stone 2002, 138). Unlike Finland's story of success, the South Korean narrative is a tale of decline. What explains this?

South Korean educators' perception of their education system can be explained by the concept of "compressed modernization" (Sato 2003, 43). After the 1960s, South Korea has developed in an extremely condensed manner within a short period of time in all aspects of society, including education (Chang 2010). East Asian countries in general are known for their state-driven high productivity, characterized by development strategies planned and implemented by state bureaucracy. This has enabled these countries to achieve what is known as "compressed industrialization." This accelerated development, coupled with a productivist urge to catch up with whomever is presumed to be ahead, has pushed the pedagogical characteristics of South Korean education toward results rather than the process itself (Ahn 2008).

In South Korea, as in many other countries, quality education has been a central theme of discussion since the 1990s. The productivist drive has led to a focus on quantitative expansion—sometimes at the expense of qualitative practice—in the public education system (KEDI 2007a). As a result, South Korean students tend to lack non-cognitive factors that contribute to educational achievement, such as motivation, interest, and creative inquiry (Kang 2008). Low self-esteem and lack of intellectual curiosity—despite high test scores—may be explained by South Korea's unique results-oriented educational culture, as well as a social structure that relies almost exclusively on individual competition (Jung 2012).

It is this self-perception that lays behind South Korean interest in the Finnish educational system, a fascination that has increased along with Finland's continued high PISA rankings since the mid-2000s (Sung and Lee 2017). This is apparent in news and journal articles, research papers produced by think tanks, and even television documentaries. Since South Korean media is a key site of educational debates, we will use this evidence—along with government policy papers, books, and magazines marketed to teaching professionals—to analyze the ways in which stakeholders turn what should be a source of pride into shame to rationalize particular policy agendas transferred from other countries.

Comparative education studies have demonstrated that policy-borrowing discourses are directly linked to the problems diagnosed in the context they are received (Steiner-Khamsi 2004). Concepts of good versus bad education are often projected from the local to outside, model countries (Waldow, Takayama, and Sung 2014). Particular directions of educational reform may be both legitimized or delegitimized in this process.

Ever since the May 31 Reform, a 1995 initiative committing the government to openness and accountability in educational policy, South Korea has been making efforts to restructure its traditionally authoritarian system. This effort has provoked ongoing debates over quality and excellence in education (KEDI 2009). Progressives have criticized the South Korean education system for its excessively competitive college entrance exams which, they argue, have hindered student-centered learning. These exams have also been blamed for an over-emphasis on rote memorization and a heavy reliance on outside tutoring, which places an economic burden on parents. Meanwhile neoliberals and conservatives argue that market-based reform should be effective in restructuring educational system (see Kim et al. 2006). This political divide determines how Finnish-style lessons are constructed and represented in South Korea.

# Perception of the East Asian Model of Education

Despite its positive results on international comparison tests, South Korea has constructed a pessimistic narrative about the present and future of education (Kim et al. 2006). Stone has described the ways in which the typical narrative structure of "decline" works in policy debates when it is said, for example, that "things were once better than they are now, and that the change for the worse causes or will soon cause suffering" (2002, 139). The narrative of decline draws on the assumption that the present system is in a state of crisis, and the future is at risk, without necessarily suggesting a return to the "good old days" of the past. What follows, according to Stone, is a warning that "unless such-and-such is done, disaster will follow" (Stone 2002, 138).

A country's historical context influences how its citizens interpret other countries' policies in order to locate legitimacy externally, to cope with domestic discontent and the crisis produced by its own history (Steiner-Khamsi 2004). The South Korean educational system has been negatively portrayed for fostering harsh competition, resulting in a shadow education system of private tutoring, and an inflated importance to higher education degrees. Manabu Sato (2003), a leading Japanese scholar-reformer, describes the end of a traditional East Asian (Taiwan, Hong Kong, Korea, and Singapore) type of education, where education was the engine of social mobility and centralized development, with schools geared toward efficiently delivering large quantities of knowledge processed through excessive competition.

One of the results of this model, as demonstrated by international measurements such as the PISA and the TIMMS (Trends in International Mathematics and Science Study), has been high achievement (OECD 2007). This success, however, has come at the cost of longer study hours, extensive homework, parental pressure, outside tutoring, and lower motivation, among other ills. East Asian educational culture has also been characterized by strict discipline, an authoritarian instructional style, rote memory, and lack of opportunity for deep processing of information—which has had a considerable influence on educational reform (Darling-Hammond 2010). Teaching high-order critical thinking skills to challenge this system has attracted great interest among South Korean education reformers and their counterparts in other East Asian countries as well.[1]

Social science research (Goodman, White, and Kwon 1998; Chang 2006) on East Asia has explored the developmental model of postwar Japan, along with the newly industrializing capitalist economies of South Korea,

Taiwan, Hong Kong, and Singapore. Johnson's (1982) term "developmental state" characterizes Japan by a strong government and effective bureaucracy practicing rational planning (Johnson 1999, 32). Many social scientists (Cumings 1999; Holliday 2000) consider the developmental strategies of Japan as deviant or unique. Esping-Andersen (1997; 1998) added Japan to his three models of European welfare states (social democratic, liberal, and conservative) as a typology which can be extended to other parts of East Asia. It is this model that countries like South Korea have followed (Cumings 1999). Meanwhile Holliday (2000) applied the term "productivist" to Japan, Korea, Taiwan, Hong Kong, and Singapore, adding yet another category to Esping-Andersen's typology (1998). According to Holliday's model, liberal worlds prioritize the market, conservative worlds are defined by status, social democratic worlds care about welfare, and a productivist world is focused on growth (Holliday 2000, 709).

The attempt to reform the high-pressure approach to education while simultaneously raising the level of excellence has led to controversies in South Korea and East Asia in general. Japan has been trying since the 1980s to reduce student anxiety over the need to succeed, and in 2002 institutionalized a low-pressure system called *Yutori* education. Perhaps unsurprisingly this has fueled heated debates over an "achievement crisis" (Tsuneyoshi 2004). The situation in South Korea is similar: Less than perfection means failure and attempts to reduce pressure increase anxiety. This is among the reasons South Koreans are so unhappy with the East Asian model (Waldow, Takayama, and Sung 2014).

## Referencing Finnish Education

This chapter examines why Finland has been chosen as a projection screen for legitimizing certain existing policy agendas in South Korea, as well as what aspects of Finnish education are presented as exemplary. In doing so, we analyze what South Koreans perceive as the reasons for Korean students' high PISA rankings, and how they inform the contemporary narrative of crisis and formulation of future solutions. We focus specially on the particular ways in which Finnish education is portrayed in South Korea by examining the content of stakeholder positions on four aspects of education that may best represent the characteristics of a country's educational system: achievement, equity, attitudes toward teachers, and quality assurance.

## Achievement

Finland and South Korea have been top-performing nations in student achievement in every round of the PISA. What distinguishes them is that Finns rarely refer to South Korea as a role model whose success they should aspire to, even as South Koreans routinely regard Finnish education as an advanced model. Furthermore, whereas Finns have systematically analyzed the factors that contributed to their high achievement in the PISA, South Koreans have downplayed the significance of their test results in domestic debates over education reform (Kim et al. 2006).

The seemingly obvious question of why South Korean fifteen-year-olds are successful in meeting the PISA standards is rarely asked at home. Professors, pundits, the media, and government think tank members already assume they know the answer: intense academic competition, extensive use of private tutoring, and test-driven recitation and drilling. Many South Korean educational scholars (Kang 2008; Kim 2011; Jung 2012) answer the question by suggesting that undesirable processes have produced desirable outcomes.

This issue is regularly covered in media accounts of South Koreans' high test scores. For example, Kim and Park (2016) of the *Chosun Daily* criticize the correlation between individual scores and the hours devoted to private tutoring, pointing out that this conjunction does not exist in Finland. Kim and Park point out that Korean students who took the PISA in 2012 received an average 4.94 hours of private tutoring per week, far more than the 11 minutes averaged by their Finnish competitors.

The South Korean image of Finnish education is shaped by the belief that they have found a way to achieve educational excellence without resorting to competitive measures. For this reason Finland has become a role model for East Asian countries in general, all of whom agonize over the perceived trade-off between high achievement and creativity (Takayama 2010). And the feature of Finnish education that attracts greatest attention is its practice of cooperation and rejection of competition as an organizing principle.

## Equity

Both Finland and South Korea have enlisted egalitarian measures to expand their public education systems. Finland's comprehensive school reforms in the 1970s resulted in an education system based on equality and cooperation. In South Korea, the equalization policy implemented in the same period abolished the old school hierarchy and paved the way for equal access (KEDI 2007b). An equalization policy developed in 1974 specifically addressed the issue of overheated competition for high school admission and promoted equal distribution of material and human resources across high schools (Seth 2002). Under this system, students were assigned to schools based on geographical proximity and grades to achieve populations as heterogeneous as possible.

The school choice controversy of the 1990s was hotly debated in terms of "equality versus excellence" in South Korean schools. On the one hand, South Korea's pursuit of equal access has been marked by egalitarianism, and education has served as an important source of social mobility. On the other hand, the education system has also been driven by its traditionally hierarchical system of differential prestige. Proponents of choice and competition argue for a more effective system based on individual differences, notably the introduction of student groupings based on ability and the creation of more schools for the gifted.

Even as Korean students excelled on international tests there has been considerable debate over a perceived diminishing of academic achievement. For example, Kim (2002), an opponent of open education and equalization who writes for the conservative *Dong-A Daily*, advocates increasing competitiveness by reintroducing of school rankings to increase competition among schools. Kim (2002) also argues that school choice for elite students is essential because it gives stronger students an education appropriate to each person's academic ability and will make them more competitive internationally. Choice proponents—primarily the elites—believe that the equalization policy lowers academic achievement by requiring strong students to learn with mediocre students under a common curriculum that is not tailored to different abilities (Lee and Lee 2004), and denies opportunities like the right to choose to attend a prestigious high school (Sung 2011).

Meanwhile progressives use Finland's success to criticize market-oriented education policies like school choice. Such concerns are given a voice when conservatives control the South Korean government, as was the case from February 2008 to May 2017, and implement neoliberal reforms. Egalitarians then counter by emphasizing the cooperative nature of Finnish education. For example Ahn (2008) argued that Finnish education provides equal opportunities for all children to realize their full potential.

> The most important thing we should learn from Finnish education is the philosophy of public education that provides quality education to all students

regardless of social background. The Finnish government has endeavored to embody the philosophy of public education that every country including South Korea has long wished to make true. This philosophy is less discussed in other countries, while in Finland, the principle of equality has contributed to successful results that suggest others could do well to adopt it. (Ahn 2008, 69)

In another progressive publication, *Hankyoreh News*, Finland is described as a country that achieved competence through cooperation, not competition (Kwon 2012). Even as conservative news media such as *Dong-A Daily* and *Chosun Daily* remain silent on the equality issue, progressive media use Finland to validate their view that equality and quality have a positive correlation. Progressives view Finnish education as a social democratic welfare model, while conservatives portray Finland as a successful capitalist country with an effective vocational education system (Takayama, Waldow, and Sung 2013). Though the tendency is more frequent among the latter than the former the one thing conservatives and progressives agree on is that Finland is better.

## Teachers

Though international standards rank South Korean teachers as highly qualified (Darling-Hammond 2010), not every Korean sees them this way. For instance, conservative media depict teacher union politics as a major challenge to excellence in South Korean education. Instead of being counted as a source of success, teachers are often blamed by market-based reform proponents for the supposedly poor quality of education in South Korea. One of the reasons for this is the progressive teachers' union, the Korean Teachers Union (KTU), founded in 1989 as the result of efforts to resist military-authoritarian rule at that time, not simply for their job protection. The KTU is now one of the largest teacher organizations in the country and conservatives portray its members as radicals opposed to market-driven neoliberal reforms (Lee 2006).

There has also been fierce debate over a teacher evaluation scheme introduced in 1995 as part of the May 31 Reform. Proponents argued that without regular evaluation teachers, secure in their tenure, would simply stagnate till retirement at age sixty-two. Teachers' unions resisted the reform, claiming that it was driven by neoliberals aiming to control teachers. Teachers who opposed both performance-based pay and evaluation cited Pasi Sahlberg's (2007) discussion of the Finnish model—which included neither bonuses for high performing teachers nor teacher evaluation—to justify their opposition (Waldow, Takayama, and Sung 2014). Yet, despite progressivists enthusiasm for Finland's system, its features have rarely been transferred into actual policy (Sung and Lee 2017).

## Quality

Quality assurance of student assessment has been as controversial as teacher evaluation. Conservatives argue that the national testing system is essential for accountability and quality control, while progressives counter that Finland lacks such a system.

In South Korea, both devolution and remote control occur simultaneously. The state monitors standards and shifts decision-making to superintendents and school officials who oversee classrooms. Though once appointed by the Ministry of Education, since 2006 superintendents at the provincial level have been directly elected by the residents of South Korea's sixteen provinces and metropolitan cities. Superintendents have decision-making power over areas ranging from school finance to establishment to personnel management (Ministry of Education, Science and Technology 2008). Decentralization however has not extended to the level that would ensure autonomy and empower to teachers.

The introduction of the 2008 national testing and publication policy, similar to the *No Child Left Behind Act* in the United States, sparked considerable controversy over the issue of accountability and quality control in schools (Ministry of Education, Science and Technology 2008). Proponents argue that parents have the right to know how well their schools perform and that such a system enables the identification of low achievers for appropriate remedial programs. Opponents counter that the publication of test results will only confirm existing inequalities based on different socioeconomic backgrounds, and that this will lower the self-esteem of the affected students and teachers. Opponents have also argued that quality assurance was already possible using sample-based tests administered to a small portion (less than 5 percent) of students. Quality assurance using such sampling achieves statistical data that allows an estimation of overall student achievement—and it was never controversial (Sung and Kang 2012).

In December 2008, seven teachers were fired for protesting mandatory testing by the Seoul Metropolitan Office of Education, because they advised their students that they could participate in alternative programs if they did not wish to take the national exam (Kang 2008). This led to intense political struggle and once again Finland was held up as an example. One of progressive educators argued that

Finland, attracting global attention as a country with an advanced education system, shows the world's best academic achievement and the smallest educational gap between the weakest and strongest students. However, it should be noted that there is no standardized national testing system in Finland. Some national assessments are carried out, but they are sample-based for the quality assurance purpose, not for the purpose of external control. The assessment aims to ensure that governments are involved in a timely manner to provide equal quality education opportunities for all schools, not to ask for accountability. (Kwon 2009)

Finland is featured as if it has defied global trends by opting out of the accountability movement and is thus portrayed as a utopia where there are neither rankings between schools nor competition among students for higher test scores. The Korean system is, in contrast, a dystopia of uninspired students learning from the sole purpose of scoring high on tests that will give no guarantee or future success, much less satisfaction.

# Conclusion

Educational policies may be borrowed from other countries because they seem better, but in South Korea the rationale is typically motivated by the politics underlying the policy-borrowing discourses (Sung 2011). References to Finnish education have been closely tied to intense struggles over domestic issues such as egalitarian schooling, mandatory standardized testing, accountability, and decentralized authority. This experience confirms Schriewer's theory (2003) that external references are used to justify positions within existing domestic political contests. Takayama (2010) has demonstrated a similar phenomenon in Japan, where Finnish success is the external authority, an increasingly common phenomenon worldwide in the wake of Finland's continued success in the PISA rankings. In South Korea, Finland is cited by competing political interests in support of opposing education policies to improve their system. In this sense Finland has become a "projection screen" onto which policy actors project their agendas (Takayama, Waldow, and Sung 2013, 307).

As discussed above, South Korean references to the Finnish education system were motivated by the desire to overcome problems with the East Asian model created by compressed modernization. So what, in fact, have the South Koreans borrowed by the Finns? Dolowitz and Marsh identify eight items that can be transferred from one political system to another: "policy goals, policy content, policy instruments, policy programs, institutions, ideologies, ideas and attitudes and negative lessons" (2000, 5). Among these, policy contents and programs have not been directly transferred from Finland to South Korea. Instead, those who want to borrow from the Finnish education system tend to focus on the relationship between its educational success and social democratic welfare system. Finland is an inspiration, not an alternative whose programs and policy instruments have been put into practice (Takayama, Waldow, and Sung 2013).

Further evidence that praise of the Finnish system is mostly rhetoric is the fact that the South Korean government continues to borrow educational policies from the United States. Why? In our earlier work (Sung and Lee 2017) we concluded this is because policy borrowing is essentially political. For decades the South Korean government held up the United States as the standard to be aspired to (Sung and Lee 2017). Though in the post-PISA era South Koreans are attracted to Finland as a role model, external referencing hinges on historical, political, and cultural experiences that transcend any one country.

# Note

An earlier version of this chapter appeared in the *KEDI Journal of Educational Policy* (2010), *7*(2), 379–401. This chapter was carefully modified to take into account the purpose of this book.

1   Although East Asian countries may appear to share a common cultural background, it is difficult to discuss regional similarities for a variety of reasons. Although the ancient Chinese civilization based on Confucianism may be a common thread, contemporary relations among the countries are not coherent and integral enough to qualify the entire region as a single analytical unit. Nevertheless, countries such as Japan, China (including Hong Kong), South Korea, and Taiwan (and Singapore in a wider context) have not only been classified into the category of "East Asia" by many social scientists (Goodman, White, and Kwon 1998; Cumings 1999; Holliday 2000; Chang 2006 ), but they also share a number of issues related to their education.

# References

Ahn, S. (2008), "How Has Finnish Education Been Successful?" *Urigyoyouk* [Our Education], *224*, 66–75.

Chang, H. J. (2006), *The East Asian Development Experience: The Miracle, the Crisis and the Future*, New York: Zed Books.

Chang, K. (2010), *South Korea under Compressed Modernity: Familial Political Economy in Transition*, London: Routledge.

Cumings, B. (1999), "Webs with No Spiders, Spiders with No Webs: The Genealogy of the Developmental State," in M. Woo-Cumings (ed.), *The Developmental State* (61–92), Ithaca: Cornell University Press.

Darling-Hammond, L. (2010), *The Flat World and Education: How America's Commitment to Equity Will Determine Our Future*, New York: Teachers College, Columbia University.

Dolowitz, D., and Marsh, D. (2000), "Learning from Abroad: The Role of Policy Transfer in Contemporary Policy-Making," *Governance: An International Journal of Policy and Administration*, 13(1), 5–24.

Esping-Andersen, G. (1997), "Hybrid or Unique? The Japanese Welfare State Between Europe and America," *Journal of European Social Policy*, 7, 179–89.

Esping-Andersen, G. (1998), *The Three Worlds of Welfare Capitalism*, Princeton: Princeton University Press.

Goodman, R., White, G., and Kwon, H. J. (1998), *The East Asian Welfare Model: Welfare Orientalism and the State*, London: Routledge.

Holliday, I. (2000), "Productivist Welfare Capitalism: Social Policy in East Asia," *Political Studies*, 48, 706–23.

Johnson, C. (1982), *MITI and the Japanese Miracle: The Growth of Industrial Policy, 1925–1975*, Stanford: Stanford University Press.

Johnson, C. (1999), "The Developmental State: Odyssey of a Concept," in M. Woo-Cumings (ed.), *The Developmental State*, 61–92, Ithaca: Cornell University Press.

Jung, I. (2012), *Characteristics and Factors of Finnish Success*, Seoul: Korean Educational Development Institute.

Kang, I. (2008), "Expulsion and Dismissal of the Seven Teachers Protested against Mandatory National Test," *The Pressian*, December 10, http://www.pressian.com/article/article.asp?article_num=60081210173040 (accessed January 10, 2018).

Kang, Y. (2008), *Finnish Public Education Reforms and Comprehensive Schools*, Seoul: Korean Educational Development Institute.

Korean Educational Development Institute = KEDI (2007a), "Education and Korea's Development," *Understanding Korean Education* (5), Seoul: Korean Educational Development Institute (KEDI).

Korean Educational Development Institute = KEDI (2007b), "School Education in Korea," *Understanding Korean Education* (3), Seoul: Korean Educational Development Institute (KEDI).

Korean Educational Development Institute = KEDI (2009), "Teacher Policy," *Understanding Korean Education* (8), Seoul: Korean Educational Development Institute (KEDI).

Kim, B. (2011), "Characteristics of Finnish Welfare System and Educational Implications," *Gyoyuk Bipyeong* [Educational Critique], *30*, 82–104.

Kim, C. S. (2002). "High School Equalization Is the Violation of the Constitution," *Dong-A Daily*, February 18, http://news.donga.com/3/all/20020217/7788789/1 (accessed January 10, 2018).

Kim, K., Park, C., Son, J., and Lee, Y. (2006), *A Diagnostic Study on the Educational Problems of Korea* (Report no. 2006–43), Seoul: Ministry of Education and Human Resource Development (MOE and HRD).

Kim, S., and Park, S. (2016), "The Secret of PISA: South Korea's Shadow Education vs. Japan's Public Education," *Chosun Daily*, March 11, http://news.chosun.com/site/data/html_dir/2016/03/11/2016031100181 (accessed January 10, 2018).

Kwon, T. (2009), "Beyond the Turmoil around Mandatory National Test," *Hankyoreh News*, September 22, http://www.hani.co.kr/arti/opinion/column/340296.html (accessed January 10, 2018).

Kwon, T. (2012,), "Education as Learning and Caring," *Hankyoreh News*, March 26, http://www.hani.co.kr/arti/society/society_general/525184.html (accessed January 10, 2018).

Lee, J., and Lee, K. (2004), "Strategies to Introduce Charter Schools," *Paper Presented at the Seminar of the Korean Forum for Educational Reform*, Seoul, South Korea.

Lee, Y. (2006), "Teachers Working for Change: Gender Equity and the Politics of Teacher Activism in South Korea," *Asia Pacific Journal of Education*, 26(2), 143–53.

Ministry of Education, Science and Technology (2008), "Implementation Plans for Enhancing School Autonomy: Towards Diversity, High-Quality, and Self-Governance in Schools, News Release," April 15.

Organization for Economic Co-operation and Development = OECD (2007), *PISA 2006: Science Competencies for Tomorrow's World*, Paris: OECD.

Sahlberg, P. (2007), "Education Policies for Raising Student Learning: The Finnish Approach," *Journal of Education Policy*, 22(2), 147–72.

Sato, M. (2003), *Children Escaping from Learning* (W. J. Son, Trans.), Seoul: Book Korea.

Schriewer, J. (2003), "Globalisation in Education: Process and Discourse," *Policy Futures in Education*, 1(2), 271–82.

Seth, M. (2002), *Education Fever: Society, Politics, and the Pursuit of Schooling in South Korea*, Honolulu: University of Hawaii Press.

Steiner-Khamsi, G. (2004), *The Global Politics of Educational Borrowing and Lending*, New York: Teachers College Press.

Stone, D. (2002). *Policy Paradox: The Art of Political Decision Making*, New York: W. W. Norton.

Sung, Y-K. (2011), "Cultivating Borrowed Futures: The Politics of Neoliberal Loanwords in South Korean Cross-National Policy Borrowing," *Comparative Education*, 47(4), 523–38.

Sung, Y.-K., and Kang, M. (2012), "The Cultural Politics of National Testing and Test Result Release Policy in South Korea: A Critical Discourse Analysis," *Asia Pacific Journal of Education*, *32*(1), 53–73.

Sung, Y.-K., and Lee, Y. (2017), "Is the United States Losing Its Status as a Reference Point for Educational Policy in the Age of Global Comparison? The Case of South Korea," *Oxford Review of Education*, *43*(2), 162–79.

Takayama, K. (2010), "Politics of Externalization Reflexive Times: Reinventing Japanese Education Reform Discourses through 'Finnish Success,'" *Comparative Education Review*, *54*(1), 51–75.

Takayama, K., Waldow, F., and Sung, Y-K. (2013), "Finland Has It All? Examining 'Finnish PISA Success' as a Multiaccentual Sign in Australia, Germany, and South Korea," *Research in Comparative and International Education*, *8*, 307–25.

Tsuneyoshi, R. (2004), "The New Japanese Educational Reforms and the Achievement 'Crisis' Debate," *Educational Policy*, *18*, 364–94.

Waldow, F., Takayama, K., and Sung, Y-K. (2014), "Rethinking the Pattern of External Policy Referencing: Media Discourses over the 'Asian Tigers'' PISA Success in Australia, Germany and South Korea," *Comparative Education*, *50*(3), 302–21.

# 12

# Conclusions: What Policy-Makers Do with PISA

Gita Steiner-Khamsi

The spectacular growth of countries participating in PISA is noticeable and deserves theorizing: forty-three countries in 2000, seventy-two countries and territories in 2015, and eighty administrative entities participated in 2018. In analyzing the explosive growth of PISA and other international large-scale assessments (ILSAs), researchers have proposed several explanations, ranging from broad ones, such as globalization and the political pressure to be part of a larger international educational space, to very concrete ones, such as an ever-increasing number of evidence-driven policy actors who rely on international comparison for measuring the quality of their educational system. Others are more contextual in their sense-making. Theirs is the intellectual project of understanding the rapid growth of standardized international comparisons against the backdrop of what is debated, contested, or at stake in a local policy context. They use the rapid growth of standardized international comparison as an opportunity for understanding why PISA resonates, or does not resonate, and how PISA results are translated or interpreted in varied policy contexts. They do not assume that PISA has a priory a salutary effect on national school reform but they rather analyze when, why and how national policy actors use PISA, or for that matter any other ILSA, for their agenda setting or policy formulation. It is this group of researchers that is represented in this edited volume.

This chapter situates the contributions in this book against the backdrop of broader debates on evidence-based policy planning and global monitoring of national developments.

## The Power of Soft Power

The fact that PISA is used for monitoring national educational systems by means of comparison catapults the ILSA into the proximity of other "soft power" tools of international organizations. International bureaucrats insist that their policies and programs are evidence-based, rational, and founded on neutral expertise. Ever since Max Weber argued, at the beginning of the last century, that bureaucratic administration means the "exercise of power by way of knowledge" (1922, 226), it has become commonplace for social scientists to evoke the crucial role of expertise as an instrument of bureaucratic power and influence. A small group of scholars has focused on the politics of expertise by international organizations (see Sending 2015; Littoz-Monnet 2017). In general, political scientists have pointed to the role of expertise in granting authority and legitimacy to actors in the global sphere, and as being an endogenous characteristic of the actual forms of governance advanced by actors (see Sending 2015).

Existing literature has granted particular attention to the politics of quantification, showing how technologies of expertise such as indicators and measurements imbue subjective assessments with objective weight (Porter 1996; Kingsbury, Engle Merry, and Davis 2015). Statistics, as an example of a numerical technology, represent reality by bringing to light relationships between previously distant and heterogeneous objects. Despite their "air of objectivity" statistics are also the product of specific political decisions (Heintz 2012, 7–8). Quantitative tools of measurement have been central to the exercise of particularly effective forms of soft power in global politics, where the possibility to formulate "hard law" is often lacking. It is through the use of highly technical knowledge (quantitative and highly specialized) that international bureaucracies can best shape the global agenda, legitimate their existence and action and establish implicit normative frameworks for collective action.

The role of international organizations in advancing governance by numbers is not to be underestimated. The expertise that international bureaucracies offer represents a specific type of soft power that draws on international comparisons, reviews and recommendations (see Littoz-Monnet 2017). In the education sector, the most discussed signposts of international soft power are the Bologna Process in higher education and PISA in secondary education (see Martens and Knodel 2014). Governments are by no mean coerced into adopting any of the recommendations of international organizations. They do so voluntarily, and in my opinion equally importantly, they do so selectively. Critical analyses of evidence-based regulation and governance by numbers are hardly new. However, most of the analyses focus on the legitimacy deficit of international organizations and examine what they do to assert power vis-à-vis national entities. Of course, there are many avenues of relevant topics that open up when the research focus is put on international bureaucracies. For example, one of them—pursued at the Graduate Institute of International and Development Studies (see Littoz-Monnet 2017)—deals with technologies of authorization and examines what international bureaucracies do to make themselves heard vis-à-vis national entities.

Authors of this book situate themselves on the flip side in that they are primarily interested in investigating the following questions: What technologies of authorization do *national* bureaucracies use to make themselves look international, that is, compatible with international standards, global "best practices" and other broadly defined features of an imagined international community. In a similar vein, how does internationality translate at the national level and what particular moment is there a receptiveness toward international technologies of authorization. In other words, what is pursued in this book is the analysis of why national governments buy into, and how they receive and translate the soft power of international organizations, such as IEA's TIMSS or OECD's PISA in ways that makes them look to be in compliance with international trends.

The shift from government to governance is commonly seen as the result of new public management policies that most OECD countries introduced in the wake of neoliberal reforms of the 1980s and 1990s. In the education sector, the shift implied a new role for the state, new ways of regulating the education system, and new tools for generating or alleviating reform pressure. The reforms were undertaken with the rhetoric of breaking the state monopoly, using market forces (demand and supply) to improve the quality of public education, and cutting inefficiency in the state bureaucracy. Regardless of whether the public education system was high or low performing, governments were under political pressure to selectively borrow new public management policies that encouraged non-state actors such as businesses, churches, communities, and families to open and operate schools with funding from public resources. Within a short period of time, the governments scaled back the role of the state in education from one in which it was the sole provider of public education to one in which it could withdraw to being only a standard-setter and regulator. Target-setting and benchmarking became the key governance tools. In education, the outcomes orientation of new public management reform triggered a proliferation of standardized student assessment. The tests have, for a variety of reasons, been utilized as the primary monitoring tool for governments to assess the quality of teachers, the school, the district, and the education system, and to make policy decisions based on these standardized assessments. The shift from government to governance has not only fueled a "governance by numbers" (Ozga 2009) but also required from governments that they engage in "network governance" (Ball and Junemann 2012) in which non-state actors, including education businesses, are not only seen as providers of goods and services but also as key partners in the policy process. The empowerment of non-state actors in the new millennium, notably businesses and philanthropies, as key policy actors has been interpreted as a clear sign of the "disarticulation and diversification of the state system" and the "destatalisation" of the policy process (Ball and Junemann 2012, 24), which neoliberal reforms of the past century intended to achieve. Of course, allowing businesses lobby for their own, for-profit cause has rightfully been criticized by many, including by several authors in this book (Lingard et al., Chapter 3 in this volume; see also Lewis 2017).

Without any doubt, the scholarship on governance by numbers has produced important theoretical insights on the changing role of the state and the soft power of international organizations. However, it is to a great extent devoid of agency. They tend to depict national governments as passive recipients of international agreements, reviews, and recommendations and fail to acknowledge that global scripts are nationally constructed. What policy actors present as an international standard or a best [international] practice varies from local context to local context. Even more crass, as the authors in this book demonstrate, the system variables that supposedly account for the high performance of league leaders (e.g., educational system of Finland) reflect more the burning issues in their own country than in the country of the league leader.

## The Main Lines of Argumentation

Arguably, any attempt to interpret PISA receptions as projections requires a comparative perspective on how policy actors in different settings explain the PISA results. It is only by way of comparison that the vastly different receptions, interpreted as idiosyncratic projections of one's own (local) context into another context, come to light. The comparative study of PISA reception, advanced in this edited volume, allows us to make sense of the growing popularity of ILSAs, and in particular PISA. In attempts to address this important question, the authors of this book (1) study the reception of international standardized comparison (as opposed to its diffusion), (2) examine incidents of externalization to PISA, (3) investigate the utility of PISA for the transnational accreditation of twenty-first-century skills, or (4) the economization of education, as reflected in the twenty-first-century skills measured in PISA.

## Reception versus Diffusion

In policy borrowing research, we differentiate between two broader interpretive frameworks that complement each other but use different angles to examine globalization in education. One group of scholars adopts a bird's eye views in order to prove the worldwide diffusion of global scripts, whereas the other group focuses on the discursive power of global scripts and analyzes at what particular moment local actors have a legitimacy deficit and therefore externalize, that is, are receptive to adopting the global script. The first set of frameworks rests on longitudinal sociological analyses to prove the existence of similar patterns, ideas, and values across a wide range of countries. Of course, there is a broad spectrum among the diffusion theorists. One group with affinity to neo-institutionalism tends to focus on positively connoted global scripts such as the global spread of human rights education or gender equality (e.g., Bromley, Buckner, and Russell 2013; Lerch et al. 2016; see Carney, Rappleye, and Silova 2012), whereas another group affiliated with political economy emphasizes the neo-liberal agenda underlying the rapid spread of the "globally structured educational agenda" (Dale 2000; see also Jules 2016). At the reception side, the theories range from sociological systems theory (see Schriewer 1990; Steiner-Khamsi and Waldow 2012) to historical institutionalism (see Verger, Fontdevila, C., and Zancajo 2016), which explain the different reasons or historical paths of why and how one and the same global script (e.g., the spread of accountability reforms, privatization in education, etc.) has been adopted and locally translated.

For innocent bystanders, the two camps may come across as dismissive vis-a-vis each other because neo-institutionalist theory consider the local variations of the global script (the main focus of sociological systems theory) simply as loose coupling and therefore irrelevant for further scrutiny. Analogously, system theorists find the preoccupation with identifying global scripts (the main focus of neo-institutionalism) futile given the semantics of globalization and the ubiquitous and inflationary use of international standards or best practices. The various explanations are, however, not mutually exclusive. On the contrary, precisely because the various interpretive frameworks differ in terms of focus or object of study, they complement each other.

It may help to illustrate the system-theoretical way of seeing things by answering the introductory question of why standardized international comparison has experienced such an exponential growth. It may be argued that the noncurriculum-based student evaluation of the PISA test design creates ample room for speculation or, more accurately, for projection. In another publication, a group of us identified the elusiveness of twenty-first-century skills as one of the reasons why PISA is so popular (Kijima and Lipscy 2015; Lockheed et al. 2015; Addey 2016; Addey et al. 2017). The test uses a decontextualized measure that enables each and every participating government, as well as different political coalitions within national governments, to project their own idiosyncratic explanations for their high, average, or low performance, respectively.

## Externalization as a Critical Event

It is important to bear in mind that many releases of ILSA results go unnoticed, either because the government purposefully suppresses the results or because the media, in anticipation of low public interest, does not report on the studies. Research on ILSA reception tends to focus on countries with excessive media reports due to "shock" or other unexpected PISA findings. As a result, these studies tend to over-estimate the impact that ILSAs have on public opinion or on educational policy. For a variety of reasons, explained by Nancy Green Saraisky (Chapter 6 in this volume), the disinterest in ILSAs is especially pronounced in the United States. However, the United States is not the only country where the release of PISA results was made with little fanfare. Even in countries, in which governments used to eagerly participate and actively used the results for domestic policy agendas (e.g., Norway, PR China), the enthusiasm for PISA is not necessarily sustained over several rounds of participations as the examples from PR China (Schulte, Chapter 9 in this volume) or Norway (Sivesind, Chapter 5 in this volume) show. For researchers interested in the reception aspect of PISA, the attention is therefore on when externalization is actually made. Methodologically, the act of externalization—reference to PISA results—is therefore not dismissed as secondary, but on the contrary is regarded as a critical event that deserves empirical scrutiny.

Drawing on Niklas Luhmann's sociological systems theory, Schriewer pioneered the concept of "externalization" for understanding the local circumstances that account for openness towards global influences (1990;

Schriewer and Martinez 2004). Systems theory is interested in the "socio-logic" of reception, that is, at what particular moments do national actors make references to experiences in other countries or to "world situations" (see Luhmann 1997)? These kind of questions, along with questions on translation, constitute the core of policy borrowing research and comparative policy studies (e.g., Steiner-Khamsi and Waldow 2012). In Norway, for example, policy actors periodically drew on OECD reviews and on PISA result whenever a fundamental reform was planned, notably for the 1996 and 2006 curriculum reforms. However, a group of us did not find any significant externalization to OECD, PISA or other ILSAs preceding incremental reforms such as the ones that were issued in 2015 and 2016 (Baek et al. 2017).

## Transnational Accreditation of Twenty-First-Century Skills

The active role of government in securing education for all is generally seen as of the great projects of the modern nation-state. In most countries compulsory education meant, at least at primary level, free public education. By default, it has been national in terms of content and organization. All along, the national orientation has not been without problems, in particular for language minorities. They found themselves left out from horizontal integration (social cohesion) as well as from the vertical integration (social mobility) that modern schooling promised to deliver. In addition, in an era of globalization, the national orientation has become in and of itself a burden to governments. Public (national) education is not doing well. In the majority of educational systems (all those that rank below the OECD average), ILSAs have exacerbated the crisis by scandalizing the poor results of public education. Noticeably, those that benefit the most from the structural constraints of (national) public education have been the most outspoken in their attacks (see Steiner-Khamsi, Appleton, and Vellani 2017): global businesses and international organizations, that is, entities that are able to provide a transnational accreditation of school exit exams.

Without any doubt, the ubiquitous talk of global markets and the reality of international student mobility has helped boost the business of transnational certifiers. If the trend continues, "global" is likely to become increasingly positively associated with cosmopolitanism and "national" with backwardness and parochialism. Strikingly, schools that claim to implement international standards are on the rise globally. Their main selling points are English as a language of instruction, technology integration, and last but not least, so-called twenty-first-century skills.

For example, the exit examinations of the International Standard Schools in Indonesia need to be accredited by one of the OECD education systems (ACDP 2013; Steiner-Khamsi 2016). In Kazakhstan, there is a network of Nazarbayev Intellectual Schools that comprises twenty-one schools. With the purpose to serve as the channels of translating best practices across the country, these schools are located in different regions of the country (see Bridges 2014). More specifically, they are based in all the seventeen major cities of Kazakhstan including Astana and Almaty. In Mongolia, there were supposed to be twenty schools tailored after the curriculum of the Cambridge International General Certificate of Secondary Education (IGCSE). Bending under pressure from civil society, however, the incoming Minister of Education and Science, reduced in 2014 that number to three schools, based in Ulaanbaatar, and highlighted the important role of these so-called Cambridge-Standards Laboratory Schools for mainstreaming competency-based curricula, the use of instructional technology, and high-stakes student tests at critical stages of their school careers. Similar to the Nazarbayev Intellectual Schools, the Cambridge-Standards Laboratory Schools in Mongolia receive technical assistance from Cambridge International Examinations or are accredited by International Baccalaureate, and have managed to implement English as a language of instruction in the STEM subjects (science, technology, engineering, and math). The spread of International Baccalaureate in Spanish speaking countries has been well documented (Resnik 2015). What is perhaps less known is the explosive growth of the IB Diploma Program in East Asia, including in educational system that by ILSA standards are high performing. The state-funded IB Diploma Program expansion in Japan represents a fascinating case of a high performing public education system that has drawn on the private sector to explicitly strengthen twenty-first-century skills, introduce critical thinking, and implement a dual language diploma (Japanese and English). The goal of the government is to roll out over a period of five years two hundred International Baccalaureate Diploma Programs (Yamamoto 2016).

With the exception of the league leaders, PISA has become a stamp of attestation that national educational systems do not teach students twenty-first-century skills. What they would need to do in terms of the curriculum in order to do so remains unclear (see Labaree 2014). Nevertheless, there is enormous political pressure on governments to have their educational systems transnationally accredited, either by excelling in PISA or by importing—as part of the public education system—International Baccalaureate Diploma Programs, Cambridge International Examination, or other transnational accreditors to assure the public that the education system is not falling behind international standards or is not failing to effectively teach twenty-first-century skills to the future workforce.

Starting in 2012, when OECD admitted territories—or what OECD likes to label "economies" (e.g., Shanghai)—rather than exclusively nations, the organization seems to have increasingly abandoned national governments as its main counterparts. OECD's counterparts in PISA 2018 include, for example, only one of the seven emirates of the United Arab Emirates (Abu Dhabi) or only five of the fifty states of the United States of America. The change in admission criterion is consequential as it signals perhaps the beginning of a new era in governance, in which transnational accreditation—real (by means of IB, IGCSE, etc.) or symbolic (by means of PISA and twenty-first-century skills)—gains further importance at the expense of a national accreditation of schools. In effect, national governments are further curtailed in their role as standard-setters and regulators in education; ultimately benefitting non-state actors in education such as education businesses and non-governmental organizations.

## The Economization of Education

The neoliberal or quasi-market educational reforms of the past two decades have revamped the way students, parents, communities, schools, and governments think about education, school choice, and school quality, and how to measure the latter. In the research literature, the transformation has been abundantly noted, documented, and analyzed. What is perhaps less discussed is the extent to which the economization of education is taken for granted. In fact, so much so that we don't see PISA as the instruments that it is: an effectiveness measure of the (future) labor force in a globalized knowledge economy.

The idea that education contributes to economic growth is a relatively new proposition that only dates back to the second half of the last century. Introduced by noted economists of the University of Chicago (Theodore Schultz, Gary Becker), the discourse of Human Capital has led to substantial resource mobilization and therefore became widely accepted, including by experts in education and in international development. It brought a windfall of resources for technical and vocational training in the 1980s, funded by the World Bank and the International Monetary Fund. The human capital approach to substantiating the need for investments in education has remained a recurring theme in policy debates. Another itineration of the approach, the Rates of Return to Education theorem (George Psacharopoulos) has had a similar positive impact on resource mobilization, in particular for the basic education sub-sector in developing countries. Based on Rates of Return analyses, the World Bank advocated in the mid-1990s for a reallocation of public spending in education, away from higher education to primary education (see World Bank 1995). Nowadays, the proposed association continues to be propelled by cost-benefit analysts (including the high social costs for low educational attainment), such as, for example, Eric Hanushek, and is used by the global education industry to enlist businesses for selling goods and services in the education sector (see Hogan, Sellar, and Lingard 2016; Steiner-Khamsi, Appleton, and Vellani 2017). Regardless of the financial benefits for the education sector, all three concepts—human capital theory, rates of return analyses, cost-benefit analyses—have been heavily criticized for assuming a linear relationship between economic growth and educational attainment (Bennell 1996; Klees, Samoff, and Stromquist 2012) and between economic growth and students' learning outcomes (Kamens 2015).

Historically, OECD used to be the primary international organization that predicted manpower needs, calculated costs and benefits of investments, and measured economic growth. These objectives were especially pronounced after the Second World War when the allied forces invested substantial amounts of financial resources to rebuild Europe. Another system theorist, Frank-Olaf Radtke, points at the economics of standardized comparison, propelled by OECD (Radtke 2016; see also Lepenies 2013; Tröhler 2014). Radtke argues that OECD has preserved its narrow focus on measuring economic growth over the past half century, first, with inventing the indicator gross domestic product (GDP) and nowadays, by means of PISA, with determining the "gross education product" (GEP). After the war, it introduced the indicator of gross domestic product to measure whether the financial investments of the Marshall Plan actually led to economic growth in post–World War II Europe. Fifty years later, OECD maintained its preoccupation which identifying factors that possibly could contribute to economic growth. They identified, among others, educational factors and in particular twenty-first-century skills that they claim to be indispensable for a globalized knowledge economy. The economistic logic of OECD —establishing a cause-effect relationship between (human) investment and economic growth—has been preserved even though the indicators for measuring investments have changed.

Seen from a systems perspective, PISA bridges two functional systems: it translates the skills, deemed relevant for globalized knowledge economies, into the language of the education system by emphasizing learning of twenty-first-century skills. The functional equivalent of knowledge economies, pursued in the economic system, is twenty-first-century skills, taught and measured in the educational system. As a result of the communication between the two functional systems, public education resembles increasingly the market, and the economic system in turn takes on educational features, as reflected in concepts such as life-long learning or learning in the workplace.

The education system is not the only (sub-)system that has been economized in the wake of the neoliberal reforms. The political system has experienced a similar fate. In particular, the politics-economy nexus is reflected in public–private partnership policies that have gone global over the past few years. Again, from the perspective of sociological systems theory, the close interaction between two distinct functional systems is noteworthy. System theorist Niels A. Andersen, for example, provides a succinct analysis of how private companies have become an integral part of the political system because they are contracted for implementing public services. Vice-versa, as part of the boundary work between the two functional systems that constantly have to communicate or interact with each other in an era of the neo-liberal Education Market Model (see Robertson and Verger 2012), the political sector has taken on private sector modes of operation (Andersen 2000, 2013).

Finally, evidence-based policy planning may also be analyzed against the backdrop of two functional systems which for the longest time were seen as separate entities and ruled by different principles: science and politics. The price we nowadays pay for the scientification of political decisions is the politicization of science, captured in the critique that, more often than not, evidence-based policy planning is (political) agenda-driven research in disguise.

## The Semantics of PISA

The stubborn resistance of national governments to acknowledge PISA's limitations in providing policy relevant information deserves greater scrutiny. Are the salutary effects of PISA great to the extent that national policy actors are prepared to downplay all the serious handicaps of the test? An example of blind belief in PISA is Vietnam's supposedly high performance in math (rank 16) and reading (rank 18) out of sixty-three countries and territories; ranks that are above the United States and the UK and much higher than any other developing country. At closer examination, the miraculous performance of fifteen-year-old students in Vietnam dissipates once it is explained in a very straightforward manner (see Glewwe, Anh Dang, Lee, and Vu 2017): From all the sixty-three participating countries, Vietnam has the third-lowest enrollment rate. Unsurprisingly, the few fifteen-years-olds that "survive" in the Vietnamese educational system are those with a higher socioeconomic status. PISA's league tables but also its sophisticated visualizations of data have been criticized for a wide range of reasons and do not need to be reiterated here.

Obviously *something* about PISA makes the test powerful. The proliferation of studies that explain the impact of PISA on national school reforms is noteworthy. Most of them problematize PISA's uncontested power as global monitoring instrument for national developments. In development studies, we have become accustomed to global monitoring of national development in the form of the Global Education Monitoring Report and annual reports of other international organizations. It has become the norm, and not the exception. In that respect, OECD and with it PISA joins the ranks of the World Bank and the International Monetary Fund who have been criticized for decades for disseminating their own portfolio of public administration reforms in the form of (funded) "best practices." In contrast to the World Bank and IMF that exert "hard power" (withholding loans and grants) if their conditions are not met at national level, the power of OECD is "soft" but nevertheless effective. A key feature of the World Bank and IMF monitoring apparatus—the overlap between analysis and prescription—is nowhere to be found in OECD reports on PISA. The influence of ILSAs on national reforms is far more subtle, less coercive, and for all of these reasons possibly more effective.

In a compelling article, Radhika Gorur draws on Actor Network Theory in order to examine the performativity of PISA (2016). She contends that PISA narrows the field of vision of policy actors in that it makes them "see like PISA," that is, makes them focus on measurable learning outcomes, rely on numbers, and use them as mechanism for accountability and regulation.

Rather than analyzing what PISA does to whom, it is also possible to inverse the object of study: what do national policy actors do with PISA? How do they use the test for their own reform agendas? This book's focus on reception or projection clearly subscribes to these kinds of questions. More concretely, PISA's potential for a triple externalization is not to be underestimated. It contributes to the power of "soft power" attributed to PISA. PISA more than other ILSAs inhabits simultaneously three external spaces which national policy actors may discursively mobilize when in need of a quasi-external reform pressure, that is, a reform pressure that is self-generated yet presented as if it is external: the economy, the concrete other (league leaders), and the generalized other ("best practices"). In that sense, PISA is polyglot, it fills a semantic space in which several languages are spoken and associations are made, notably with the economy, globalization, and international mobility.

As mentioned above and elsewhere (Addey et al. 2017), PISA's disregard for national curricula may be viewed as a strength, not a weakness. Precisely because the test is meaningless in terms of national curricula, policy actors are able to fill this vacuum by providing their own explanations of why their system is not preparing the students for twenty-first-century skills. PISA is an empty vessel that policy actors may use as leverage for generating reform pressure and mobilizing resources, including more technology integration and introducing English as a language of instruction. The dilemma is, however, that the private sector is much better equipped than the public sector for scaling up technology and for bypassing national languages. For all the reasons explained in this conclusions chapter and several other chapters of the book, the test propels besides Seeing Like PISA, also a destatalization and possibly, as a corollary, a privatization of education.

# References

ACDP (2013), *Evaluation of International Standards School in Indonesia*, Jakarta: ACDP (Education Sector Analytical and Capacity Development Partnership).

Addey, C. (2016), "Participating in International Literacy Assessments in Lao PDR and Mongolia: A Global Ritual of Belonging," in M. Hamilton, B. Maddox, and C. Addey (eds.), *Literacy as Numbers: Researching the Politics and Practices of International Literacy Assessment*, 147–65, Cambridge: Cambridge University Press.

Addey, C., Sellar, S., Steiner-Khamsi, G., Lingard, B., and Verger, A. (2017), "Forum Discussion: The Rise of International Large-Scale Assessments and Rationales for Participation," *Compare*, 47(3), 434–52.

Andersen, N. A. (2000), "Public Market—Political Firms," *Acta Sociologica*, 43(1), 43–61.

Andersen, N. A. (2013), "Contract as a Form of Intersystemic Communication," in A. Febbrajo and G. Harste (eds.), *Laws and Intersystemic Communication: Understanding 'Structural Coupling'*, 129–54, Surrey: Ashgate.

Ball, S. J., and Junemann, C. (2012), *Networks, New Governance and Education*, Bristol: University of Bristol and Policy Press.

Baek. C., Hörmann, B., Karseth, B., Pizmony-Levy, O., Sivesind, K., and Steiner-Khamsi, G. (2017), "Policy Learning in Norwegian School Reform: A Social Network Analysis of the 2020 Incremental Reform," *Nordic Journal of Studies in Educational Policy*, doi: 10.1080/20020317.2017.1412747.

Bennell, P. (1996), "Using and Abusing Rates of Return: A Critique of the World Bank's 1995 Education Sector Review," *International Journal of Educational Development, 16*(3), 235–48, doi: 10.1016/0738-0593(96)00016-8.

Bridges, D. (2014), *Educational Reform and Internationalisation: The Case of School Reform in Kazakhstan*, Cambridge: Cambridge University Press.

Buckner E., and Russell, S. G. (2013), "Portraying the Global: Cross-National Trends in Textbooks' Portrayal of Globalization and Global Citizenship," *International Studies Quarterly, 57*(4), 738–50.

Carney, S., Rappleye, J., and Silova, I. (2012), "Between Faith and Science: World Culture Theory and Comparative Education," *Comparative Education Review, 56*(3), 366–93.

Dale, R. (2000), "Globalization and Education: Demonstrating a 'Common World Education Culture' or Locating a 'Globally Structured Educational Agenda'?" *Educational Theory, 50*(4), 427–48, doi:10.1111/j.1741-5446.2000.00427.x.

Glewwe, P., Anh Dang, H., Lee, J., and Vu, K. (2017), "What Explains Vietnams Exceptional Performance in Education Relative to Other Countries? Analysis of the 2012 PISA Data," https://www.apec.umn.edu/sites/apec.umn.edu/files/pisa_vn4.pdf.

Gorur, R. (2016), "Seeing Like PISA: A Cautionary Tale about the Performativity of International Assessments," *European Educational Research Journal, 15*(5), 598–616.

Heintz, B. (2012), "Welterzeugung durch Zahlen: Modelle politischer Differenzierung in internationalen Statistiken, 1948–2010" [Creating a World through Numbers: Models of Political Differentiation in International Statistics], *Soziale Systeme, 18*(1+2), 7–39.

Hogan, A., Sellar, S., and Lingard, B. (2016), "Commercialising Comparison: Pearson Puts the TLC in Soft Capitalism," *Journal of Education Policy, 31*(3), 243–58.

Jules, T. D. (ed.) (2016), *Global Education Policy Environment in the Fourth Industrial Revolution: Gated, Regulated, and Governed*, Bingley: Emerald.

Kamens, D. (2015), "A Maturing Global Testing Regime Meets the World Economy: Test Scores and Economic Growth, 1960–2012," *Comparative Education Review, 59*(3), 420–46.

Kijima, R. and Lipscy, P. Y. (2017), "The Politics of International Testing," http:ssrn.com/abstract=2995226.

Klees, S. J., Samoff, J., and Stromquist, N. P. (eds.) (2012), *The World Bank and Education: Critiques and Alternatives*, Rotterdam: Sense.

Kingsbury, B., Engle Merry, S., and Davis, K. (2015), *The Quiet Power of Indicators: Measuring Governance, Corruption, and Rule of Law*, New York: Cambridge University Press.

Labaree, D. F. (2014), "Let's Measure What No One Teaches: PISA, NCLB, and the Shrinking Aims of Education," *Teachers College Record, 116*(9), 1–14.

Lepenies, P. (2013), *Die Macht der einen Zahl: Eine politische Geschichte des Bruttoinlandproduktes* [The Power of a Single Number: A Political History of GDP], Frankfurt a. M.: Suhrkamp.

Lerch, J., Bromley, P., Meyer, J. W., and Ramirez, F. O. (2016), "The Rise of Individual Agency in Conceptions of Society: Textbooks Worldwide, 1950–2011," *International Sociology*, 3(5), 38–60.

Lewis, S. (2017), "Policy, Philanthropy and Profit: The OECD's PISA for Schools and New Modes of Heterarchical Educational Governance," *Comparative Education*, 53(4), 518–37.

Littoz-Monnet, A. (2017), *The Politics of Expertise in International Organizations: How International Bureaucracies Produce and Mobilize Knowledge*, London: Routledge.

Lockheed, M. E., Prokic-Breuer T., and Shadrova A. (2015), *The Experience of Middle-Income Countries Participating in PISA 2000–2015*, Paris and Washington: OECD and World Bank Group.

Luhmann, N. (1997), "Globalization or World Society: How to Conceive of Modern Society?" *International Review of Sociology*, 7(1), 67–79.

Martens, K., and Knodel, P. (eds.) (2014), *Internationalization of Education Policy: A New Constellation of Statehood in Education?* New York: Palgrave Macmillan.

Ozga, J. (2009), "Governing Education through Data in England: From Regulation to Self-Evaluation," *Journal of Education Policy*, 24(2), 261–72.

Porter, T. M. (1996), *Trust in Numbers: The Pursuit of Objectivity in Science and Public Life*, Princeton: Princeton University Press.

Radtke, F.-O. (2016), "Konditionierte Strukturverbesserung" [Conditioned Structural Improvement], *Zeitschrift für Pädagogik*, 62(5), 707–31.

Resnik, J. (2015), "The Development of the International Baccalaureate in Spanish Speaking Countries: A Global Comparative Approach," *Globalisation Societies and Education*, 14(2), 298–325, doi: 10.1080/14767724.2015.1051951.

Robertson, S. L., and Verger, A. (2012), "Governing Education through Public Private Partnership," in S. L. Robertson, K. Mundy, A. Verger and F. Menashy (eds.), *Public Private Partnership in Education. New Actors and Modes of Governance in a Globalizing World*, 21–42, Cheltenham: Edward Elgar.

Sending, O. J. (2015), *The Politics of Expertise: Competing for Authority in Global Governance*, Ann Arbor: University of Michigan Press.

Schriewer, J (1990), "The Method of Comparison and the Need for Externalization: Methodological Criteria and Sociological Concepts," in J. Schriewer in cooperation with Brian Holmes (ed.), *Theories and Methods in Comparative Education*, 25–83, Frankfurt a. M.: Peter Lang.

Schriewer, J., and Martinez, C. (2004), "Constructions of Internationality in Education," in G. Steiner-Khamsi (ed.), *The Global Politics of Educational Borrowing and Lending*, 29–53, New York: Teachers College Press.

Steiner-Khamsi, G. (2016), "Standards are Good (for) Business: Standardised Comparison and the Private Sector in Education," *Globalisation, Societies, and Education*, 14(2), 161–82.

Steiner-Khamsi, G., Appleton, M., and Vellani, S. (2017), "Understanding Business Interests in International Large-Scale Student Assessments: A Media Analysis of The

Economist, Financial Times, and Wall Street Journal," *Oxford Review of Education*, *44*(2), 190–203.

Steiner-Khamsi, G., and Waldow, F. (eds.) (2012), *Policy Borrowing and Lending: 2014 World Yearbook of Education*, Oxford: Routledge.

Tröhler, D. (2013), "Change Management in the Governance of Schooling: The Rise of Experts, Planners, and Statistics in the Early OECD," *Teachers College Record*, *116*(9), 1–26.

Verger, A., Fontdevila, C., and Zancajo, A. (2016), *The Privatization of Education: A Political Economy of Global Education Reform*, New York: Teachers College Press.

Weber, M. (1922), *Wirtschaft und Gesellschaft* [Economy and Society], Tübingen: Mohr Siebeck.

World Bank (1995), *Priorities and Strategies for Education: A World Bank Review*, Washington: World Bank.

Yamamoto, B. A. (ed.) (2016), *Implementation and Impact of the Dual Language IB DP Programme in Japanese Secondary Schools: Final Report June 16, 2016*, Osaka: Osaka University.

# Index

Yang, H. 188
Yelland, N. 55
You, Y. 190
*Yutori* education 222

Zeng, K. 12–13

Zhang Minxuan 178, 180,
　186
Zhou, D. 182, 183
Zhu, X. 183
Zhu Yongxin 188
Zymek, B. 4

CPSIA information can be obtained
at www.ICGtesting.com
Printed in the USA
LVHW080207301019
635794LV00004B/12/P